FORTH
An Applications Approach

David L. Toppen, Ph.D.
California State University, Northridge

McGraw-Hill Book Company

New York St. Louis San Francisco Auckland Bogotá
Hamburg Johannesburg London Madrid
Mexico Montreal New Delhi Panama
Paris São Paulo Singapore
Sydney Tokyo Toronto

Library of Congress Cataloging in Publication Data

Toppen, David L.
  Forth, an applications approach.

  Includes index.
  1. FORTH (Computer program language)   I. Title.
QA76.73.F24T67   1985   001.64′24   84-14432
ISBN 0-07-064975-8 (pbk.)

Copyright © 1985 by McGraw-Hill, Inc. All rights reserved.
Printed in the United States of America. Except as permitted
under the United States Copyright Act of 1976, no part of this
publication may be reproduced or distributed in any form or by
any means, or stored in a data base or retrieval system, without
the prior written permission of the publisher.

1 2 3 4 5 6 7 8 9 0   DOC/DOC   8 9 8 7 6 5

ISBN 0-07-064975-8

The editors for this book were Tyler G. Hicks and Ruth L. Weine;
the designer was Elliot Epstein;
and the production supervisor was Teresa F. Leaden.
It was set in Century Schoolbook by University Graphics, Inc.

Printed and bound by R. R. Donnelley & Sons, Inc.

Contents

Preface, vii
Acknowledgments, ix

Part I. The Forth Language   1

1. The Stack   5
    1.1 Introduction, 5
    1.2 The Stack, 6
    1.3 Keeping Track of the Stack's Contents, 9
    1.4 Forth Words that Manipulate the Stack, 11
    1.5 Problems, 14

2. Words: The Forth Dictionary   16
    2.1 The Forth Word, 16
    2.2 The Forth Dictionary, 22
        Rules for Naming Forth Words, 23
        Dictionary Structure, 25
    2.3 Controlling the Dictionary, 26
        Redefinition, 27
        Advanced FORGETTING, 28
    2.4 Forth Vocabularies, 29
        Run-Time versus Compile-Time Behavior, 30
        Immediate Words, 31
        Interlingual Applications of Forth's Dictionary, 33
    2.5 Problems, 34

3. Numbers   36
    3.1 Number Concepts, 36
        Binary Numbers, 37
        Unfamiliar Radices, 37
    3.2 Nondecimal Arithmetic Operations, 39
        Binary Arithmetic, 39

Octal Arithmetic, 39
Hexadecimal Arithmetic, 39
3.3 Storage of Numbers in Memory, 40
3.4 Binary Representations, 42
Octal Encoding, 42
Hexadecimal Encoding, 43
3.5 Signed Numbers, 43
3.6 Single-Integer Mathematics, 46
3.7 32-Bit Number Representations, 48
Double-Length Integers, 49
Floating-Point Numbers, 49
Number-Input Conventions in Forth, 51
3.8 Floating-Point Mathematics, 52
Stack Effects of Floating-Point Forth Words, 52
Floating-Point Input and Output Conventions, 53
Floating-Point Stack Manipulations, 54
3.9 Creating Forth Words that Use Floating-Point Mathematics, 55
3.10 Double-Length Integer Mathematics, 58
3.11 Radix Conversions, 61
3.12 Problems, 62

4. Variables, Constants, and Arrays — 64
4.1 Variables, 64
4.2 Memory Allocation for Variables and Constants, 66
Reinitialization, 71
4.3 Constants, 73
4.4 Double-Length Variables and Constants, 74
32-Bit Integer Variables, 74
Double-Length Constants, 75
4.5 Floating-Point Variables and Constants, 76
4.6 User Variables, 78
4.7 Arrays, 79
4.8 Double-Integer and Floating-Point Arrays, 82
4.9 Byte Arrays, 83
4.10 Problems, 84

5. Decisions, Loops, and Logic — 85
5.1 Decisions, 85
Comparison Operations, 86
Conditionals, 87
Alternate Execution, 88
Nested Conditionals, 89
5.2 Loops, 90
Definite Loops, 90
The Return Stack, 91
Early Loop Termination, 93
5.3 Loops Containing 32-Bit Arithmetic, 94
5.4 +LOOP, 95
5.5 Indefinite Loops, 96
Begin . . . Until Loops, 97
Begin . . . While . . . Repeat Loops, 98

5.6 More Logic, 98
    Boolean Operations, 99
    Logic, Bit by Bit, 101
5.7 Problems, 103

6. Input-Output Editor and Disk — 105

6.1 Character Representations, 105
    The ASCII Code, 105
    Nonprinting Characters, 106
    Printing Characters, 109

6.2 Single-Character Input, 110
    Forth's Scratchpad, 111
    Buffers, 111
    Writing on the Pad, 112
    Reading the Contents of the Pad, 114

6.3 Multiple-Character Input, 116
    WORD, 116
    COUNT, 118
    Moving Characters in Memory, 118
    TEXT, 119

6.4 Disk Storage and Virtual Memory, 120
    Listing Forth Blocks, 121
    Indexing Forth Blocks, 123
    BLOCK, 125

6.5 The Skeleton Editor, 126
    Using the Editor to Enter the Editor, 127
    Saving Blocks on the Disk, 129

6.6 Loading Forth Definitions from the Disk, 131

6.7 Numeric Output, 133

6.8 Formatted Output, 137
    Right-Justified Output, 138
    Formatting Output with .WITH, 139
    32-Bit Integer Formatted Output, 141

6.9 Problems, 142

Part II. Hardware Control with Forth — 145

Introduction — 145

7. Introduction to Hardware: Input-Output — 147

7.1 Computer Organization, 147

7.2 Memory Organization, 150
    PDP-11 Memory Geography, 151
    Forth Geography, 152

7.3 Peripheral Devices and Communications Protocol, 153
    Parallel versus Serial I/O, 153
    The Electronics Industry Association Standard: RS232C, 155
    Baud Rate, 156

7.4 Accessing the Printer, 156
    I/O Interface, 156
    A Top-Down Approach to Creating a Printer Application, 157

Contents

7.5 Hardware Input-Output, 160
    Input Operations, 162
    Output Operations, 163
    `W!`, A Hardware-Specific Interface Word, 165
    Printing Blocks on the Printer, 166
7.6 Escape Sequences, 166
    Video Hardware Escape Sequences, 168
    The ANSI Standard, 169
    Hard-Copy Escape Sequences, 172
7.7 Problems, 173

8. Analog Signals: Data Acquisition and Device Control   174
8.1 Digital-to-Analog Conversion, 174
    Forth and DAC, 177
    Waveforms, 178
    Repeating Waveforms, 180
    A Question of Time, 180
    Slowing Forth Down, 180
    Fast Conversions, 183
    Nonlinear Waveforms, 186
8.2 Analog-to-Digital Conversion, 186
    Forth Voltmeter, 191
8.3 Saving Data on the Disk, 192
    Storing Data in an Array, 192
    Saving Binary Data on the Disk, 194
8.4 Problems, 195

9. Signal-Processing Fundamentals   197
9.1 The Sampling Theorem, 197
9.2 Noise, 199
9.3 Forth in Identification of Peaks, 201
    Calculation of Mean Noise, 205
    `ADJUST`ing an Array, 205
    Identifying Peaks, 206
    Peak Integration, 207

Appendixes

A	Software Tools	210
B	Floating-Point Support	212
C	Forth Dialects	213
D	Number Formatting	215
E	The Universal Screen Editor	217
F	A Forth Assembler	222
	Index	227

Preface

This book began life as a project to facilitate the introduction of Forth into the environments of scientific and engineering applications programming. The original intent was to focus specifically on areas where micro and minicomputer resources are traditionally used for real time, online data acquisition and device control. As the project evolved, however, it became increasingly clear that Forth affords its users a far richer potential for creative system design than even the author had envisioned. Forth extends to its practiced users the dual benefits of an intrinsically structured programming environment and an economy of code that is virtually unequaled in contemporary computer languages. Consequently, the thrust of the book was broadened to emphasize both Forth's incisive approach to fundamental programming tasks and its facility in the data-acquisition regimen.

The first part of the book focuses on the fundamentals of the Forth programming environment. Presupposing no programming expertise on the part of the reader, these chapters lay the foundation for an understanding of Forth's unique approach while covering the hardware-independent aspects of Forth programming. Numerous examples and solved problems are included.

Part II addresses hardware-specific aspects of Forth programming. Using examples derived from the laboratory environment, these chapters provide the reader with the programming tools to create and control the interface between his or her computer and real-world devices such as printers, plotters, and spectrometers. An extensive treatment of digital-to-analog and analog-to-digital conversion (and converters) is included, for example, as is a chapter devoted to the fundamentals of signal processing in a Forth programming context.

The Digital Equipment Corporation (DEC) PDP-11 computer system has been extensively used in this work as the illustrative hardware environment. Beyond the fact that DEC has been traditionally supportive of academic scientific computing activities, the selection of PDP-11 hardware is a consequence of the original intent underlying the book's creation, i.e., the demonstration of Forth's usefulness in the realm of device control and data acquisition, domains where PDP-11s have historically played a dominant role.

In the computing world it has been long established that no specific language or computer system can best handle every programming or computational problem. This is certainly true of Forth, and it is true of the PDP-11 computer as well. Similarly, in the academic world it is a given that a single book can never provide all the information necessary for mastery of a particular discipline, and this book is, of course, no exception. But it does provide a broad coverage of the principles of thoughtful programming in the framework of a structured language. Thus, this book is of value to a far broader spectrum of readers than was originally intended.

In the scientific and engineering disciplines, a reader who is armed with the manuals that accompany his or her computer and external devices and who uses the powerful interfacing tool that Forth has proven itself to be, should be able to readily handle a wide variety of interface applications with relative ease and programming efficiency.

David L. Toppen

Acknowledgments

This book would not exist were it not for the support given the author by his colleagues in the Department of Chemistry, California State University, Northridge. For their patience and tolerance of my computer whimsy, Professors Ricardo A. Silva, Kenneth I. Hardcastle, and Dean O. Skovlin deserve special thanks, as do Jerry Boles and Jeff Craig of the CSUN Computer Center.

The encouragement of Max Schwartz, who showed me how a book is conceived, is gratefully acknowledged.

I am especially grateful to David Crawford for his illuminating descriptions of both hardware and software details and for his patient willingness to read much of this book and fearlessly comment on it.

Finally, I wish to thank my wife, Nina Alexis Klein, whose patience and loving support have made this book a reality.

About the Author

David Livingstone Toppen founded the Data Acquisition Laboratory at California State University, Northridge, and created the NetForth, a multiprocessor extension of the Forth programming environment. He is currently University Planner for Instructional Computing at CSU Northridge.

For the past several years, Professor Toppen's major research interests have been laboratory automation, computer networking, data acquisition, and device control.

Professor Toppen has published over twenty papers in the journals of the American Chemical Society and the IEEE Computer Society. This is his first book.

Part

I

The Forth Language

Introduction

Computers have become indispensable tools in the business world, as well as in engineering and in the sciences. They are an inescapable attribute of modern society. Computing machines of all shapes and sizes are found nearly everywhere, in diverse applications ranging from very large "number-crunching" mainframes to tiny microprocessor-based device controllers in medical implants. The entry of minicomputers into the scientific laboratory, for example, along with the development of low-cost interfaces between instruments and computers, has liberated scientists and technicians from many of the time-consuming tasks of acquiring data from their equipment. The burgeoning use of micro- and minicomputers in industry has led to the development of such marvels as the robot assembly line and the talking automobile dashboard. On the domestic front, many families now have their own small computers which are used for entertainment as well as business-oriented applications.

But we can all remember when it was not like this, and some of us can even remember back to the earliest applications of computers, when the user of a computer had to physically carry programs and data back and forth to the machine. Usually information had to be prepared for the computer in some relatively inconvenient form like punched cards or paper tape. Back then, turn-around time was measured in hours; and direct, or hard-wired, connections between a computer and a scientific instrument or a manufacturing process were almost always too expensive to be practical. Just a decade ago the idea of computer-based consumer items was viewed more as science fiction than as future fact.

2 The Forth Language

The advent of the microprocessor changed everything. Today, with suitable interface hardware and appropriate programming, a fairly inexpensive computer system can automate an entire laboratory. Robot assembly lines are becoming more and more common, and more paychecks are computer-printed than not. In laboratories and process-control facilities in factories, the time lag between data gathering and desk-top results analysis is now measured in seconds rather than hours, and punched cards and paper tape have become nearly extinct, giving way to bubble memory, magnetic disks, and magnetic tape.

In spite of all these changes, most business, technical, and scientific people lack a firm foundation in principles of computer operations. This is especially true in areas of interface between computers and so-called real-world devices, an area loosely called "data acquisition and device control."

In the midst of all the technological progress in hardware design in the past few years, spurred largely by incredibly rapid advances in solid state techniques, the growing mismatch between the capabilities of the hardware available to the scientist and the software which can be used to control the hardware is becoming increasingly clear. Increasingly, computer applications in science and industry require a *direct* connection between the computer and another device, with the human operator freed from the tasks of data gathering and adjustment of device parameters. Unfortunately, the early scientific languages, FORTRAN and ALGOL, though elegant and powerful in their role as computational tools, were never designed to provide for such connections. Indeed, as usually implemented, they contain elaborate safeguards to prevent a programmer from ever gaining control of any direct connection to anything other than a printer or terminal. Computers using such languages usually leave device-control applications to be written in the machine language specific to the particular computer.

The advent of the microcomputer, usually based on microprocessors such as the Intel 8080, the Rockwell 6502, and their successors, spurred an explosion in computing in the late 1970s and 1980s. Languages like BASIC and PASCAL, minicousins of FORTRAN and ALGOL, have become very popular, and some versions of these languages have been extended or modified to support hardware interfacing to some extent. Even so, the writing of programs for efficient control of instruments and devices has usually involved learning the assembly language of the particular computer involved, a process for which relatively few people have had either the time or the patience.

What is obviously needed is a computer language designed specifically for device-control and data-acquisition applications, a language which gives the programmer the ability to work efficiently in a format that can be transported from one type of computer to another. Fortunately, such a language exists. It is called "Forth."

Forth is the brainchild of Charles H. Moore, who developed it over a period of years beginning at the National Radio Astronomy Observatory in Charlottesville, Virginia. Moore was dissatisfied with the applicability of available languages to the problems of observatory automation: telescope control, spectral analysis, stellar observation, image processing, interferometric calculations, and the like. He viewed the development of his new language as an interface between himself and the computers he programmed, and he wanted it to be not only powerful, but flexible and easy to use as well. Also important to Moore was the intent to design into the language the ability to allow a programmer to add to the language whatever capabilities would later become necessary. Indeed, the very structure of Forth can be modified by a programmer to accomplish a given goal.

The origin of the name Forth is amusing. When Moore first accumulated his ideas into a functional programming tool, he was using an IBM model 1130, a so-called third-generation computer. The new, "fourth-generation" language needed a name, but the 1130 allowed only five characters for this purpose. Thus "Forth" was born.

This book is about Forth, how it works, and how to use it to write programming applications in a scientific, industrial, or engineering environment. That is Forth's heritage, after all. But the applicability of Forth is certainly not limited to device control and data acquisition. In Chap. 6 you will see how a very fast and sophisticated video editor has been written in Forth. Just for fun you will see how commercial vendors have been quietly using Forth to create video games, you will get a taste of Forth's ability to communicate in many human languages other than English, and you will see how Forth can be used in intercomputer communications, through a facility called the "Net-Forth."

But the best way to fully appreciate Forth's flexibility, and to really learn "how it works," is to have access to a running Forth system. Reading books about programming is a necessary beginning, of course, but the full flavor of a language, human or machine, cannot be appreciated without an opportunity to speak it. So get yourself to a terminal and speak Forth, starting with the demonstrations and examples in Chap. 1.

Chapter 1

The Stack

Keep the terminal in the "CAPS"-on mode; FORTH differentiates between small and capital letters. E.G. ".s" ≠ ".S". The latter is the word dot ess; the former is undefined.

1.1 Introduction

Computer languages were invented to provide their users or programmers with a relatively easy way to use a computing device to obtain results for a particular type of calculation or decision-making process. Some languages, those which are traditionally called *high-level*—examples are FORTRAN, BASIC, and PASCAL—were designed to allow programmers to create programs that carry out sophisticated calculations without ever being concerned with any of the details about the structure, organization, or location of the computer's hardware. For languages like these, one of the language designer's foremost goals has been to render the hardware aspects of the machine virtually transparent to the programmer.

Low-level, or *machine,* languages represent the opposite extreme. These languages are characterized by a design philosophy that necessarily centers on the programmer's need to clearly grasp the details of the computer's inner workings, down to the levels at which individual numbers are stored and manipulated, and data are transferred from one device to another.

High-level languages are designed to incorporate terminology which is closely aligned with human tongues and algebraic expressions, ensuring that the computer can be effectively used by individuals who would prefer to expend their intellectual skills on the problem at hand, rather than to devote a career to the arts and sciences of machine-level programming. In this regard Forth is possibly the highest-level language of all.

Machine languages operate at the level of the hardware itself, allowing the programmer to interact directly with the memory and devices that compose the particular computer. By virtue of its firm commitment to allow the programmer access to *all* the computer's resources, including the "nuts and bolts," Forth easily qualifies as a low-level language as well.

As you become proficient in the applications of Forth, you will become increasingly aware of Forth's unique ability to remain firmly planted in both these camps, low-level and high-level. Indeed, it is this obvious ambivalence, this deliberate, premeditated adherence to no previously defined tradition in computer language design, which makes Forth so useful to the users and programmers of computers that do more than just "compute," that interact with external devices as well. One of the reasons that Forth works so well as a computer language is that it allows the programmer to have direct access to a particular feature of the computer's architecture, the *stack*.

1.2 The Stack

The stack is an active area within the computer's memory in which Forth keeps numbers and character representations that are being used in the current computational process. This area is called the "stack" because Forth stores parameters in this region of the computer's memory in much the same way that the face-down pile of playing cards in a rummy game holds the discards. Each value added to the stack increases the "depth" of the stack by 1. Only the value most recently added to the stack is directly available (without changing the order of the values on the stack), just as the top card is the only one available to the next card player. For these reasons, the stack is called a LIFO (or last-in, first-out) data structure.

The concept of a stack is certainly not unique to Forth. FORTRAN, BASIC, and other high-level languages all use an internal LIFO stack to hold numbers as they are processed. The programmer cannot access or in any *direct* way affect the stack in these languages, however. As will become obvious, what makes Forth so powerful and unique is the design philosophy that not only requires but virtually demands that a Forth programmer use the stack *directly* in creating Forth programs.

> Although there are at least two stacks in any Forth system, the *parameter* stack is the one we are discussing here. There is also another LIFO area called the *return* stack which Forth uses as a sort of roadmap as it winds its way through an application. More about this stack later.

In computer jargon, addition of a value to the stack is called a *push*, whereas removal of a value is called a *pop*. Fortunately, the Forth programmer rarely needs to use these terms, since Forth does the pushes and pops automatically. Let us see how it works.

Enter the following line at your terminal:

47 54 + .<ret> 101 ok

where <ret> represents the key labeled "return" or "enter" on your terminal and Forth's response is underlined. You should see the sum of the two values you entered displayed, and a message from Forth that all is OK. (i.e., as far as *Forth* is concerned, you have not done anything wrong).

Here is what happened. While there is nothing else to do, Forth monitors the terminal keyboard, waiting for you to give it something to do. This waiting state is called Forth's *quit loop* (i.e., in the absence of things to do, Forth quits doing anything). Whenever you enter something at your terminal, a Forth structure called INTERPRET inspects the incoming typed information and, based on the nature of what you have entered, causes the computer to take an appropriate action.

1. INTERPRET first checks the list of valid Forth commands to determine whether your entry is *executable* (whether it gives Forth something to *do*). If so, it does what you have commanded.
2. If your entry is not executable, INTERPRET checks it to determine whether it is a valid number. If so, INTERPRET gets Forth to push it onto the stack.
3. If your entry is neither a valid Forth command nor a recognizable number, INTERPRET alerts Forth of an error condition, and Forth prints an error message.

In the example above, INTERPRET first encountered 47. Since 47 is not a predefined Forth command but is a valid number, INTERPRET promptly pushed it onto the stack. Similarly, 54 is a number, not a command, and it too was pushed onto the stack. INTERPRET next found + (pronounced "plus") in the incoming typed information. At this point the response differed, because INTERPRET recognized + as a valid Forth command. As previously determined, plus (+) causes the top two values to pop from the stack, adds them together, and pushes the sum onto the stack. The stack is one value less deep after this operation.

Finally, INTERPRET spotted . (pronounced "dot," not "period") in the input stream. Dot (.) causes the top value to pop from the stack and displays it on the user's terminal. The stack is one value less deep after this operation. The overall effects of these operations on the Forth stack are shown in Fig. 1.1.

Until this point we have been calling predefined Forth structures like . (dot) and + (plus) "commands." In actual fact, this term is not the correct one to use when dealing with Forth. Predetermined executable structures in Forth are properly called "words" and the collection of words [like + (plus) and . (dot)] that make up Forth is the Forth *dictionary*. Learning Forth entails learning how to use the words in the dictionary to create new words to add to the dictionary, so that these new words can be later used to create yet more words that can ultimately be used to solve a

8 The Forth Language

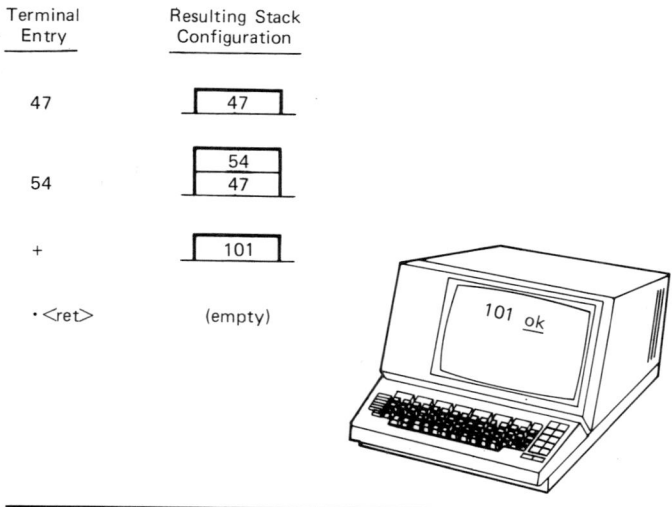

Figure 1.1 Stack effects of a simple integer addition

problem. In this regard, Forth is unlike any other computer language. Whereas languages like BASIC and FORTRAN use lines of "code" to create applications, branching about in response to explicit or implicit GO TO instructions, Forth defines its processes in these very short words. Most revealing to the new Forth programmer is the realization that Forth has no GO TO at all (and no line numbers either).

Before we get into the process of creating new words, let us look at a few more examples of Forth's use of the stack. Try these at your terminal:

24 3 / . <ret> 8 ok

17 17 * . <ret> 289 ok

29 40 − . <ret> −11 ok

Several important features of Forth are illustrated in these very simple examples.

1. *Forth is interactive.* You can get results immediately following entry of your parameters without need for outside help from "compilers" or "assemblers."

2. *Forth uses postfix notation.* Data precede the identity of the desired operation. If you were to enter 54 + 47 . in the first example, + would not have both the requisite values on the stack when INTERPRET encountered it.

3. *Forth uses spaces as delimiters.* If the entry has been 5447+.,
   INTERPRET would not have recognized it as either a word or a number.
   When that happens, INTERPRET just gives up and prints Forth's error
   message: ? (pronounced "huh?"). The spaces between the numbers
   and words are the telltale signs in the stream of information flowing to
   the interpreter that signify to Forth the difference between valid
   words, numbers, and gibberish.

Problem

Predict the effects on the stack when the following line is entered:

7 3 2 1 17 + + + + .<ret>

Solution

```
      17
   1  1  18
 2  2  2   2  20
 3  3  3   3   3  23
 7  7  7   7   7   7  7  30 ... (empty after .)
```

Remember, + (plus) adds the top two values and replaces them with their sum.

1.3 Keeping Track of the Stack's Contents

All Forth words use, affect, or manipulate the stack in one way or another.
The effect of the Forth word * (pronounced "star") is to reduce the stack
depth by one value as it replaces the top two values with their product. +
(plus), − (minus), and / (slash) have the identical effects on the stack
depth, but the values remaining after their action are the sum, difference,
and quotient, respectively.

One of the Forth programmers' most important responsibilities is keeping track of the stack, in terms of both depth and content. To aid in this, most Forth systems include a special, nondestructive, stack copy word called .S (pronounced "dot ess"). Try it.

1 2 3 .S<ret> 1 2 3 ok

7 5 19 243 .S<ret> 1 2 3 7 5 19 243 ok

If your system does not have a .S (dot ess), see App. A, "Software Tools," for instructions on how to add it to your system.

You may find a pair of values on the bottom of the stack that you did not put there. They were pushed onto the stack by an error routine earlier. Do not worry about them now.

Once you have used Forth to push a bunch of values onto the stack, you may realize that you do not want them there any longer. How do you get all those values *off* your stack? You can dot them off individually:

`.<ret> 243 ok`

`.S<ret> 1 2 3 7 5 19 ok`

`.<ret> 19 ok`

`.S<ret> 1 2 3 7 5 ok`

or even in pairs:

`. .<ret> 5 7 ok`

`.S<ret> 1 2 3 ok`

Note the order!

But this method is time-consuming and inelegant, particularly when there are lots of values involved. Remember `INTERPRET`? Whenever something is entered on the sack that `INTERPRET` cannot recognize, an error message `?` (huh?) is printed, *and the stack is cleared.*

`.S<ret> 1 2 3 4 7 ok`

`//<ret> // ?`

`.S<ret> 0 2 ok` *Z-80 FORTH does not push 0 & 2 onto the stack.*

Note: The 0 and 2 were pushed onto the stack by the error-handling words, and // (slash slash) is definitely *not* OK.

Until the introduction of the utility word `.S` (dot ess), we used the vertical stack representation:

```
1 2
6 3
 4
2 1
```

This method probably is the best way to represent the stack contents, but it is wasteful of space and paper in computer printouts (and in books like this one as well).

On the other hand, the horizontal format, as displayed by .s (dot ess),

```
21 4 63 12
```

with the top of the stack at the right, saves space on the terminal screen and is best suited for illustration of the stack effect of Forth words. We can use this type of notation as a general technique to catalog the stack effects of the Forth words we have encountered thus far. The general form is:

```
WORD ( before ... after )
```

where "before" represents the values on the stack before execution of the word, and "after" describes the contents after. Remember, the top of the stack is on the right, just as printed by .s (dot ess). Examples:

```
*   ( n1 n2 ... prod )
/   ( n1 n2 ... quot )
+   ( n1 n2 ... sum )
.   ( n ... )
```

1.4 Forth Words that Manipulate the Stack

Since Forth insists that the programmer learn to use the stack in operating on the data, it must also provide software tools to make that use of the stack both easy and effective. To demonstrate, enter this:

```
22 DUP<ret>
.S<ret>
```

<u>22 22 ok</u>

DUP (pronounced "dupe"), is for "duplicate," one of the words provided in Forth systems to handle the stack. DUP's function is the duplication of the value on top of the stack, increasing the number of values on the stack by 1 in the process. In the list of predefined Forth words appears an arsenal of such words, the *stack-manipulation tools*. These are words that alter the order of the items on the stack (and allow one to deal from the bottom, as it were). These words give Forth much of its flexibility. Using the stack representation presented above, we can easily visualize the operation of these words, as presented in Table 1.1.

12 The Forth Language

Table 1.1 Forth's Stack-Manipulation Words

Word	Stack notation	Manipulation
DUP	(n1 ... n1 n1)	Duplicates the top number, increasing depth by one.
DROP	(n ...)	Drops the top value, decreasing depth by one.
SWAP	(n1 n2 ... n2 n1)	Swaps the top two numbers; no changes in depth.
ROT	(n1 n2 n3 ... n2 n3 n1)	Copies the third number to the top, moving the top two down.
OVER	(n1 n2 ... n1 n2 n1)	Copies the second value to the top, increasing depth by one.
2DUP	(n1 n2 ... n1 n2 n1 n2)	Duplicates the top two values, increasing depth by two.
2DROP	(n1 n2 ...)	Drops two; depth decreases correspondingly.
2SWAP	(n1 n2 n3 n4 ... n3 n4 n1 n2)	Swaps the top two numbers with the two beneath.
2OVER	(n1 n2 n3 n4 ... n1 n2 n3 n4 n1 n2)	Copies the 3d and 4th numbers to the top.
2ROT	(n1 n2 n3 n4 n5 n6 ... n3 n4 n5 n6 n1 n2)	Rotates the 5th and 6th numbers to the top, moving the others down.

The first five stack-manipulation words operate on individual numbers, and the rest operate on the contents of the stack in pairs. The latter words will prove specially useful later, when we deal with double-length numbers and scientific notation. For now we will focus on the first five.

Suppose you needed to evaluate $Y = A + AX^2$, given A and X on the stack in the order (A, X). Here is how to obtain the answer:

	A X
DUP	A X X
*	A X^2
OVER	A X^2 A
*	A AX^2
+	A + AX^2

The answer is now on the stack. Try it, assuming $A = 15$ and $X = 9$:

15 9 DUP * OVER * + . <ret> 1230 ok

What if the values were reversed on the stack, but the same problem wanted solution? Just precede the line with SWAP.

9 15 SWAP DUP * OVER * + . <ret> 1230 ok

Now for a tougher one. Evaluate $A + BX + CX^2$, given the initial stack order A B C X. Here is a solution which illustrates the usefulness of ROT (pronounced "rote," by the way).

```
        A B C X
DUP     A B C X X
ROT     A B X X C
 *      A B X CX
ROT     A X CX B
 +      A X (CX+B)
 *      A X(CX+B)
 +      A + X(CX+B)
```

which is equivalent to A + BX + CX². Try it:

7 2 9 5 DUP ROT * ROT + * + . <ret> 242 ok

If these solutions seem at first to entail a lot of work employing rather alien terminology, that is OK. Bear with them a little longer. The use of the stack gives Forth its speed and power. Charles Moore would not have been inspired to invent Forth if it were faster, or more efficient, to accomplish this last problem with

```
10 A=7.
20 B=2.
30 C=9.
40 X=5.
50 Y=A+(B*X)+C*(X^2)
60 PRINT Y or TYPE *, Y
```

14 The Forth Language

Besides, in the next chapter you will learn how to combine all the above into a Forth word of your own, so that you will have to type in the DUP s and SWAP s only once per application.

Although the foregoing examples may well be a bit bewildering at first, do bear with them. As is true of most of the better things in this life, a greater investment is required for a greater return. In the case of Forth, the simple algebraic representations that became so familiar to you in seventh grade are not used. *Postfix notation* is used instead. That is the price Forth programmers pay for the speed and power of their language. In the long run, you will find that a typical Forth application will almost "write itself," especially after you have gone through the next several chapters.

As already indicated, the task of learning a new language (or *any* skill, for that matter) is best accomplished by initially forcing oneself to practice it. That is particularly true of the approach used in this book. The problems at the end of each chapter are intended to be a vital part of the learning experience. Some Forth concepts appear *only* in the problems, particularly in the later chapters, and all are directed at the introduction of data processing as well as Forth and scientific principles. Some of the problems are even fun, and in one way or another, all of them will contribute to your understanding of computers and computer languages—but only if you do them.

1.5 Problems

1. Predict the final contents of the stack after entry of the following sequences:

   a. 47 DUP *

   b. 10 20 30 40 * 2SWAP + +   *No way to predict this!*

   c. 89 13 152 −712 ROT DROP ROT

   d. 21417 19258 DUP − DROP

   e. 21417 19258 DUP DROP −

   f. 21417 19258 DROP − DUP   ?

   g. 21417 19258 DROP DUP −   0

   h. 21417 19258 − DUP DROP   2159

   i. 21417 19258 − DROP DUP   ??? 12594

   j. 1 2 3 ROT ROT

2. Use stack notation to prove that 2DUP does not have the same effect as DUP DUP.

3. Write a sequence of Forth words to accomplish the following:

a. (1 2 3 4 ... 4 3 2 1)
   b. (11 22 ... 44 22)
   c. (3 2 1 ... $1^3\ 2^3\ 3^3$)
4. Given $A = 16$, $B = -11$ and $f(x) = A + BX + BX^2$, use Forth to calculate $f(x)$ for $x = 21$.
5. Give a one-word replacement for OVER OVER.

Chapter

2

Words: The Forth Dictionary

A computer's usefulness lies in its ability to do simple, repetitive tasks quickly and easily. The greatest usefulness of a good computer *language*, on the other hand, lies in its ability to identify and execute the sequence of simple jobs which constitute the more complex task desired by the user. Forth's power lies in the manner in which it associates a given task with a series of simple procedures. Forth links these tasks together into a programming structure called a word. Forth words can be linked together to form more complex words, and these new words can then be further linked to form even more powerful and complex words. There is virtually no limit to the complexity of a Forth word.

2.1 The Forth Word

Suppose you need to regularly compute the area and perimeter of a rectangular space. If you need to do it often enough, it will be useful to create a computer procedure to do the job for you. In Forth, you accomplish this by "defining" a Forth "word," a process analogous to "writing" a program in other languages. You would then "execute" your word, a process akin to "running" a program. In the present example, we could call our first word AREA and define it thus:

    : AREA * . ;

First we must inform Forth that we are about to define a new word. That is the function of the leading colon (:) in the definition; : (colon) is a Forth word too. It was defined as part of the Forth system. When

`INTERPRET` (another of Forth's predefined words) encounters : (colon) in the incoming stream of characters, it alerts Forth to begin the process of defining a new word.*

Following the space required to set the colon apart comes the name of the new word, `AREA`, followed by the preexisting Forth words that define `AREA`'s behavior. Finally the semicolon (;) terminates the definition, telling Forth to stop creating a new word and to enter it into Forth's dictionary, the list of words that composes Forth. The dictionary will now be longer by one word, `AREA`, than it was before, and this new word, like any other preexisting Forth word, can be used in the definition of more complex words.

Try typing in the definition:

`: AREA * . ;` <u>ok</u>

Note that Forth did not calculate any area for us, but that it did respond <u>ok</u>. We've just compiled `AREA` into the dictionary. To execute `AREA`, just enter a pair of values onto the stack and follow them with the name of the word to be executed.

`21 14 AREA` <u>294 ok</u>

`7 13 AREA` <u>91 ok</u>

Be careful. Do not just type in the word `AREA` without first providing a pair of values. As we have defined it, `AREA` removes two values from the stack. If there are no values on the stack when `AREA` is executed, an `Empty Stack!` error will result.

A fancier (but not necessarily better) version of `AREA` is

`: AREA * ." the area is " . ;`

where between the * (star) and the . (dot) in the definition we have inserted the Forth word ." (dot quote), a word whose job is to type to the screen whatever follows it, up to the next " (quote) found in the definition. As you will see, the usefulness of ." is enormous.

Enter the definition

`: AREA * ." the area is " . ;` <u>AREA has already been defined. ok</u>

AREA is redefined ok — Z80 FORTH

---

*In most Forth systems, either uppercase or lowercase characters can be used to form the words. In this book, uppercase characters will be used, although later on, in examples and applications, lowercase characters will also appear.

18   The Forth Language

The message occurs because we have now compiled two definitions with the same name into the dictionary. This is not necessarily bad, and it will not bother us here.

Enter a pair of values and execute AREA. *Z80 FORTH redefines the word.*

```
20 20 AREA the area is 400 ok
```

It is a good practice, particularly when first learning Forth, to follow the configuration of the stack through the execution of a new Forth word like AREA. When the word is first executed, there will already be two values on the stack:

```
21   21
14   14   294   (294)=>screen,
     AREA  *            .
```

The ." (dot quote) and " (quote) words have no overall effect on the stack, and the net stack effect of AREA is the removal of two values and the appearance of their product (along with a message) on the screen.

What about the perimeter? Enter this definition:

```
: PERIMETER + 2 * . " the perimeter is " . ;
```

Execute it.

```
14 21 PERIMETER the perimeter is 70 ok
```

It is simple. PERIMETER calculates the sum of the long and short sides, doubles the sum, and "dots" it off the stack to the terminal.

The following table is another way to represent the flow of values to and from the stack during the execution of a Forth word:

Word	Value	Flow
PERIMETER	14 21	At execution time 2 values reside on the stack, 21 on top.
+	35	+ (plus) the first word in the definition of PERIMETER, adds the two values together.
2	35 2	2 is pushed onto the stack.
*	70	The top two values are multiplied.
.	(empty)	And the product is sent to the screen.

Now that we have compiled definitions of area and perimeter into the Forth dictionary, we can use these words to define newer, more powerful, higher-level words, like `SPECS`.

    : SPECS 2DUP AREA ." and " PERIMETER ;

Enter and try it.

    42 17 SPECS the area is 714 and the perimeter is 118 ok

Recall that `2DUP` is a predefined Forth word which duplicates the top two values on the stack. In this example its use allows both `AREA` and `PERIMETER` to have values to use.

    SPECS   42 17
    2DUP   42 17 42 17
    AREA   42 17   (714) => screen
    PERIMETER   (118) => screen

Here we show only the overall effects of `AREA` and `PERIMETER` on the stack, each removing the top two values and sending their respective answers to the output device. Again, the dot quote ... quote words have no effect on the stack depth, and they do not have to be shown here.

Words we define, such as `AREA`, should be reusable. If they are, we can use them any time we have the need for area or perimeter calculations for rectangular objects. Consider the following problem:

Problem

Given the dimensions, calculate the cost of aluminizing and trimming a rectangular mirror flat. The aluminizing costs $22 per square meter and trimming costs $3 per meter. Define a word, `PRICE`, to do the calculation.

Solution

Assuming that the dimensions of the flat will be on the stack when `PRICE` is executed, `PRICE` will have to:

1. Compute the area.
2. Determine the aluminizing cost.
3. Compute the perimeter.
4. Determine the trimming cost.
5. Add the costs together and print the results.

Unfortunately, our words `AREA` and `PERIMETER` are useless in this application. We made them too complex. They not only compute their respective parameters, they output them as well, popping them from the stack, rendering these values unavailable to following words within a higher-level definition. There are at least two important lessons to be learned here.

> *Rule 1*   *Keep it simple.* The simpler the word, the greater the likelihood it will be reusable.
>
> *Rule 2*   *Consider the needs of the highest-level words before writing the low-level words.* Do not write words that destroy their output parameters unless you are finished with them.

We would never have allowed `AREA` and `PERIMETER` to send their results to the terminal if we had known that we would need them later for `PRICE`.

Let us forget our old words `AREA` and `PERIMETER` and redefine them with the intent of enhancing reusability.

```
FORGET SPECS ok

FORGET PERIMETER ok

: AREA * ; ok

: PERIMETER + 2 * ; ok

: SPECS 2DUP AREA ." the area is " . PERIMETER ." and the
 perimeter is " . ; ok
```

When `SPECS` is executed, the result is identical to that observed earlier, but in this case the output operations are all done by the high-level word. The amount of typing is the same (actually a bit less), and the words `AREA` and `PERIMETER` do no more than their names imply, calculating the relevant parameter and leaving its value on the stack.

What about `PRICE`?

```
: PRICE 2DUP AREA 22 *ROT ROT PERIMETER 3 * + ; ok
```

This word does not print out anything at all. But it *does* calculate the total cost of aluminizing and trimming, leaving the result on the stack.

```
PRICE           17    24
2DUP            17    24    17    24
AREA            17    24    408
22              17    24    408   22
*               17    24    8976
ROT             24    8976  17
ROT             8976  17    24
PERIMETER       8976  82
3               8976  82    3
*               8976  246
+               9222
```

Now we need to define a set of high-level output words that can use our simpler words such as AREA or PRICE.

```
: .AREA AREA ." the area is " . ;
: .PERIMETER PERIMETER ." the perimeter is " . ;
: .PRICE PRICE ." the total cost is $" . ;
```

Since Forth uses . (pronounced "dot") as the word to "print" something to the screen, a useful convention is to choose names beginning with a period for words which output values. Each of our "dot words" has a name which clearly identifies its purpose, and each relieves a lower-level word of the responsibility for output, making the lower-level word reusable. Try them.

52 19 .AREA the area is ~~1178~~ 988 ok

23 11 .PRICE the total cost is $ 5770 ok

Let us review the words that we have defined thus far, along with their respective stack effects.

```
AREA            ( length width ... area )
PERIMETER       ( length width ... perimeter )
PRICE           ( length width ... price )
.AREA           ( area ... )
.PERIMETER      ( perimeter ... )
.PRICE          ( price ... )
```

2.2 The Forth Dictionary

Whenever a new Forth word is defined, it is automatically entered into Forth's dictionary. The contents of the dictionary are the words which constitute Forth. One of the phenomenal features of Forth, and the source of its compactness and much of its power, is its ability to "extend" itself. This term means that new Forth words, defined in terms of old Forth words, become old words themselves, at least as far as even newer words are concerned. They can be used to define new words which can be subsequently used in the definition of even newer words which can be used in the definitions of more advanced words, *ad infinitum*.

Another, almost accurate way of expressing this phenomenon is: "Forth is written in Forth." Let us see how that works.

At your terminal enter the Forth word VLIST, followed by a return. You will see a display on your terminal like Fig. 2.1. This is Forth's *vocabulary list*. It begins with the most recently defined word, which in our configuration is .PRICE. Words which are familiar to us have been shaded.

At the base of the dictionary are the earliest, or oldest, definitions—fundamental words used in the definitions of all other words. LIT, for

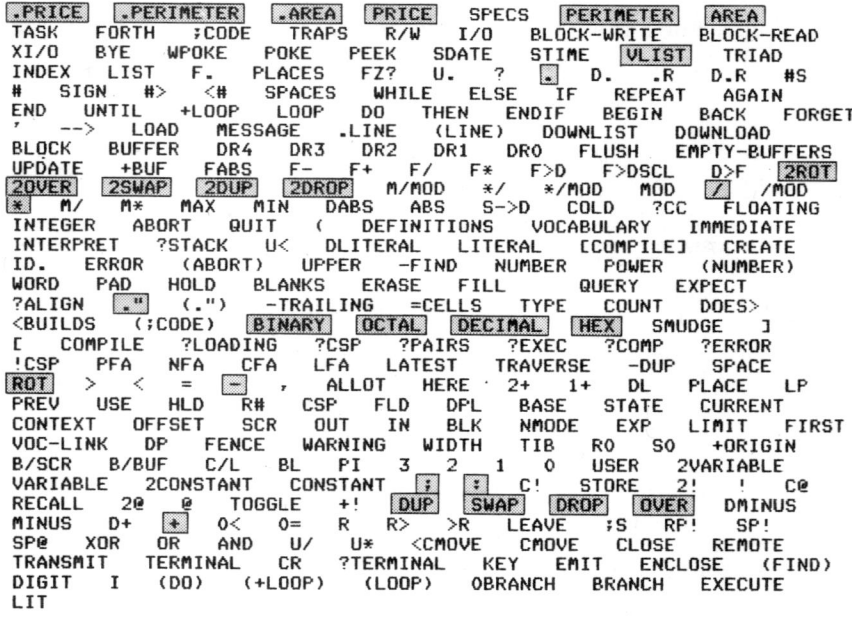

VLIST is replaced by WORDS in Z80 FORTH

The Z80 word list is essentially different, and contains 418 words, not at all in the order shown.

Figure 2.1 The Forth dictionary VLIST

instance, is essentially a stack push. EXECUTE initiates execution of a word, and BRANCH determines the direction of execution in decision-making words.

Every Forth word traces its roots back to these 45 or so words. They are the very essence of Forth. They are *not* written in terms of one another, but they have been defined in the machine code of the computer being used. They are called the "primitives."

Beginning with : (colon) and extending upward to the newest definitions, the dictionary contains words which have been written in terms of both the primitives and other previously defined words. Here is the definition of 2SWAP, for example.

: 2SWAP ROT >R ROT R> ;

Do not be concerned about the definitions of >R and R>. They are primitives which use a special stack called the return stack. Rather, note that 2SWAP is defined in terms of words all of which appear farther down, or earlier in the dictionary. Of the set of five single-number stack-manipulation words we learned previously, all were primitives except for ROT. Its definition is : ROT >R SWAP R> SWAP ; —all primitives.

Highest-level definitions (those at the top of the vocabulary list, and those that you will soon be writing) are usually a blend of high-level words and primitives. In general, the higher the level of the definition, the fewer primitives are employed. Here is the definition of TYPE, a word we shall soon be using to type messages to the terminal.

: TYPE −DUP IF OVER + SWAP DO I C@ EMIT LOOP ELSE DROP THEN ;

Again, the content of the definition is unimportant at this time. Just note that the definition of TYPE contains a fair distribution of primitives and higher-level words.

Now that you have had a chance to examine a VLIST display, you may have been impressed by the variety of names that identify Forth words. It is appropriate at this point to look more closely at the rules about Forth words' names.

Rules for Naming Forth Words

When you define a new Forth word, a new entry for your word is compiled into the dictionary. Since the "name" you select for your word will be used as a label in subsequent dictionary searches, it is imperative that you clearly understand Forth's naming conventions. Forth's own, internal version of the name you have chosen for your new word is incorporated into the Forth dictionary entry in a region called the "name field."

In some Forth systems, poly-Forth and Kitt Peak Forth in particular, the name-field portion of the dictionary entry for the name of your word will consist of:

1. The number of characters in the name you have chosen, followed by
2. The first three characters of the name

In these systems, the name-field portion of a particular dictionary entry cannot exceed four characters (three from the name and the leading count). Even if your choice of a name has many more than three characters, only the character count and the three characters will be used. For example, suppose you compose a Forth application consisting of the words .AREA and PERIMETER. The respective dictionary name-field entries for these words would be 5.AR and 9PER. (*You* would continue to refer to these words by their "given" names of .AREA and PERIMETER, of course.)

The advantage of limiting names to a count and three characters lies in economical use of the computer's memory. The shorter the average name length, the more memory available for data and programs. The disadvantage is greater risk of ambiguity. Suppose your application uses words you have named NINA and NINE. Both are four-character names beginning with NIN. Both will be stored in the dictionary as 4NIN, and whichever was defined most recently will be the only accessible definition, regardless of which the word programmer actually calls for, NINA or NINE.

One way to avoid name ambiguity problems in these Forth systems is to be sure to include numeric identifiers at the *beginning* of your names, rather than at the end. Thus TEST1 and TEST2 would both be identified as 5TES by these systems, whereas 1TEST and 2TEST would be labeled as 51TE and 52TE, respectively.

In other Forth systems, ambiguity is rarely a problem. Most use the convention that the stored representation of the word's name will include a character count, just as above, followed by as many as 31 of the assigned name's characters. If you can safely assume that your Forth applications will not be running on poly-Forth or other three-character-name Forth systems, be as free as you wish with your words' names. On the other hand, if you run a three-character-name system, or if the applications you write may be destined to run on such a system, try to restrict yourself to fairly terse names for your words. Your dictionary will be all the more manageable for your labors.

Whatever your system, there is one delightful feature of Forth names that is infrequently encountered in other computer languages. Within the confines of the rules just presented, you can use just about any of your terminal's symbols to call your words anything you want. If you feel inclined to define a new word with the name [[<<>>]], go right ahead. Forth will accept that just as readily as 1DEMO or TESTPROG. Of course, if you use too many bizarre names, you may have trouble later, when you need to remember what you called a definition. Furthermore, until you have a bit more experience, you should avoid using your terminal's special characters in defining names—and you should especially avoid the "control," "offline," and "break" keys in this context.

Now that you have a good grasp of the naming of the words in the dictionary, we can more closely examine the actual structure of the dictionary. Although most of the details of the structure will have to wait until you have a better grasp of the concepts of addresses and pointers, we can now take our first look at the way in which Forth creates a *threaded* code structure in creating its dictionary.

Dictionary Structure

Every time you define a new word, your Forth system prepares a series of commands and data that will be added to the dictionary as a Forth dictionary entry. Among other things, each dictionary entry consists of:

1. The name of the word
2. The computer code describing what the word is supposed to do.
3. A "pointer" to the word previously defined in the dictionary.

It is this last feature that makes the Forth dictionary so useful to us. In computer jargon, the Forth dictionary is a *linked list*. When the INTERPRETer encounters a name of a Forth word in the stream of characters coming in from the terminal, it begins to search the dictionary for a region labeled with that name. The search begins at the "top" of the dictionary, with the most recent definitions. Forth tries to match the name in the dictionary with the name of the word for which it is looking. If the search fails at the first, or most recent, word, Forth proceeds to the next most recent word. It finds that word using the pointer stored in the just-examined word.

Since Forth dictionary entries come in a wide variety of sizes (our word AREA takes up a lot less dictionary space than does SPECS, for example), the search routines must know how to get from the entry for one word to the corresponding part of the next. For that reason, the design of Forth requires that every word "point to" its predecessor in the dictionary.

Once Forth finds the entry it seeks, it executes the code that it finds in that dictionary entry, and goes on to find the next word in the current

26 The Forth Language

definition. In this way, the running Forth system can thread its way through entry after entry, executing the code that characterizes the definition.

Assuming that you have entered all the example words that we have presented thus far, your dictionary will have the structure represented in Fig. 2.1. Now you need to learn the tricks required to keep the size of your dictionary managable.

2.3 Controlling the Dictionary

The amount of a computer's memory that is occupied by programming information sets a limit on the amount of data that can be stored or processed by the computer. In Forth systems the dictionary is used for both program storage (Forth words) and data storage (variables, constants, and arrays, as discussed in Chap. 4). The amount of memory available for the dictionary is a function of the type of computer used and the amount of memory used by the computer's operating system. The Forth word ROOM can be used to determine the amount of memory available for additions to the dictionary. Try it. If your system lacks ROOM, see App. A, "Software Tools," for its definition.

ROOM<ret> 24944 bytes available ok

ROOM does not exist as a Z-80 word, and I can not find any comparable word.

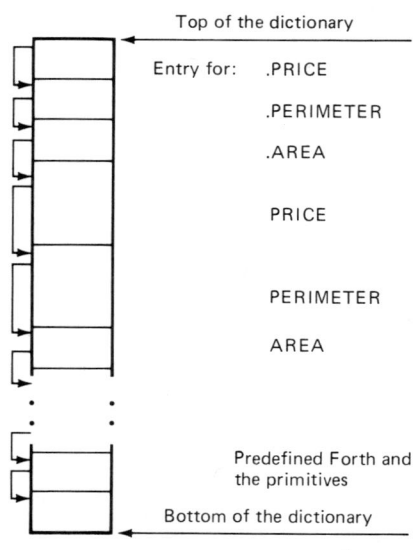

Figure 2.2 Forth Dictionary structure

If you do not know what a byte is as yet, do not worry. We will be covering that concept in Chap. 3. For now, remember that one typed character requires one byte for storage. At this point, nearly 25,000 bytes are available on the PDP-11 used to prepare the examples for this book. How many will be used up by entering a new word? Enter one and find out.

```
: WISH ." I speak Forth fluently " ;<ret> ok

ROM<ret> 24906 bytes available ok

24944 24906 - .<ret> 38 ok
```

Thirty-eight bytes; the new word takes up very little space in the dictionary, and execution of our new word gives the expected result.

```
WISH<ret> I speak Forth fluently ok
```

Redefinition

The structure of the Forth compiler system includes a provision that checks the dictionary as a new word is being defined. If that name has already been used, Forth lets you know. Try redefining WISH.

```
: WISH ." I'm a Sphinx and I speak in riddles " ; <ret>
WISH has already been defined! ok
```

The redefinition is OK, but Forth wants you to know, just in case your choice of duplicate names was inadvertent. Now execute WISH.

```
WISH<ret> I'm a Sphinx and I speak in riddles ok
```

When you type a Forth word, the system searches the dictionary from the top down, starting at the most recent definition. The old definition is still there, however, as you can see with a VLIST:

```
VLIST<ret>

WISH WISH .PRICE .PERIMETER .AREA .. .. . .
```

However, it cannot be executed. To get to the earlier definition, you must tell Forth to FORGET the most recently defined version.

```
FORGET WISH<ret> ok

WISH<ret> I speak Forth fluently ok
```

28   The Forth Language

`FORGET` forgets not only the word you tell it to forget, but all words defined subsequently as well.

```
FORGET .AREA<ret> ok

VLIST<ret>

PRICE PERIMETER AREA TASK ... etc.
```

If you try to execute any of the words `WISH`, `.AREA`, `.PERIMETER`, and `.PRICE`, Forth will not recognize them. They have truly been forgotten. Now that you have mastered the basics of `FORGET`, it is time to get into the details of `FORGET` at an advanced level. At the same time, we will take this opportunity to further explore the structure of the dictionary.

Advanced `FORGET`ting

Now and then you will forget a crucial part of a definition while you are entering it. This most commonly occurs when you are entering a complex set of words which must appear in a definition as a matched set. As you will see in Chap. 5, the words `DO` and `LOOP` compose such a set. In a definition, the appearance of `DO` must be followed by `LOOP` someplace later. Sometimes, a programmer leaves out one of these words (usually `LOOP`).

When such a programming blunder occurs, Forth prints a cryptic error message, and in some systems, the interpreter refuses to mark the definition of the new, "flawed" word as complete. No other word will be able to use the flawed word in a definition, because incomplete words are not found as the interpreter builds a new dictionary definition.

If, by using the flaky word in a definition or by attempting to execute it directly, you stubbornly attempt to force Forth to accept the flawed word ("What does this computer know about what I want to do, anyway?"), yet another error message will appear. Either `Dictionary search failed` or the suspect word's name, followed by a question mark, will be printed.

```
RUBBISH<ret> RUBBISH?
```

At the same time, though, a `VLIST` will show the *name* of the word on the top of the dictionary, right where you thought you had put it.

```
VLIST<ret> RUBBISH TRASH DETRITUS . . . . . ok
```

This feature of some Forth interpreters is intended to prevent the inadvertent use of syntactically flawed words in otherwise OK definitions. The obvious intent is to keep the "debugging" of programs to a minimum.

Words   29

When you have created such a nonfunctional word, the easiest solution to the situation is to simply FORGET the unsatisfactory version of the word, and then redefine it. But in the midst of all this cleverness, an interesting quandary emerges. How can Forth FORGET a word that cannot be found in the dictionary? FORGET uses the same dictionary-search tricks as do all the other Forth words. The solution lies in the actions of another Forth word that goes by the unlikely name of SMUDGE.

SMUDGE<ret> ok

SMUDGE is supported in Z-80 FORTH, but is not listed in the glossary (also UNSMUDGE).

SMUDGE marks the *last* word defined, flawed or not, as complete. In those systems where its use is required, it works only on the most recent word, thereby avoiding the need to know the last word's name. Once SMUDGEd, even a bad word can then be forgotten with FORGET.

FORGET RUBBISH<ret> ok

Your system may not need SMUDGE. If you are curious, you can look closely at your VLIST to see if it is listed; or you can wait until you need to forget an incomplete word.

If you are either incredibly good or incredibly careful, you may never need SMUDGE and FORGET. More likely, though, you will use these words (at least FORGET) frequently. It has been said that programmers have not even begun to learn Forth until they have learned to "forget" properly. Indeed, as you will see, the ability to FORGET an entire portion of the dictionary, as dreadful as that may sound, gives the Forth programmer a useful tool in controlling the size of the dictionary, allowing efficient use of the computer's memory.

In Chap. 3 we will take a much closer look at the way the computer does math. Now that you can compile new words into the dictionary, arithmetic operations will become almost enjoyably easy. Before going on to the worlds of Forth math, however, we will continue to explore the Forth dictionary. And before you go much farther into the inner workings of the language, you must begin to understand Forth's *multicontext vocabulary*.

2.4 Forth Vocabularies

Without going into the details of its operation, enter the following Forth phrase at your terminal:

7 EMIT<ret> ok

You should have heard the ring of your terminal bell. Try it again. In Chap. 6 you will learn all the details of EMIT. For now, just note that

EMIT has the responsibility of sending to your terminal the "codes" for the characters that make up the communications system between you, Forth, and your computer. The value of 7 happens to correspond to the code for the terminal's bell. What will happen if the 7 EMIT phrase is included within a definition? Finding the answer to that question will take you a long way toward understanding one of the more perplexing aspects of computer programming, the difference between *execution*-time behavior and *compile*-time behavior.

Run-Time versus Compile-Time Behavior

Enter this definition:

: TOOT 7 EMIT ; <ret> ok

The 7 EMIT phrase is part of the stream of commands flowing from your terminal to Forth, just as it was above. This time, however, when you passed Forth the phrase *within a definition,* the bell did *not* ring.

Obviously, the colon preceding the 7 EMIT phrase did something to prevent 7 EMIT from "executing" as the Forth words constituting the phrase passed through the interpretive process.

▶ *Indeed, colon's principal task is to alert Forth that subsequent incoming words are to be "compiled" into the dictionary, rather than "executed."*

This concept is neither new nor unique to Forth. In BASIC, for example, if you were to enter

PRINT CHR$(7)

the terminal bell would also ring. But if you were to enter

10 PRINT CHR$(7)

nothing audible would occur. Rather, BASIC would enter this line into the program you were composing. Like Forth, BASIC is interactive (slower and far less flexible, to be sure, but interactive, nonetheless). To BASIC's interpreter, a line beginning with a (statement) number is a signal to enter a mode in which BASIC infers that incoming information is to be collected in an intelligent fashion for *later* use.

In much the same way, Forth is alerted by : (colon) to enter the COMPILE state, a mode of operation in which nothing is actually executed, but in which new dictionary definitions are neatly interwoven from the incoming sequential references to older words. It is the semicolon (;), counterfoil to colon, that "turns off" the COMPILE mode and returns Forth to EXECUTION state.

As you have seen, to execute a Forth word, all you need to do is enter its name.

TOOT<ret> ok

Obviously, TOOT is the equivalent of 7 EMIT.

But there are times when we need to have a word execute while Forth is still in its COMPILE state. Indeed, the most important word that has to actually *do something* while Forth is in its COMPILE state is ; (semicolon). What the semicolon *does,* of course, is to return the system to EXECUTION state.

Imagine what would transpire if there were no Forth word that actually *did* anything other than create dictionary entries while in COMPILE state. There could never be any escape from the COMPILE state, nor would there be anything for the Forth system to do with incoming information except to create an ever-increasing but unusable dictionary.

Immediate Words

There is something obviously different about ; (semicolon) and the other words that can actually do useful work even while Forth is in its COMPILE state. (Such words are *immediate* words, by the way.) The design of Forth allows you to actually create your own immediate words. To assist you, a special Forth word has been created expressly for this purpose. Its name is IMMEDIATE, and its task is straightforward.

▶ IMMEDIATE *marks the last word defined as an immediate word.*

Try it with TOOT.

: TOOT 7 EMIT ; IMMEDIATE<ret> ok

Now, if you use TOOT in another definition, you will actually hear the bell ringing at compile time, during the creation of the dictionary entry, rather than later, at execution time. Try this definition:

: HARK TOOT ." I Can Hear Again! " ;<ret< ok

This time you should actually hear TOOT's toot right after you depress the <return> key.

You might ask what will happen to an immediate word during subsequent execution of a word which contained it at compile time. You can do the experiment yourself. Just execute `HARK`.

```
HARK<ret> I Can Hear Again! ok
```

Maybe so, but you certainly did not hear the terminal bell—not this time.

The bell rang at *compile time*. It will not ring again at *execution time*. Indeed, when you have learned how, a close examination of the dictionary entry for `HARK` will reveal that *no references to the immediate word* `TOOT` *were included in the compilation of* `HARK`.

You do not get to have it both ways. Either a word is immediate and it executes at compile time, or it is not immediate and it executes at *run time*. In later chapters you will encounter other immediate words. In this chapter, the one area where immediate words are of great importance involves the generation of separate but parallel vocabularies.

Enter these phrases:

```
VOCABULARY ENGLISH IMMEDIATE<ret> ok

VOCABULARY SPANISH IMMEDIATE<ret> ok
```

Do you have other favorite languages? Whatever they are, enter them:

```
VOCABULARY FRENCH IMMEDIATE<ret> ok

VOCABULARY PIG-LATIN IMMEDIATE<ret> ok
```

You can define as many vocabularies as you wish. Indeed, none of the names of the human languages that we have chosen to use as examples here have been predefined in Forth. Rather, `VOCABULARY`, like : (colon), is a defining word. It enters new definitions into the dictionary, definitions of a very special sort. These words define the context of the entries to the dictionary.

The words which follow `VOCABULARY` in the above entries become the names of new vocabularies in the Forth dictionary. Execution of any one of these names alerts Forth that incoming definitions will belong to that particular vocabulary, at least until there is a switch of context. As is so often the case, the best way to appreciate these concepts is through example. Enter these phrases:

```
ENGLISH DEFINITIONS<ret> ok

 : GREETING ." Hello " ; <ret> ok

 : FAREWELL ." Goodbye " ;<ret> ok
```

```
SPANISH DEFINITIONS<ret> ok
: GREETING ." Buenos Dias ." ;<ret> GREETING has already been defined! ok
: FAREWELL ." Vaya con Dios ." ; <ret> FAREWELL has already been defined!
ok
PIG-LATIN DEFINITIONS<ret> ok
: GREETING ." ello-Hay" ;<ret> GREETING has already been defined! ok
: FAREWELL ." Oodgay Eyebay " ;<ret· FAREWELL has already been defined! ok
FRENCH DEFINITIONS<ret> ok
: GREETING ." Bon Jour " ; <ret> GREETING has already been defined! ok
: FAREWELL ." Au Revoir " ; <ret> FAREWELL has already been defined! ok
FORTH DEFINITIONS ok
```

[handwritten annotation: In Z-80 FORTH, the second (and succeeding) same names in different vocabularies are just compiled without comment.]

The word DEFINITIONS selects the particular vocabulary into which the word will be entered. From that time on, even if two words have the same name, there will be no ambiguities *at run time*, as long as the programmer has been careful to choose the correct vocabulary when composing the word in the first place.

Interlingual Applications of Forth's Dictionary

Although interlingual translations were not by any means the original purpose of Forth, it is obviously ideal for them, as we can now demonstrate:

```
ENGLISH GREETING Hello ok
PIG-LATIN FAREWELL Oodgay Eyebay ok
SPANISH GREETING Buenos Dias ok
FRENCH FAREWELL Au Revoir ok
```

No wonder that Forth was chosen by a worldwide microelectronics firm for the control of its hand-held language translator. As you will see in Part II, the same techniques can even be used first to write high-level technical applications in one language and then to link them to a different human vocabulary, making Forth a truly universal computer communications system.

When exploring different vocabularies, always remember to reset the current system vocabulary to Forth before going on to other tasks.

34 The Forth Language

```
FORTH DEFINITIONS<ret> ok
```

In all Forth systems, `FORTH` is the base vocabulary. When you define a word in another vocabulary, that list of dictionary entries will be searched first, but thereafter, the Forth vocabulary will be searched as well. In this way, it is said that "all vocabularies chain to Forth." Indeed, almost all Forth systems have two other vocabularies, the `EDITOR` vocabulary and the `ASSEMBLER` vocabulary. More on the former in Chap. 6. The latter will have to wait until Part II, when you have more experience in programming in Forth.

One final note on vocabularies: When you use `FORGET` to forget a defintion, Forth will `FORGET` the contents of the dictionary beginning at the word forgotten, and extending through *all* the newer words, regardless of the vocabulary in which they were originally defined. The underlying reasons for this will become obvious when you learn more about the structure of the dictionary, and the uses of a Forth variable called the *dictionary pointer*.

2.5 Problems

1. Define a word called `CUBED` to type out the cube of the top number on the stack. Your word should behave like this:

   ```
   2 CUBED<ret> 8 ok
   ```

   (When you test your new word, the answer you obtain may appear to be incorrect if the value on the top of the stack is greater than 31. That is a function of the way in which computers store numbers. In Chap. 3 you will learn how to get around this limitation.)

2. Define a word called `SECONDS` which computes the distance a dropped object will fall toward the Earth in the number of seconds which is on the stack at the time the word is executed. In case you have forgotten, distance = $gt^2/2$ where g = 10 m/sec² or g = 32 ft/s². If you use USCS (U.S. customary system) units, your word will work like this:

   ```
   2 SECONDS<ret> Fall 64 feet ok

   4 SECONDS<ret> Fall 256 feet ok

   10 SECONDS<ret> Fall 1600 feet ok
   ```

   and the metric version should operate thus:

   ```
   2 SECONDS<ret> Fall 20 meters ok

   10 SECONDS<ret> Fall 500 meters ok
   ```

3. a. Define a word VOLTS to calculate the IR drop across a resistor of resistance R (in ohms) carrying current I (in amperes). The word should have the following stack effects:

$$V = IR$$

VOLTS (R I ... I V)

b. Using VOLTS in the definition, calculate the power dissipation of the same resistor with a new word called POWER. This word can dot the results to the terminal. In case you have forgotten:

> Twinkle, twinkle little star,
> Power equals I squared R."

4. Explain what would happen in Prob. 3b if the stack effects of VOLTS had been

VOLTS (R I ... V)

Chapter

3

Numbers

In one way or another, all computer applications are manipulations of either numbers or numerical representations. Indeed, this generalization is even true of text-editing and word-processing applications, for individual characters are actually stored in the computer memory as numerically coded values. It follows that, to be proficient, a programmer must be well versed in the ways in which computers deal with numbers.

3.1 Number Concepts

Although the exact details of the techniques of data encoding vary from machine to machine, all contemporary computer systems store and process information in a binary (or base-two) format. To those accustomed to a decimal (or base-ten) world, the computer designer's choice of a binary numbering system for data storage probably seems peculiar. But the binary numeric system is ideally suited for machine processing of information.

In many areas, not only computer applications, the simplest judgments can always be made when one has to deal with quantized phenomena which exhibit a minimum number of clearly differing states. When there are no more than two possibilities, these sorts of phenomena are called "binary quantities." The spin quantum number of an arbitrarily chosen electron, for instance, must be either $+\frac{1}{2}$ or $-\frac{1}{2}$, nothing else. A light switch is either on or off; no in-between state applies. And there are no more than two options for the hopeful mother; she is either pregnant or not pregnant.

The *design* and *fabrication* of a device to store information and to process data are greatly simplified if the device need never discriminate between more than two distinct states in any single decision-making process, even though the ultimate *use* of such a device may well be complicated by such a design decision.

In the context of this book, it is especially important for the user or programmer of a data-acquisition computer system to clearly understand the realities of computer design, for the process of data gathering and reduction requires that the information being processed undergo a (usually rapid) conversion from instrument format to machine-compatible format. Inasmuch as all computer systems store incoming data in a binary format, it is appropriate to begin the study of computer numbers with an introduction to the binary numbering system.

Binary Numbers

The binary numbering system follows the same rules as the decimal numbering system, even though there are fewer possibilities for the value of a given digit. In the familiar decimal system, each digit represents an integer value ranging from zero to nine. In the binary system, however, the only allowed values a digit can have are zero and one. So it follows that the binary representation of a particular quantity will require more digits than the decimal representation of the same quantity. We will soon see how this aspect of "computer numerology" affects Forth's number-handling methodology.

Counting in binary proceeds thus: 0, 1, 10, 11, 100, 101, 110, 111, 1000, 1001, 1010, 1011, 1100, 1101, 1110, 1111, 10000, etc. It does seem weird to the uninitiated, but rest assured that you will become comfortable with it.

The value used as the *base* of a number system is called the *radix* of that system. Thus, ten is the radix of the decimal system and two is the radix in binary operations. In addition to binary, however, several other number systems are commonly used in computer applications. Table 3.1 illustrates various ways of representing numbers in several radices. The number systems used by the Romans and the domino system are included for historical interest, not because they find any widespread applications in contemporary computer systems.

Unfamiliar Radices

Having learned to count in decimal in our early years, most of us rarely give any thought to the way in which we customarily represent numbers. But when we are forced to do so, some puzzling facts emerge. For instance, why is there no *single* symbol for "ten," the base of our familiar number system? For that matter, why are there no symbols for "two" in binary, "eight" in octal, and "sixteen" in hexadecimal?

Table 3.1 Comparison of Numbering Schemes for Various Bases

Domino	Roman	Binary	Quartal	Octal	Decimal	Hexadecimal
		0	0	0	0	0
.	I	1	1	1	1	1
:	II	10	2	2	2	2
...	III	11	3	3	3	3
: :	IV	100	10	4	4	4
: ·:	V	101	11	5	5	5
: : :	VI	110	12	6	6	6
: : : ·	VII	111	13	7	7	7
: : : :	VIII	1000	20	10	8	8
: : : : ·	IX	1001	21	11	9	9
: : : : :	X	1010	22	12	10	A
: : : : : ·	XI	1011	23	13	11	B
: : : : : :	XII	1100	30	14	12	C
: : : : : : ·	XIII	1101	31	15	13	D
: : : : : : :	XIV	1110	32	16	14	E
: : : : : : : ·	XV	1111	33	17	15	F
: : : : : : : :	XVI	0000	100	20	16	10
: : : : : : : : ·	XVII	10001	101	21	17	11

The answer lies at the foundation of number theory. The largest single character representation of a quantity in a single-base number system is 1 less than the base; 9 in decimal, 1 in binary, 3 in quartal, and so on. In each system the base number turns out to be the smallest quantity requiring two digits for representation.

In binary that quantity is expressed as 10 (pronounced "one zero"; see Table 3.1). In octal that quantity is also expressed as 10 (again pronounced "one zero," *not* "ten"), and in hexadecimal the base is again expressed as "one zero." The pronunciation "ten" is reserved for use with decimal numbers.

This ambiguity, resulting from most people's obviously understandable identification of "10" with "ten" is a common problem in introductory computer science courses. Indeed, even experienced programmers occasionally forget to specify the base of the relevant numbering system when citing or using a possibly ambiguous value or number.

To avoid the possibility of confusion, programmers traditionally express the base of the numbering system with subscripts. The base of the octal system is expressed as 10_8 to avoid confusion with the base of the decimal system. Likewise, 10_2 represents the base of the binary system, and 10_{16} represents the base of the hexadecimal system. In this context, incidentally, unless specified otherwise the subscript is always assumed to be decimal.

3.2 Nondecimal Arithmetic Operations

In computer programming operations it is frequently useful for the programmer to be able to carry out arithmetic operations in binary and other nondecimal radices.

Binary Arithmetic

Addition of two binary numbers, for instance, is straightforward. Just remember to add vertically and to "carry" whenever the sum of the digits equals or exceeds the base. The key here is $0 + 1 = 1$ but $1 + 1 = 10_2$.

Binary	Decimal	Binary	Decimal
1011	11	11101	29
+ 1100	+12	+01001	+9
10111	= 23	100110	= 38

Subtraction is equally simple, provided borrowing is done carefully.

Binary	Decimal
1011	11
−100	−4
111	= 7

Although the computer stores and manipulates all its numbers in binary, programmers usually use octal or hexadecimal representations of numbers, as discussed in Sec. 3.4.

Octal Arithmetic

Here again, remember to carry whenever the sum of the digits exceeds the base, in this case eight. The key is $7 + 1 = 10_8$.

```
  777      2367     177170
 +123     + 417   −   7171
 ----     -----    ------
 1122     3006     167777
```

Hexadecimal Arithmetic

The inclusion of the representations A through F in the number set makes hexadecimal (hex) math seem harder at first, but with practice it too becomes straightforward. As shown below, nearly all computer manufacturers have adopted the hexadecimal system for representing the computer's binary number system. Thus, understanding hex math takes on an added importance.

Remember that $A = 9_{16} + 1$ and that $F + 1 = 10_{16}$.

Also, always represent 10_{10} as 0A rather than A to avoid confusion with the *letter* A, 11_{10} as 0B rather than just B, and so on.

Hex	Decimal	Hex	Decimal
4A	74	1F0A	7946
+321	801	+1B3E	6974
36B	875	3A48	14920

You will be doing some practice arithmetic in hexadecimal and octal shortly. Before delving more deeply into the methods with which computers carry out arithmetic operations, you need to consider the manner in which computer systems store numeric representations.

3.3 Storage of Numbers in Memory

Modern computing equipment uses solid-state memory devices which consist of large arrays of information-storage locations. Each individual location stores an electrical image of an individual *binary digit*, or *bit*. Collections of storage locations are required for the representation of numbers bigger than 1, obviously, and the design and fabrication of solid-state computer memory chips is a very important facet of the contemporary electronics industry.

In Part II we will look closely at hardware aspects of such memory systems. For now, however, we need to concentrate on their applications in number representation and storage.

One design parameter which characterizes a particular computer is the number of individual locations, or bits, allocated for the storage of one number. One binary digit can be represented by the state of one individual location, 0 or 1. Numbers larger than 1 obviously require more than one location. For example, the state of each two locations could represent two bits corresponding to any decimal digit from 0 to 3:

0 0   0
0 1   1
1 0   2
1 1   3

This is still too few bits to be useful for most scientific computations.

Indeed, the single most descriptive attribute of any computer system is the number of bits allocated by the designer for the manipulation of numbers in the system's registers and memory locations. This value is the *word length* of the computer (not to be confused with Forth's special use of the word "word"). Regardless of the hardware designer's design, the implementation of Forth on a particular computer is predicated on the storage of numbers in groups of individual storage locations 16_{10} bits in length. These groups are called *16-bit cells*.

Forth's use of a 16-bit cell length explains the popularity of this language on computer systems designed to use 16-bit words, such as the Digital Equipment Corporation PDP-11 or the Motorola 68000, and on the 8-bit microprocessors such as the Intel 8080, Zilog Z-80, and Rockwell 6502, where two 8-bit words are combined to represent a 16-bit Forth cell.

The individual bits in a cell are numbered from 0 to 15, with the least significant bit on the right.

For some operations, half a cell is enough. Character representations, in particular, need only 8 bits to represent any letter, punctuation mark, or numeral. Almost all computer systems, regardless of word length, can operate in 8-bit groupings called "bytes." The lower bits, those numbered 0 through 7, compose the lower byte of a cell, and bits 8 through 15 are the upper byte. The relationship between bits, bytes, and cells is shown in Fig. 3.1.

Within a 16-bit cell it is possible to represent binary numbers ranging from

    0000000000000000 through 1111111111111111

in binary or

    0 through 65,535

in decimal. Since each bit conveys so little information, binary numbers tend to be long and difficult to use. It is therefore convenient to use shorthand methods to represent binary numbers. The first of these, familiar to users of Digital Equipment Corporation equipment, encodes binary into octal. The other commonly employed system encodes binary into hexadecimal.

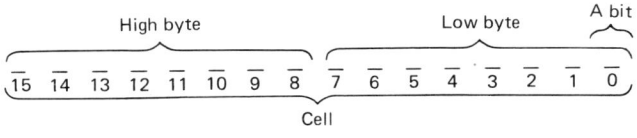

Figure 3.1 A 16-bit cell

3.4 Binary Representations

A computer has absolutely no trouble distinguishing between the binary values 00001000010 and 000000100010. That these fairly long strings of binary digits look very similar to a human observer is of no consequence to a computer. Because it is intrinsically poor at pattern recognition, the computer simply interprets these as differing numbers. On the other hand, a human observer, much better at pattern recognition than a machine, would first be struck by the obvious similarities between the bit patterns in these binary values. To such an observer the differences would appear only after a fairly close inspection of the long strings of digits.

It is therefore not surprising that human programmers programming in binary make lots of mistakes. To avoid these inevitable errors, all computer manufacturers and language designers prefer to use numbering systems with base values greater than two. Furthermore, conversion from one radix to another is enormously simplified if the number bases of the two systems are powers of some common radix. Unfortunately, that qualification eliminates decimal, but it opens the door for both octal and hexadecimal encoding processes. Here is how they work.

Consider a 3-bit binary number. The possible values such a number can have range from 000 to 111_2 or 0 through 7_8.

Binary*	Octal
000	0
001	1
010	2
011	3
100	4
101	5
110	6
111	7

*Bit 0 is the 2^0 place. Bit 1 is the 2^1 place. Bit 2 is the 2^2 place.

Thus, 101 is $2^0 + 2^2 = 1 + 4 = 5$ and $010 = 2^1 = 2$.

Octal Encoding

If we divide a 16-bit number into groups of 3 bits each, beginning at the right and leaving the most significant bit as a group of 1, we can use the above technique to "code" each group of bits into one octal digit.

$$\frac{1}{1} \quad \frac{111}{7} \quad \frac{101}{5} \quad \frac{001}{1} \quad \frac{110}{6} \quad \text{corresponds to in octal}$$

The key is to remember that, going from right to left within a group, the three binary digits correspond to 1, 2, and 4, respectively.

Decoding is simply the reverse. Remember, the most significant bit stands alone in octal encoding. The leftmost digit in the octal representation of a 16-bit number *must* be either 1 or 0, nothing else. Octal encoding is used exclusively by Digital Equipment Corporation; all other companies use hexadecimal.

Hexadecimal Encoding

If a 16-bit cell is divided into 4 groups of 4 bits each, encoding into hexadecimal proceeds in an equally straightforward fashion. Within a group, again proceeding from right to left, the individual bits correspond to 1, 2, 4, and 8, respectively.

$$\frac{1111}{F} \quad \frac{1011}{B} \quad \frac{1000}{8} \quad \frac{0100}{4}$$

Decoding is equally easy. Try decoding a few cells. Later in this chapter a method for using Forth to check your work will be described.

3.5 Signed Numbers

The representation of a value within a 16-bit cell limits the range of possible values a number can have from 0 to $2^{16} - 1$ (1111111111111111_2 or 177777_8 or $FFFF_{16}$). If negative numbers are also to be represented, there must be some provision for representing them as well. The convention used by most computer systems to represent negative numbers is called "two's complementing."

The binary representation of the process of subtraction of 1 from 0 looks like this:

$$\begin{array}{r} 0\,0\,0\,0\,0\,0\,0\,0\,0\,0\,0\,0\,0\,0\,0\,0 \\ -0\,0\,0\,0\,0\,0\,0\,0\,0\,0\,0\,0\,0\,0\,0\,1 \\ \hline 1\,1\,1\,1\,1\,1\,1\,1\,1\,1\,1\,1\,1\,1\,1\,1 = 177777_8 \end{array}$$

At every step we must borrow from the position to the left until, at the leftmost bit, we borrow from an imaginary 17th bit. Since we have actually written another way of representing $0 - 1$, this must also be an alternative representation of -1. If that is the case, adding this binary representation to another value should actually decrease the other value by 1. Calculate $7 - 1$ by *adding* the binary representation of -1 to the corresponding representation of 7.

$$0\ 0\ 0\ 0\ 0\ 0\ 0\ 0\ 0\ 0\ 0\ 0\ 0\ 1\ 1\ 1 = 7_8$$
$$+\ 1\ 1\ 1\ 1\ 1\ 1\ 1\ 1\ 1\ 1\ 1\ 1\ 1\ 1\ 1\ 1 = 177777_8 = -1_{10}$$
$$\text{Carry bit}\quad (1)\ 0\ 0\ 0\ 0\ 0\ 0\ 0\ 0\ 0\ 0\ 0\ 0\ 0\ 1\ 1\ 0 = 6_8$$

At the left end we see that addition propagated a carry of the last place leftward out of the 16-bit number field. As far as our representation of the sum is concerned, that bit is gone, and the rightmost 16 bits hold the binary representation of the correct sum, 6. In fact, the carry to the left is recognized by the computer hardware, which sets a special bit called the "carry bit" in the hardware whenever the result of an addition causes a carry condition. Some of the machine's internal processes use this bit, but we will not need to be concerned with it at this time.

It is important to recognize that computers do not do subtraction in the common sense of the word. Rather, two's-complement *addition* is employed.

For example, the Forth phrase:

```
24 15 - . <ret> 9 ok
```

is executed by the computer by

1. Pushing 24 onto the stack
2. Pushing 15 onto the stack
3. Two's complementing the top stack value (15) and *adding* it to the one below
4. Dotting off the difference

The Forth word − (pronounced "minus") then, is seen in a new light. Its responsibility is twofold, generating the representation of the negative value and then adding the top two values.

Similarly, INTERPRET has a part to play in this business as well. In the Forth phrase

```
24 -15 + . <ret> 9 ok
```

NUMBER, the Forth word that INTERPRET uses to push numbers onto the stack, will automatically push the two's complement of 15 onto the stack when it spots the minus sign in the stream of incoming characters.

The most significant consequence of the two's-complement system becomes obvious when we consider binary representations of several values.

Decimal	Two's-complement binary representation
24	0000000000011000
−24	1111111111101000
512	0000001000000000
−512	1111111000000000
20000	0100111000100000
−20000	1011000111100000

Note that every negative value has a 1 in bit 15. Indeed, the two's-complement notation not only allows the computer to do its subtractions and additions with only an addition instruction, it also allows use of the most significant bit as a *sign bit*. To determine whether a number is negative, the computer need only check the value of bit 15. Figure 3.2 illustrates this use of the sign bit.

It is important to recognize that the representation of negative numbers is more complicated than simply setting bit 15. If it were that easy, −1 would be represented as $100001_{(8)}$, rather than $177777_{(8)}$.

The useful way to appreciate this method of representing negative numbers is to consider a familiar example, the counter on an audio tape recorder. Such a device is usually a 3-digit decimal counter which advances as the tape plays. On rewind the counter runs backward. When it reaches 0, the next number to appear is 999, corresponding to −1; 998 corresponds to −2 and so on. The obvious conclusion is that $0 - 1 = 999$, just as in the octal computer representation $0 - 1 = 177777$.

Always remember that both positive and negative numbers are represented as strings of binary digits. There is no special state or representation for negative values. To demonstrate this, enter the following at your terminal:

	Unsigned Numbers		
Hexadecimal	0	7FFF	FFFF
Decimal	0	32767	65535
Octal	0	077777	177777
	Signed Numbers		
Hexadecimal	8000	FFFF	7FFF
Decimal	−32768	−1	32767
Octal	100000	177777	077777

Figure 3.2 Two's-complement representation

46 The Forth Language

```
-1 .<ret> -1 ok

-1 U.<ret> 65535  ok
```

U. (pronounced "you dot") is the Forth word that outputs a 16-bit number under the assumption that bit 15 does not represent the sign but is just another significant binary digit. Its name means "unsigned print."

Prove it in binary.

```
BINARY<ret> ok

-1 .<ret> -1 ok

-1 U.<ret> 1111111111111111 ok

DECIMAL ok
```

This is the first time we have used BINARY and DECIMAL, which are Forth words that change the base or radix of Forth's input and output routines. If your system does not seem to have BINARY, see App. A, "Software Tools," for a quick fix. Forth responded to U. by putting the binary representation of −1 on the stack with a string of 1s, the machine's representation of *both* −1 and 65535. This apparent abiguity will not be as burdensome as might first appear, since we will be using signed numbers most of the time, and Forth will take care of the signs.

3.6 Single-Integer Mathematics

The math words + (plus), − (minus), * (star), and / (slash) were first used in Chap. 1. At that point it was inappropriate to elaborate on the inner workings of such words, but now that you understand the techniques used by the computer to store numbers, we can further explore their capabilities and limitations.

Enter this phrase at your terminal.

```
1000 1000 *.<ret> 16960 ok
```

Everyone knows that 1000 × 1000 = 1000000, not 16960. What happened?

The binary representation of 1000000_{10} is 11110100001001000000, a 20-binary-digit value which cannot be represented in less than 20 bits. When * (star) carried out its multiplication of the top two stack values, only the rightmost 16 bits of the product were retained on the top of the stack.

*I think $1,000,000_{10}$ should be:

11110000110101000000000$_2$ yet this does not work out — the right 16 bits then = $27,146_{10}$, not $16,960_{10}$ which FORTH gives. Something else must happen.

Numbers 47

The left 4 bits were lost. The remaining part, 0100001001000000, is the binary representation of 16960, the value duly presented to the terminal by dot.

There is a simple solution to this dilemma, however. The next section will introduce special Forth "double-integer" words which greatly expand the system's ability to handle large numbers.

Here is a pair of phrases to enter:

37 3 / . 12 ok

38 3 / . 12 ok

Slash produces only the quotient of the division, in this case 12. The remainders, 1 in the first case and 2 in the second, are lost altogether. But Forth provides several division operators, not just / (slash). For example, try this phrase:

38 3 /MOD . . <ret> 2 12 ok *If the quotient is on top, it should appear first — as it does in Z-80 FORTH (i.e. 12 2 ok)*

The Forth word /MOD (slash mod) carries out the division just as / (slash) does, but it returns the quotient *and* the remainder, with the quotient on top.

38 3 MOD . <ret> 2 ok

Like /MOD, MOD produces the remainder, but it discards the quotient. When you begin to write Forth words that perform branching operations, you will see effective uses for MOD.

The stack effects of these two new division operators are

/MOD   (u1 u2 ... uremainder uquotient)

MOD   (u1 u2 ... uremainder)

Unlike / (slash), the values to undergo division, both numerator and denominator, must be unsigned numbers. This is designated in the stack notation with the lowercase u prefix.

Forth, unlike other computer languages, allows the programmer to get very close to the operations of the system. That is why words like /MOD and MOD are included in the primitives. They will be seen to be very useful. But first you have to understand the way in which Forth handles 32-bit numbers.

3.7 32-Bit Number Representations

As you have seen, a range of −32768 to 32767 (or 0 to 65535) is sufficient for most applications, but sometimes a greater range is desired. This can occur when the magnitude of a parameter exceeds the capacity of a 16-bit word or when the number of significant figures required for a particular application is greater than the 5 or 6 figures available in a 16-bit word. (The largest unsigned integer expressible in 16 bits is decimal 65535, a value having 5 *decimal* significant figures.)

Forth has two different ways of using 32 bits to store and manipulate numbers. Both techniques provide a much greater range of possible values than can be accommodated in 16 bits. As shown below, one of these techniques has a more limited data range than the other, but it encodes data in a fashion more consistent with rapid arithmetic calculations. The other technique offers the widest possible range of data values at the expense of computer speed.

The first technique allows representation of numbers ranging from 0 through $2^{32} - 1$ (4,294,967,296) in unsigned format. These types of numbers are called "double-length integers" to distinguish them from the "single-length integers" we have dealt with thus far. Double-length integers are stored in two consecutive 16-bit cells but are treated by Forth as though they were stored in a 32-bit "super cell." Bit 31, the most significant bit, either is used as a sign bit or, as in the case of 16-bit unsigned numbers, holds a data bit. Figure 3.3 illustrates the bit allocation in a double-length integer.

In the event that even the broad range of double-length integers is inadequate for a particular application, some Forth systems allow the use of 32-bit *floating-point* numbers. This representation corresponds to the computer equivalent of scientific notation. Since it involves an elaborate encoding process for every number, its use tends to slow down the performance of the computer, but it is often incredibly useful, as a few examples from engineering, physics, and chemistry will demonstrate.

Since the Forth stack is oriented toward 16-bit integers, pushes and pops involving 32-bit numbers are a bit more involved than in the case of single-length numbers. The special set of double-length stack-manipulation words discussed in Chap. 1 are used for such operations, as shown below.

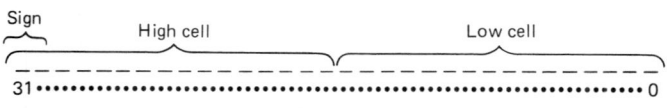

Figure 3.3 The double-integer format

Numbers

We will begin looking at 32-bit representations with an introduction to 32-bit integer math.

Double-Length Integers

Suppose you wanted to determine the product of 22400 and 398. If you naively entered the Forth phrase

22400 398 * . 2304 ok

the result would obviously be in error. This unexpected result stems from the limitations of normal 16-bit integers. The actual product, 8915200, is clearly much larger than 65535, the largest possible unsigned 16-bit number.

We need some Forth words that will enable us to use Forth's ability to store numbers in 32-bit double cells. Here are some such words.

```
D+    (d1 d2 ... d_sum)
D-    (d1 d2 ... d_diff)
M*    (n1 n2 ... d_product)
M/    (d n ... n_quotient)     Not included in Z-80 FORTH. Instead, Z-80
M/MOD                          FORTH uses M/MOD (d n ... rem, quot.)
D.    (d ...)
```

Whereas we have used lowercase n to represent 16-bit integers to this point, the stack notation for double integers is lowercase d.

D+ and D- do double-integer addition and subtraction, 32-bit analogs of + (plus) and - (minus). As the stack notation indicates, M* multiplies two single integers, leaving the product as a 32-bit number on the stack. D. , as its name implies, is the double-integer equivalent of . (dot), D-dotting the 32-bit number off the top of the stack. M/ requires a double-length numerator and a single-length denominator, leaving a 16-bit quotient on the stack. Their use is straightforward. For example,

22400 398 M*D. 8915200 ok

We will try some of the others after introducing floating-point numbers.

Floating-Point Numbers

All the numbers we have encountered thus far have fallen into the category of *fixed-point* numbers. They have all been integers. Indeed, even the problems that have been assigned have always used only integer values. No decimal points have appeared anywhere.

However, if you are a curious type, you may have already tried to enter a sequence like this:

```
22.0 7.0 / . <ret>
```

with rather alarming results. Let us see why.

The Forth math operations that we have used so far have all been designed to handle integer-type 16- or 32-bit numbers. But even double-length numbers are too limited in scope to accommodate common scientific parameters such as Avogadro's number, 6.02×10^{23} or the charge on an electron, 1.60×10^{-19} coulombs.

Furthermore, we frequently need to represent decimal fractions such as 3.14159, 2.1414, or 22.4 in the course of evaluating a problem, another impossible representation for either single- or double-length numbers.

Computers handle such representations with a binary floating-point representation, the two-base equivalent of scientific notation. Like double-length numbers, floating-point values are stored in memory using two 16-bit cells. The bits are allocated as shown in Fig. 3.4. Bit 31 is the sign bit, followed by eight exponent bits. The remainder of the bits are used to represent the fractional part of the number.

Since both the exponent and the fractional part of the number can be negative, there must be two signs encoded into the floating-point representation. Thus, -0.1217×10^{-05} would have bit 31 set, and the negative exponent would be stored in the exponent bits.

The sign of the exponent is included in a clever way. The eight exponent bits correspond to exponents ranging from 00000000 to 11111111, or 2^0 to 2^{256}. This corresponds to a decimal range of 10^0 to about 10^{76}. Offsetting the binary exponent by 128_{10} gives a range of about 10^{-38} to 10^{38}.

Fortunately, the Forth programmer does not need to be concerned about the process of encoding numbers into floating-point format. Forth does it automatically, as you will see in Sec. 3.8.

As an option, some systems also allow floating-point numbers to occupy four 16-bit cells in a *double-precision* representation. We will cover only the 32-bit floating-point representation here.

It is important to note here that, in most Forth systems, single- and

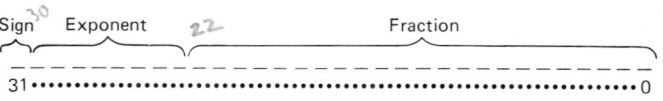

Figure 3.4 The floating-point format

double-length integer representations and their corresponding math words are all that are available. Indeed, many Forth programmers enjoy the challenge of finding ways to do complicated arithmetic operations without the aid and benefit of floating-point words.

Though it is true that floating-point math operations are generally slower than single- or even double-integer calculations (because of the complexities of the encoding as well as the necessity of keeping track of the exponents), floating-point words are very convenient. This will become apparent as we examine some examples using floating-point math. But first you need to learn the tricks that Forth uses to determine which of the three kinds of numbers you mean when you enter a value at your terminal.

Number-Input Conventions in Forth

NUMBER, the Forth word used by INTERPRET to push numbers onto the stack, has already been mentioned. NUMBER has the job of determining which kind of value is to be pushed onto the stack, single- or double-integer or floating-point value. In Forth systems which have no floating-point features, NUMBER's job is fairly easy. In such systems, by convention, if the incoming number contains punctuation, either decimal point or comma, NUMBER pushes a 32-bit double integer onto the stack. If there is no punctuation, a 16-bit single integer is pushed.

Forth systems which use floating-point words must have a more elegant version of NUMBER. The most sophisticated systems use Forth words FLOATING and INTEGER to inform NUMBER of the programmer's intentions. In these systems, if the programmer enters

FLOATING ok   *FLOATING is undefined in Z-80 FORTH (without the special f-point package).*

NUMBER will convert any incoming number which contains punctuation into floating-point format. This includes the character E in scientific notation. This CONVERSION mode remains in effect until the programmer enters

INTEGER ok   *INTEGER is undefined in Z-80 FORTH*

whereupon numbers containing punctuation will be pushed as 32-bit double integers. FLOATING turns INTEGER mode off (and vice versa).

> ▶ *Regardless of NUMBER's CONVERSION mode, values entered without punctuation will be pushed as 16-bit single integers. This is the standard practice in all Forth systems.*

52   The Forth Language

If your system does not have floating-point support (or if you are not sure just how your version of `NUMBER` works), do not despair. There are some very sophisticated 32-bit integer functions that will do almost as well in most circumstances.

On the other hand, if you do have floating-point capability, App. B. "Floating-Point Support," gives additional floating-point routines you can add to your system after you have gained a bit more sophistication by reading a few more chapters and working the problems at the ends of the chapters. For now, let us look at the fundamentals of floating-point math.

3.8 Floating-Point Mathematics

Floating-point addition, subtraction, division, and multiplication are the responsibility of the Forth words `F+`, `F−`, `F/`, and `F*`, respectively. In order for you to use any of them, there must be a pair of floating-point numbers on the stack. We will assume you are using a "smart" version of `NUMBER` which is in the `FLOATING` mode.

Enter the following:

```
22. 7. F/ F. 3.1428E0 ok
```

`F.` is the floating-point output word equivalent to dot (`.`).

Stack Effects of Floating-Point Forth Words

The stack effects of the four simple floating-point math operators are summarized in Table 3.2. Since these words operate on numbers which each occupy 32 bits, the stack notation employed must reflect this difference. In Chap. 1 we used n1, n2, etc., to represent numbers in the stack notation for math words. Thus,

```
* ( n1 n2 ... prod )
```

clearly indicates that the single-length multiply operation results in the replacement of the top two 16-bit numbers on the stack with a 16-bit product.

Table 3.2   Floating-Point Mathematics

`F*`	(f1 f2 . . . fprod)
`F+`	(f1 f2 . . . fsum)
`F−`	(f1 f2 . . . fdiff)
`F/`	(f1 f2 . . . fquot)
`F.`	(f1 . . .)

Floating-point stack notation uses lowercase f to represent floating-point values. When you enter floating-point values you must pay close attention to the input conventions. If you forget one or the other of the decimal points, for instance, an erroneous result will appear; however, depending on the depth of the stack when you goof, Forth may not inform you of the error.

`22 7 F/ F. Stack Underflow!`

In fact, the error occurred even before F. was encountered. Here, in stack notation, we can see why:

Entered	Stack contents	Comments
22	22	First value
7	22 7	Second value
F/	(empty)	F/ needs two 32-bit numbers

Again, to use floating-point math, you must be sure that the values you enter are in an appropriate floating-point format.

Scientific notation is perfectly acceptable. For example, enter

`6.02E23 1.60E-19 F*F. 9.6319E4 ok`

to obtain the value of the charge of Avogadro's number of electrons (1 Faraday).

Floating-Point Input and Output Conventions

The number of decimal places in the value entered has no effect on the number of significant figures in the answer. Either

`.08206 273.15 F* F. 2.2414E1 ok`

or

`8.206E-2 273.1500 F* F. 2.2414E1 ok`

gives the same result.

The output of F. defaults to four places to the right of the decimal point, or five significant figures. That can be changed with the word PLACES, if your system has it. Try it.

6 PLACES ok

22. 7. F/ F. 3.142857E0 ok

Floating-Point Stack Manipulations

Suppose you have to DUP a floating-point number on your stack. Remembering that a floating-point number resides in two 16-bit cells, you could try to duplicate it with

OVER OVER

and that would work perfectly. Try it yourself.

121. OVER OVER F. F. 1.2100E2 1.2100E2 ok

To see how a 32-bit floating-point number can be duped into being DUPed by OVER, consider the contents of the stack in terms of 16-bit values.

Enter	Stack	Comments
121.	f1 (or n1 n2)	32-bit floating-point number
OVER	n1 n2 n1	First half over
OVER	n1 n2 n1 n2 (or f1 f1)	Next half
F.	n1 n2 (or f1)	Print the copy
F.	empty	Print the original

The important thing to realize here is that the single-length, 16-bit operators can operate on half a 32-bit number, but that we usually do not need to use them in this way.

Consider the definition of 2DUP.

: 2DUP OVER OVER ;

This is *exactly* what we need to DUP a floating-point number (or *any* double-length number). The entire set of double-length stack words, which were discussed briefly in Chap. 1, can be used to handle the stack tasks in floating-point math in just the same way that the single-length stack tools are an aid in problems using single-length numbers. Let us review them, this time using floating-point stack notation.

2SWAP (f1 f2 ... f2 f1)

2DUP (f1 ... f1 f1)

```
2OVER  ( f1 f2 ... f1 f2 f1 )
2DROP  ( f1 ... )
2ROT   ( f1 f2 f3 ... f2 f3 f1 )
```

We can now use these stack tools to write Forth words containing floating-point operations.

3.9 Creating Forth Words that Use Floating-Point Mathematics

We created new Forth words to handle various types of problems in Chap. 2. Now that we have control of the floating-point operations, we are no longer limited to integer or double-length integer numbers. Let us look at a few problems which demonstrate the usefulness of Forth's floating-point facility.

Problem

One of the problems addressed in Chap. 2 involved falling bodies. Write a Forth word, PLUNGE, which computes the distance through which a rock falls in the time (seconds) on the stack. Use 9.8 m/s^2.

Solution

```
: PLUNGE   2DUP 2DUP 9.8 F* 2. F/ F. ." meters in " F. ." seconds "
```

Execute it.

```
1.1 PLUNGE 5.929E0 meters in 1.1000E0 seconds ok
```

Without floating-point capability this would have been a difficult problem (although not impossible, as shown below). The next problem would be even more challenging.

Problem

How long will it take an object to fall through a distance of d meters, where d is a floating-point value on the stack? Even if you are tempted, do not call the word DROP. (Why not?)

Solution

The formula we need is $t = (2d/g)^{1/2}$. This problem will illustrate an important naming convention in Forth. We need to write a word that "converts" distance into the corresponding time of falling. The terminal keyboard has a pair of keys (< and >) which have the usual "less-than" and "greater-than" significance in Forth *when they are used alone*. But when imbedded within a Forth word, they are just characters; they have no special meaning. The right-facing arrow, or greater-than symbol, when used within a Forth word signals conversion of some kind. In this problem, for example, let us call the new word D>T, for distance to time.

The stack effects of our D>T should be consistent with the name:

D>T (fdistance ... ftime) .

Here is the definition of D>T:

: D>T 2. F* 9.8 F/ FSQRT ;

There is not much to it, but it has two notable features:

1. D>T does not output anything. We will leave that task to a higher-level word. If you do not see why, review Chap. 2.
2. This marks the first appearance of FSQRT, a Forth word whose job is to take the square root of the floating number on top of the stack.

FSQRT (f ... f$^{1/2}$)

The stack effects of the new word are trivial: D>T (dist ... time). In keeping with good Forth practice, we can define a higher-level word to take care of the input-output operations. Call it METERS-FALL.

: METERS-FALL D>T ." Requires " F. ." seconds " ;

which, on execution, gives:

2.5 METERS-FALL Requires 7.1428E-1 seconds ok

This result is pleasant and useful, but it is not the best we can do. Indeed, we have outsmarted ourselves again. Although the name does not hint at it, the word D>T only works with metric units. A USCS engineering problem cannot use D>T as we have defined it. Let us start over, forgetting D>T and specifically defining conversion words with more informative names.

: METERS>SECONDS 2. F* 9.8 F/ FSQRT ; (dist$_{met}$ ... time$_{sec}$)
: FEET>SEC 2. F* 32.0 F/ FSQRT ; (dist$_{ft}$ ... time$_{sec}$)

```
and : METERS-FALL METERS>SECONDS ." Requires " f. .." seconds " ;

: FEET-FALL FEET>SEC ." Requires "f. .." seconds " ;
```

A process called *vectored* exeuction, discussed below, will allow us to use only one definition for either metric or USCS units. We will now go on to a more substantial example.

Example: Stefan's Law

From John Tyndall's early measurements, Josef Stefan concluded that the rate of emission of radiation from the surface of a body could be expressed as:

$$R = eST^4$$

where R is the rate of emission in watts per square meter, e is the emissivity of the body, the constant S has a vlaue of 5.672×10^{-8} in mks (meter-kilogram-second) units, and T is the absolute temperature. Values of the emissivity range from zero for highly polished substances to unity for perfect blackbody emitters.

Calculate the rate of energy emission from a square meter of polished brass ($e = 0.035$) held at a constant temperature given in °C.

Solution

Write a Forth word to calculate the absolute temperature first, then use it in your new word RADIATE. Finally, write a word to output the result.

The stack effects of RADIATE should be (T °C ... power)

```
: C>K 273.15 F+ ;  ( T °C ... T K )

: RADIATE C>K 2DUP F* 0.035 F* 5.672E-8 F*;

: .RADIATE 2DUP ." At" F. ." degrees" RADIATE F. ." watts " ;
```

Try it:

```
200. .RADIATE At 200 degrees 9.9459E1 watts ok
```

The sequence 2DUP F* 2DUP F* in RADIATE executes faster than the more obvious 2DUP 2DUP 2DUP F* F* F*. In Chap. 4 you will learn how to define words like BRASS that will push the emissivity of various materials onto the stack, making words like RADIATE *much* more versatile. Below is another example involving a familiar concept from hydraulics, flow of fluid through a pipe.

Example: Reynolds Number, Floating-Point Version

There are four factors which establish whether flow of a viscous fluid through a pipe is turbulent or laminar. The Reynolds' number, a unitless parameter, is defined as

$$N_r = SDd/V$$

where d is the density of the fluid, S represents the average flow velocity, D is the pipe diameter, and V is the fluid's viscosity. If the value of N_r exceeds 3000, flow is always observed to be turbulent. A value of N_r less than 2000 is characteristic of laminar flow. Between lies a transition region where either type of flow may be observed.

Solution

Write a Forth word, NREYNOLDS, to push onto the stack the Reynolds number for water flowing with velocity S through a pipe of diameter D at 20.0°C (viscosity = 0.0101 dyne·s/cm^2 and density = 1.0 g/cc). Your word should expect S and D to be already on the stack in floating-point format when it is executed.

```
: NREYNOLDS 1.0 0.0101 F/ F* F* ;
```

Try it.

```
10.1 NREYNOLDS f. 9.9009E2 ok
```

At 10 cm/s, flow through a 1.0-cm pipe will be laminar.
This example is fairly trivial, and its presence here serves more to introduce the concept of integer scaling than to illuminate the subtleties of floating-point math.

3.10 Double-Length Integer Mathematics

Suppose that your Forth system has no floating-point words and that you have not had the time to install the floating-point routines given in App. B.

Example: Reynolds Number, Integer Version

You can still do the preceding example. Even though it contains a decimal fraction, 0.0101, the viscosity of water at 20.0°C, Forth integer math can still solve the problem.

Solution

Here is a definition of NREYNOLDS which uses only integer arithmetic. Enter it.

`: NREYNOLDS 10000 101 */ * ;  NREYNOLDS has already been defined ok`

Try it, this time preceding NREYNOLDS with single-length integer values for the flow velocity and the diameter.

`10 1 NREYNOLDS . 990 ok`

This method is quicker and simpler than the floating-point version. Here is how it works.

The secret is the math word */ (pronounced "star slash"). The obvious stumbling block that arises when we attempt to use integer arithmetic in Forth words like NREYNOLDS is their inability to handle decimal fractions, or floating-point numbers. However, if we could represent a decimal fraction as an integer fraction, we could get by with integer math words.

The decimal fraction 1/0.0101 can also be represented as 10000/101. To divide some value *directly* by 0.0101 requires floating-point routines. But multiplication by 10000 followed by division by 101 uses only integers. That is where */ (star slash) comes in. Here is its stack notation:

`*/ ( n1 n2 n3 ... n1*n2/n3 )`

Star slash first multiplies, and then divides. But it differs from the Forth phrase * / (star and then slash; note the space) in one crucial respect. Star slash uses a 32-bit intermediate product. That is, n1*n2 is held in a double-integer format until it is divided by n3. That is important because a single-length-integer intermediate result would be limited to a maximum range of only ± 32767. With the 32-bit intermediate, */ (star slash) allows us to do some pretty fancy arithmetic without using floating-point math.

Example: Volume of a Sphere

In Chap. 2 you wrote Forth words to calculate the areas of rectangular spaces. Up to this point, you have not had the tools available to enable you to do any more sophisticated geometry calculations unless you used floating point. But */ (star slash) opens up a whole new area of calculations.

Remember the old approximation for π; $22/7$? Let us define a Forth word, VOLUME, to calculate the volume of a sphere, given its diameter on the stack. Use the formula $V = \frac{4}{3}\pi r^3$.

: VOLUME DUP DUP * * 4 3 */ 22 7 */ ;

Solution

Try it, assuming a radius of 2 in.

2 VOLUME . 31 ok

If you have trouble seeing how the word works, note that the DUP DUP * * phrase calculates r^3, the 4 3 */ phrase takes care of multiplying by $\frac{4}{3}$, and the 22 7 */ phrase represents our integer approximation of π.

The floating-point version looks like this:

: VOLUME 2DUP 2 DUP F* F* 1.3333 F* PI F* ;

(PI is not a Forth word even on all-floating-point systems. You can also put 3.14159 on the stack if you wish.)

2. VOLUME F. 3.3509E1 ok

Obviously the floating-point version gives a more accurate result, since we have a much better value of π to work with. But what if there was a better approximation to π than $22/7$? It turns out there is. Surprisingly, $355/113$ is an incredibly good approximation to π. Try defining VOLUME using this pair of integers in place of $22/7$.

: VOLUME DUP DUP * * 4 3 */ 355 113 */ ;

[handwritten: I still obtain 31, not 33]

It is not unreasonable to wonder why anyone would use floating-point words at all with */ (star slash) available. But we have been choosing examples designed to emphasize the power of these integer-scaling operations without addressing their limits. The integer version of VOLUME will be hard-pressed to compute the volume of a sphere of radius 1.80×10^{-10} m, for example, without some elaborate prescaling of input parameters. And there may not always be an easy integer approximation for the constant you need for a particular operation. Sometimes it is just a lot easier to use floating point.

All things considered, though, these integer operations demonstrate one of the finest features of Forth, its elegant simplicity. As you become more comfortable with Forth, you will find yourself turning more frequently to these simple integer math tools.

3.11 Radix Conversions

Now that you have been exposed to the various ways in which computers store and manipulate numbers, and have practiced some conversions between binary, octal, decimal, and hexadecimal systems, you are ready to be dazzled by the ease with which Forth can perform such transformations. Try these:

100 OCTAL . DECIMAL<ret> 144 ok

512 HEX . DECIMAL<ret> 200 ok

59 BINARY . DECIMAL<ret> 111011 ok

In each example, the number pushed onto the stack was treated by NUMBER as a decimal value. The binary representation of the number was accordingly pushed to the stack. The Forth words BINARY, OCTAL, DECIMAL, and HEX set the input-output (I/O) conversion routines to their respective radix. When . (dot) is charged with outputting a value, it does so in the current I/O radix.

Let us use these words to check some of the nondecimal arithmetic problems encountered earlier in this chapter. Enter

HEX<ret> ok

4A 321 + .<ret> 36B ok

1F0A 1B3E + .<ret> 3A48 ok

All Forth number conversions will be in radix 16 as long as HEX is in effect. To change it, enter another radix word:

OCTAL ok

I don't think this is correct — 177170 oct. is a negative number in Z80 FORTH, and the addition comes out to -10000. Z80 FORTH converts the value to a negative value on the stack (e.g. 177170 is pushed on as -392 (= FE78 h))

177170 7170 - .<ret> 167777 ok

It is very easy to forget the switch back to decimal after a long session in another base.

DECIMAL<ret> ok

The radix switching words can be used *within* another Forth word, of course, with powerful results. Let us create a Forth word that converts decimal values to binary, prints them, and then switches the base back to decimal. We will use the unsigned print version of dot so that we can get another look at the two's-complement conventions. Most if not all Forth systems have HEX, by the way. Some have OCTAL and BINARY. Installing them is very simple. Again, refer to App. A, "Software Tools."

```
: B. BINARY U. DECIMAL ;<ret> ok

64 B.<ret> 100000 ok

-64 B.<ret> 1111111111000000 ok
```

We included DECIMAL in our word so that it would automatically switch the system back to base ten, but it could have been switched to any other base. Words that help convert between binary and octal or hex, for instance, are very effective tools in understanding the encoding processes.

```
: OB. BINARY U. OCTAL ;<ret> ok
```

This word resets the system to base eight, rather than decimal. Be sure that the system is set to octal before using it, and that the system is reset to decimal afterward.

```
177170 OB. 1111111001111000 ok

42 OB. 110010 ok

DECIMAL ok
```

3.12 Problems

1. Write a Forth word that produces a list of binary, octal, and hexadecimal equivalents for any decimal value entered. The word should work like this:

   ```
   10 .CBASES<ret>
   
   Binary = 1010
   
   Octal = 12
   
   Hexadecimal = 0A ok
   ```

2. Relativistic mass: As the velocity of an object (relative to some observer) approaches the velocity of light in a vacuum, 3.0×10^8 m/s, its mass (as measured by the observer) increases dramatically. The observed mass is given by

$$m = m_0 / (1 - (v^2 / c^2))^{1/2}$$

Define a floating-point Forth word REL-MASS (mass velocity ... rel-mass) that calculates the observed mass as a function of rest mass and velocity. The resultant mass should be left on the stack.

3. a. Volume of a sample of a gas: According to the ideal gas law, the volume of a sample of a gas is given by:

$$V = \frac{nRT}{P}$$

where n is the quantity of the gas (in moles), R has a value of 0.8206 (L atm)/(mol K), T is the absolute temperature, and P is the pressure. Write a floating-point Forth word that calculates the volume of a gas sample given the initial stack contents (n T P). Test your word. One mole of gas should occupy 22.4 liters at 0.0°C (273 K).

b. Write a double-length integer version of your word and test it.

4. Rewrite FEET-FALL and METERS-FALL as double-integer Forth words. Test your words.

5. One of the neatest uses of Forth's */ (star slash) arises in unit-factor conversions. For example, the word : M>F 3937 1200 */ ; converts meters to feet by multiplying the length in meters on the stack by 39.37 in/m and then dividing by 12.00 in/ft (39.37/12.00 = 3937/1200). Write Forth words to carry out the following conversions (in both directions):

a. Gallons to liters

b. Degrees F to degrees C

c. Degrees F to kelvins

d. Pounds to kilograms

Chapter 4

Variables, Constants, and Arrays

As your Forth programming skills improve, our Forth definitions will become increasingly sophisticated. As you attack more and more difficult programming tasks, it will quickly become obvious that using only the preexisting Forth words you have learned thus far would restrict your ability to write the most general possible definitions. For instance, the only techniques by which we can include a value (such as the acceleration of a freely falling body) in a computation are (1) to leave the value on the stack before executing the word or (2) to incorporate the value within the definition itself. The first approach uses the stack as a data-storage system for the value, and the second uses the portion of memory allocated for the computer's storage of the contents of your defined word. Although both have worked well thus far, there is a better way.

Within the structure of Forth there is a set of words that enables us to save values in memory locations which are neither on the stack nor defined parts of executable Forth words of the sort we have used up until now. Rather, these new words are expressly designed for data storage and retrieval. The first of these is the word **VARIABLE**.

4.1 Variables

Consider, for example, how you would write a simple Forth word designed to calculate the electrical resistance of a wire, given the length and cross-sectional area of the wire on the stack. We shall call the word **RESISTANCE**. To formulate a Forth word for computing resistance, we need to have a value for ρ, the specific resistance of the material. Commercial annealed copper, for instance, has a specific resistance of 17 $\mu\Omega \cdot$mm, and the corresponding value for tungsten is 55 $\mu\Omega \cdot$mm. Insulators have much higher specific resistances, of course; fused quartz exhibits a value of about 7×10^{26} $\mu\Omega \cdot$mm. How do we get these values into the definition?

The relevant equation is simply

$$\text{Resistance} = \frac{\rho(\text{length})}{\text{area}}$$

One approach might lead to a definition like this:

: RESISTANCE */ ; (area length rho ... resistance)

In this technique, the value of ρ is expected to be on the stack along with the other parameters when the word is executed. On the other hand, we could incorporate the value of the specific resistance within the definition:

: RESISTANCE 55 */ ; (area length ... resistance)

The first version has the advantage of generality. It can be used for any material, provided the appropriate value for ρ is poised on top of the stack when the word is executed. But it has the disadvantage of requiring the direct entry of ρ every time it is used. If this version of the word were used in another Forth word, the task of providing a value of ρ on top of the stack could be foisted off on this "outer" word, but the fact remains, the value has to come from somewhere.

The second version of **RESISTANCE** involves an approach we have employed before. The value of the parameter is included in the word, obviating the necessity of providing it on the stack every time the word is executed and simultaneously restricting the usefulness of the word to calculations involving only tungsten, or any other material with a specific resistance of 55 $\mu\Omega\cdot$mm.

What is needed is a facility that lets us store values in labeled memory locations and provides the means for us to fetch those values as we need them in the course of our computations. Forth provides this facility through use of the word **VARIABLE**. Let us see how it does so.

Enter this*:

55 VARIABLE RHO<ret> ok

---

*This is the Forth Interest Group (FIG) convention. If you are using a Forth-79 or poly-Forth system, you should enter

VARIABLE RHO 55 RHO !<ret>

and then refer to App. C, "Forth Dialects," for an explanation. Briefly, there are a few words which operationally differ between Forth dialects. VARIABLE is one of them.

You have just extended Forth's dictionary in a new and powerful way. A new entry in Forth's dictionary has been created by `VARIABLE`. You can confirm the presence of this addition to the dictionary with `VLIST`. Up to this point, the only way to add something to the dictionary was with `:` (colon), but now you have another way.

Now, enter this expression, including the `@` (the symbol for "at," pronounced "fetch")

```
RHO @ . <ret> 55 ok
```

When you entered the phrase `RHO @`, the Forth system pushed the value stored in the variable `RHO` onto the stack.

```
17 RHO ! <ret> ok

RHO @ . <ret> 17 ok
```

The number pushed onto the stack when you entered `RHO @` has become 17. Obviously, the first phrase above modified `RHO` so that `RHO @` pushed a new value onto the stack. The Forth words `!` (pronounced "store," not "exclamation point") and `@` (fetch) are the utility words that work with dictionary entries created by `VARIABLE`. To understand them, you need to learn more about the ways Forth uses memory.

4.2 Memory Allocation for Variables and Constants

Chapter 3 introduced the techniques Forth uses to store values in the computer's memory. Recall that Forth stores single-length integers in 16-bit cells, and that 32 bits are used to store double-length integers and floating-point values. Even though Forth and other computer languages use a minimum of 16 bits to carry out almost all their math operations, the basic unit of computer memory is the 8-bit byte.

We can visualize the computer's memory as a long column of 8-bit byte pairs, each of which corresponds to a single-integer cell, as in Fig. 4.1.

Each memory byte is numbered, beginning with byte 0 and running to the highest value available on the computer being used. Any particular byte can be located in memory on the basis of its byte number or "address." Similarly, any 16-bit cell is uniquely identified in memory by the address of its even-numbered byte. The cell at address 4 consists of bytes 4 and 5, bytes 7170 and 7171 compose cell 7170, and so on. The even-numbered byte in a cell is sometimes called the *right* byte, but more often it is referred to as the *low* byte. Obviously, the odd-numbered byte in a cell must then be the cell's *high* byte.

Contents	Cell	Bytes
10101111 00000000	0	1,0
00000000 10000011	2	3,2
00000000 00000001	4	5,4
....		
....		
11111111 10010010	7170	7171,7170
00000000 01010101	7172	7173,7172
....		

Figure 4.1 Addressing cells and bytes

▶ *As a consequence of this addressing scheme, bytes can have either even or odd addresses, but cells always have an even address.*

Two parameters are associated with every byte and every cell in the computer's memory. Every storage location has both an address and a value which is stored at that address, the *contents* of the byte or cell. In Fig. 4.1, for example, the contents of the *byte* at address 7170 is 10010010_2 whereas the contents of the *cell* at 7170 is 1111111110010010_2. Although the distinction between address and content appears trivially simple at this stage, it will become more challenging later, when we use cells at particular addresses to store addresses of other cells. The *contents* of one cell may thus become the *address* of another.

For now, though, we are ready to return to look closely at the workings of VARIABLE. Enter this:

RHO .<ret> 23422 ok

Leave out @ (fetch) this time. The value dotted off the stack had been pushed there by RHO. (You will undoubtedly see a different value from this one.) It is obviously not a specific resistance value. Rather, it is the *address* of a cell set aside for storing a value. This is the way in which words created by VARIABLE operate. When executed, all they do is push onto the stack the address of a particular cell. The specific address that gets pushed was included in the definition of the word by VARIABLE at the time the word was created.

The stack description of RHO, or *any* word created by VARIABLE, is

RHO (... add)

In this context, add represents a 16-bit address. As far as subsequent Forth operations are concerned, there is nothing special about this number. For instance, we can DROP or DUP it as we do any other value.

The jobs of storing data in the cell and fetching values from the cell fall upon the two words introduced earlier, ! (store) and @ (fetch). Here are their stack effects:

```
@ ( add ... n )
! ( n add ... )
```

Used together, RHO and ! (store) provide a means to store values in a specific location, whereas RHO and @ (fetch) work to retrieve values from that location. ! (store) always puts the value second from the top of the stack into the address pointed to by the value on the stack top, replacing the value that previously occupied that location.

Oftentimes we need to *accumulate* data in a variable. If every entry destroys the previous value, accumulation becomes difficult. To handle this situation, there is another version of ! (store) which *adds* the second value on the stack to the contents of the address on top. It is called +! (pronounced "plus store"). The stack effects of +! (plus store) are the same as those of ! (store), but the result is addition rather than replacement. Enter:

```
0 VARIABLE TOTAL<ret> ok

22 TOTAL +! 72 TOTAL +! TOTAL @ . <ret> 94 ok
```

We shall use both store and plus store in the example below.

(Programmers familiar with other languages will recognize the respective similarities in function between @ (fetch) and ! (store) in Forth and PEEK and POKE in some versions of BASIC and FORTRAN. Most high-level languages do not provide a facility corresponding to +! (plus store), however.)

Example: Behavior of Gases

Dalton's law of partial pressures states that the total pressure in a mixture of gases is the sum of the individual pressures of the constituents of the mixture:

$$P_t = P_a + P_b + P_c + ... + P_i$$

The ideal gas law allows computation of the volume of a gas mixture, given the *total* pressure of the mixture, the total number of moles of gas and the absolute temperature.

$$P_t = nRT/V$$

Suppose we need to define a set of Forth words that compute the overall pressure *and* all the individual partial pressures within a container of known volume at some particular temperature. We would like to be able to vary the temperature and volume parameters to suit the needs of a variety of conditions. In developing the requisite set of Forth words, we shall use variables whenever it seems appropriate.

Solution

Suppose our mixture can potentially consist of molecular oxygen, nitrogen, and helium. First we need locations for variables in which to store the individual quantities of each gas.

0 VARIABLE OXYGEN<ret> ok

0 VARIABLE NITROGEN<ret> ok

0 VARIABLE HELIUM<ret> ok

We also need some locations for volume, temperature, and total moles.

0 VARIABLE VOLUME<ret> ok

0 VARIABLE TEMP<ret> ok

0 VARIABLE TOTAL<ret> ok

We need a word that stores data in the appropriate location as values are entered. Such a word might look like this:

: MOLES OVER TOTAL +! ! ;

so that we could use MOLES in this way:

3 NITROGEN MOLES<ret> ok

4 HELIUM MOLES<ret> ok

which would result in the contents of the variables NITROGEN, HELIUM, and TOTAL being modified as follows:

NITROGEN @ . <ret> 3 ok

HELIUM @ . <ret> 4 ok

TOTAL @ . <ret> 7 ok

If you do not see immediately how `MOLES` works, that's OK. The inner workings of Forth words are not always obvious when first read. You should write a stack-effects diagram for `MOLES`, remembering that the word expects a count and an address on the stack.

Next we need to write a word to store the volume of the container.

```
: LITERS VOLUME ! ;
```

This word is easily understood. It works like this:

```
44 LITERS<ret> ok
```

To check, enter

```
VOLUME @ . <ret> 44 ok
```

We also need a similar word to save the temperature.

```
: DEGREES TEMP ! ;
```

We can now enter

```
500 DEGREES<ret> ok
```

and confirm with

```
TEMP @ . <ret> 500 ok
```

At last we are ready to write a word to compute the pressure in the container. Since we will want the word to work for either the *total* pressure or any *partial* pressure we might select, we should plan on designing a word which expects to find a number of moles on the stack, rather than having the word go looking for a value among the many variables already defined.

Here is how we calculate the pressure. Remember, we shall use the ideal gas law, $P = nRT/V$, with a value of 62.4 (L·torr)/(mol·K) for R.

```
: PRESSURE @ TEMP @ VOLUME @ */ 624 10 */ . ." Torr " ;
```

This is how we can use it:

```
500 DEGREES 20 LITERS<ret> ok

2 HELIUM MOLES 5 NITROGEN MOLES 3 OXYGEN MOLES<ret> ok
```

```
TOTAL PRESSURE<ret> 15600 Torr ok

HELIUM PRESSURE<ret> 3120 Torr ok

OXYGEN PRESSURE<ret> 4680 Torr ok

NITROGEN PRESSURE<ret> 7800 Torr ok
```

The order of data entry is unimportant, and any number of variables can be altered if we wish. If we compress the gas sample to half the previous volume without altering the temperature or quantity of gas, we can see the direct consequences of Boyle's law:

```
10 LITERS HELIUM PRESSURE<ret> 6240 torr ok
```

The partial pressure of helium has doubled. If we increase the temperature without altering the other parameters, we can see Charles' law at work as well:

```
20 LITERS 1000 DEGREES
NITROGEN PRESSURE<ret> 15600 Torr ok
```

Expansion at this higher temperature leads to a decrease in all the pressures:

```
50 LITERS<ret> ok

NITROGEN PRESSURE<ret> 6240 Torr ok

HELIUM PRESSURE<ret> 2496 Torr ok

OXYGEN PRESSURE<ret> 3744 Torr ok

TOTAL PRESSURE<ret> 12480 Torr ok
```

Reinitialization

We also need a Forth word to "reinitialize" the system. MOLES uses +! (plus store), remember. We need a word to clear the contents of TOTAL and the other variables. Enter

```
: CLEAR 0 OXYGEN ! 0 NITROGEN ! 0 HELIUM ! 0 TOTAL ! ;<ret>
```

This set of words describing the behavior of gases is an example of a computer programming *application*. Taken together, the various words we have defined work to provide answers to a set of problems pertaining to ideal gases. A well-written application should be reusable, self-documenting, and simple. Furthermore, it should be accessible without the necessity of retyping every time we need to use it. For example, Fig. 4.2 illustrates the application we have just entered from the keyboard in the form of a Forth "block," a magnetic disk image of the series of words we have constructed, available for use over and over without retyping. To use a previously written application, all we have to do is tell Forth to LOAD it from the disk rather than from the keyboard. In Chap. 6 we shall learn how to save our applications on the disk and how to alter them when the need arises.

Below is the definition of another Forth word, ? (pronounced "question mark"), that is very useful. It is so simple and so useful that you may have already thought of it. Since it is already a part of your system, you do not have to enter it.

```
: ? @ . ;
```

(Imagine the bewilderment of a browser who happened to open the book to this page, trying to get a feeling for Forth, and spotted this string of punctuation marks.)

Rather than entering

```
TEMP @ .<ret> 500 ok
```

we can use

```
TEMP ?<ret> 500 ok
```

The contents of the address at which the variable is stored are unaffected:

```
Block  # 104
   0 ( Ideal Gas Law, Integer Version, Forth Applications )
   1
   2 0 VARIABLE OXYGEN          0 VARIABLE VOLUME ( Liters )
   3 0 VARIABLE NITROGEN        0 VARIABLE TEMP   ( Degrees Kelvin )
   4 0 VARIABLE HELIUM          0 VARIABLE TOTAL  ( Total moles )
   5
   6 : MOLES OVER TOTAL +! ! ;  ( Calc's n[i], accumulates in TOTAL)
   7 : LITERS VOLUME ! ;        ( Stores volume in variable VOLUME )
   8 : DEGREES TEMP ! ;         ( Stores the temperature )
   9
  10
  11 : PRESSURE   @ TEMP @ VOLUME @ */ 624 10 */ . ." Torr " ;
  12
  13 : CLEAR   0 OXYGEN ! 0 NITROGEN ! 0 HELIUM ! 0 TOTAL ! ;
  14
  15
```

Figure 4.2 A Forth disk block

TEMP ? TEMP ? TEMP ?<ret> 500 500 500 ok

Numerous uses of ? (question mark) will appear as we develop more interesting applications in Forth programming. But now we need to turn our attention to a Forth feature that simplifies the process of storing and retrieving values that we do not expect to ever need to change. Such constant values are dealt with using Forth's CONSTANT.

4.3 Constants

In one of the problems at the end of Chap. 2 we defined a word to compute the distance through which an object falls toward the Earth in a specified number of seconds. We used the formula $d = \frac{1}{2} gt^2$, with a value of $g = 32$ ft/s^2. Using CONSTANT, we can write a more sophisticated version of that word, storing the value of g in a memory location. Enter

32 CONSTANT G<ret> ok

Like VARIABLE, CONSTANT expands Forth's dictionary with the addition of a new word, G. Unlike VARIABLE, however, CONSTANT creates words which push the *content* of a location onto the stack, not the *address*.

G .<ret> 32 ok

We can include G in any word that needs a value of g on the stack. In the present example, we need to write a word that expects a time (in seconds) on the stack, and computes the corresponding distance.

: FALL DUP * G 2 */ . ." Feet " ;

Enter the word and try it. The constant G must have been defined first, remember.

2 FALL<ret> 64 Feet ok

We will use constants whenever we are sure that the values we need to store will not change during the application. We do not need to know the address of the value, since we will never be storing anything there. One of the most useful applications of CONSTANT will emerge in Part II, where we shall use constants to store the addresses of some devices that Forth will be used to interface with. Until then, experiment with CONSTANT, but be careful not to make the mistake that tempts all Forth programmers at one time or another:

▶ *Do not use* ! *to change the value of a constant.*

4.4 Double-Length Variables and Constants

A pair of Forth words that create dictionary entries that are used to hold 32-bit numbers are `2VARIABLE` and `2CONSTANT`. As you might expect, they work the same way as `VARIABLE` and `CONSTANT`. We shall consider `2VARIABLE` first.

As you learned earlier, Forth systems have two different formats in which 32 bits can be employed to store numbers, double-length integers, and floating-point representations. We shall begin with double integers.

▶ *If you are working at a terminal and your Forth system has a version of* `NUMBER` *which can accept either floating-point or double integers, be sure to set the* `INTEGER` *mode (see Chap. 2) before going further.*

32-bit Integer Variables

Double integers can be stored in variable locations as follows:

`40000. 2VARIABLE MASS<ret>` <u>ok</u>

Entering `MASS` will bring the address of the 32-bit variable to the stack, but *you cannot use* `@` *(fetch) to fetch a 32-bit value.* The Forth word that does that is `2@` (pronounced "two fetch"). Enter

`MASS 2@ D.<ret>` <u>40000 ok</u>

Storing a 32-bit value in a memory location is the work of `2!` (that's right, pronounced "two store").

`10000. MASS 2!<ret>` <u>ok</u>

`MASS 2@ D.<ret>` <u>10000 ok</u>

The stack effects of `2@` (two fetch) and `2!` (two store) are analogous to those of `@` (fetch) and `!` (store).

`2@ ( add ... d )`

`2! ( d add ... )`

Variables, Constants, and Arrays

Most Forth systems do not have 32-bit versions of ? (question mark) and +! (plus store) but you can create such words for your system, if you wish. For example, the definition of D? is

```
: D? 2@ D. ;
```

Double-Length Constants

If you want to save a double-length integer that will not change, 2CONSTANT is the word to use to create the dictionary entry and its associated storage location:

```
96494. 2CONSTANT FARADAY<ret> ok
```

To fetch the value of the constant, merely enter the name of the double constant. 2@ is not required, just as we do not need @ to obtain the contents of a 16-bit constant.

```
FARADAY D.<ret> 96494 ok
```

One of the slickest uses of double constants appears when we remember that we can store a pair of 16-bit values in a 32-bit double-integer location. Enter this:

```
624 10 2CONSTANT RG<ret> ok
```

You have created a new dictionary entry which has stored the single-length numbers 624 and 10 in a pair of adjoining locations affiliated with the name R. The execution of RG, or any word created by 2CONSTANT, results in the contents of a particular 32-bit location being pushed to the stack. In this case the 32-bit location contains the 16-bit representations of two useful numbers.

Remember PRESSURE earlier in this chapter? Its definition was

```
: PRESSURE @ TEMP @ VOLUME @ */ 624 10 */ .." Torr " ;
```

where the values 624 and 10 represented the ideal gas constant, 62.4 (L·torr)/(mol·K).

Now that we have defined RG as a word which fetches these values to the stack, we can redefine PRESSURE as

```
: PRESSURE @ TEMP @ VOLUME @ */ RG */ .." Torr " ;
```

a much more pleasing definition. [Were it not that R is already a Forth word that does something else (see Chap. 5), we could have used R as the name of this 32-bit constant, leading to an even more pleasing definition.]

You can use such double-length integer constants to store single-length integer pairs to work with */ (star slash). This is especially useful when you want to use integer arithmetic to carry out some calculation involving an irrational constant. You have already seen that 355/113 is an excellent approximation to π, for example.

```
355 113 2CONSTANT PI (error < 10⁻⁷)
```

Here are some more such approximations:

```
19601 13860 2CONSTANT SQRT2   (1.414... error < 10⁻⁸ )
18817 10864 2CONSTANT SQRT3   (1.732... error < 10⁻⁸ )
22936  7253 2CONSTANT SQRT10  (3.162... error < 10⁻⁸ )
```

Thus the circumference of a circle of known diameter is readily computed with this definition:

```
: Circum PI */ ;
```

4.5 Floating-Point Variables and Constants

If your system has floating-point capability, you will want to be able to store and fetch values which have been encoded into floating-point format. Fortunately, no new words are required.

Just as 2CONSTANT was equally adept at handling either a pair of 16-bit constants or a single 32-bit integer, it can also create words that store and produce floating-point values on demand. Likewise, 2VARIABLE creates dictionary entries that produce the address of a 32-bit storage location on execution. And 2@ and 2! are just as good at dealing with 32-bit floating-point representations as they are at dealing with 32-bit integer representations. Indeed, to all these words, 32 bits are just 32 bits, regardless of the history of their contents.

Set your version of NUMBER to FLOATING, if appropriate, to do the following example.

Example

Using floating point, write a series of words to compute the density of a sample of a particular gas.

Solution

Use the formula

Density = $(P \times MW)/(R \times T)$

where R = 0.0821 (L·atm)/(mol·K).

FLOATING\<ret\> <u>ok</u>	(Optional, depending on your system)
2.016 2CONSTANT HYDROGEN\<ret\> <u>ok</u>	
32.00 2CONSTANT OXYGEN\<ret\> <u>ok</u>	
28.02 2CONSTANT NITROGEN\<ret\> <u>ok</u>	
24.02 2CONSTANT CARBON\<ret\> <u>ok</u>	
16.04 2CONSTANT METHANE\<ret\> <u>ok</u>	
0.0821 2CONSTANT RG\<ret\> <u>ok</u>	

These floating-point constants will provide the molecular weights of the named elements as needed. Any number of such floating-point constants could be entered, of course. This time, use floating-point variables for pressure and temperature. Here is the list of definitions:

1. 2VARIABLE PRESSURE 273.15 2VARIABLE TEMP	(We shall initialize at standard conditions of temperature and pressure, STP.)
: DENSITY PRESSURE 2@ F* RG F/ TEMP 2@ F/ ;	(Evaluate the density.)
: .DENSITY DENSITY F. ." grams/liter " ;	(Print the density.)
: DEGREES TEMP 2! ;	(Store the temperature as desired.)

Try them:

HYDROGEN .DENSITY\<ret\> 8.9897E-2 grams/liter <u>ok</u>

700. DEGREES HYDROGEN .DENSITY\<ret\> 3.5079E-2 grams/liter <u>ok</u>

OXYGEN .DENSITY\<ret\> 5.5680E-1 grams/liter <u>ok</u>

TEMP 2@ F. \<ret\> 7.0000E2 <u>ok</u>

You may also vary the pressure and have `.DENSITY` determine the vapor density under varying pressure conditions.

Experiment with these words, and practice using floating-point variables and constants in your own definitions. Just be careful always to include a decimal point when entering a value to be stored in a location created by `2VARIABLE` or `2CONSTANT`.

4.6 User Variables

Although you did not know it at the time, when you examined Forth's *vocabulary list* (`VLIST`) in Chap. 2, you encountered several predefined Forth variables which are necessary components of your Forth system. They are called *user* variables because time-sharing Forth systems keep a separate "copy" of each of these variables for each user. Some of the important ones follow.

DP   The *d*ictionary *p*ointer, this variable contains the address of the next available space in the dictionary. When you create a new word, or enter a new variable or constant, Forth adds to the dictionary starting at the address stored in this variable. When the entry is complete, Forth advances the value of `DP` in anticipation of subsequent entries.

S0   The address of the base of the stack. The Forth word `.S` uses `S0`.

BASE   The current radix relevant for numeric input and output operations. The definition of `OCTAL` is `8 BASE !`, for example. `DECIMAL` is obviously defined as `10 BASE !`.

Forth systems may have as many as a couple of dozen such variables, many of which are never *directly* obvious to the Forth programmer. But some of these variables are useful in helping us understand the ways in which Forth manages to accomplish the things it does. For example, enter

`DP ?<ret> 11584 ok`

`0 VARIABLE VALUE<ret> ok`

`DP ?<ret> 11596 ok`

The addition of the variable `VALUE` to the dictionary altered the contents of `DP` to point to the next available cell for addition of subsequent dictionary entries. The difference between the initial and final values of `DP` tells us the exact size of the new entry. `VALUE` occupies 12 bytes, or `six` 16-bit cells. One cell is allocated for data storage, and the remaining `five` are storage locations for the name of the variable (each letter occupies one byte) and the address of the Forth procedure which dictates what variables do when their names are EXECUTEd. (The address of the value is pushed to the stack.)

Now enter this:

100 ALLOT<ret> ok

DP ?<ret> 11696 ok

The dictionary pointer has been advanced by 100 bytes. Since the last two bytes in the dictionary entry for VALUE were allocated by Forth for the storage of one 16-bit value, the action of ALLOT, effectively tacking an additional block of number storage area onto the end VALUE's storage area makes the word now capable of storing an additional fifty 16-bit entries.

We can use ALLOT to modify variable entries to enable them to store an almost unlimited number of values under one name. Such a collection of values constitutes an *array*. In scientific, business, and engineering applications, such arrays are very commonly employed to collect and organize large blocks of closely related data.

4.7 Arrays

If you have not already done so, FORGET VALUE and enter

0 VARIABLE POINTS 100 ALLOT<ret> ok

Now that this new array has been created, we need Forth words to allow us to store and fetch values to and from locations within the array. Enter

: SAVE 2 * POINTS + ! ;<ret>

: GET 2 * POINTS + ? ;<ret>

Here is how these are used. Suppose we wanted Forth to store a list of values that we had obtained during the course of monitoring the atmospheric nitrogen oxide (NO_x) levels in a particular area. We may wish to calculate the mean NO_x levels, or we may want Forth to print the dates when the levels exceeded a particular limit. Whatever the ultimate reason, we'll need to store and retrieve a bunch of data. Suppose the NO_x levels for the first 15 days of August were as tabulated on page 80.

Date	NO$_x$ level(noon), ppm
1	22
2	27
3	18
4	29
5	9
6	5
7	16
9	23
10	33
11	27
12	19
13	19
14	14
15	22

Entering the values into the array is SAVE's job. To SAVE the first value, you must tell Forth both the value's *magnitude* and its *position* in the array. Enter the values

```
22 1 SAVE<ret> ok
27 2 SAVE<ret> ok
18 3 SAVE<ret> ok
29 4 SAVE<ret> ok
        .
        .
        .
14 14 SAVE<ret> ok
22 15 SAVE<ret> ok
```

To get them back, all you need to do is enter the date followed by GET, and the value appears. You can GET any value you want. The order in which you retrieve the data is unimportant.

```
15 GET<ret> 22 ok

3  GET<ret> 18 ok
```

Indeed, you could have entered the data in any order as well, and you can alter it even now. Let us revise the entry for August 14:

```
17 14 SAVE<ret> ok

14 GET<ret> 17 ok
```

Variables, Constants, and Arrays 81

Of course, you can use any name you wish for your words that manipulate the data in your array; the names GET and SAVE are too general for most uses. Here is a stack notation description to help illustrate how words like these work with VARIABLE and ALLOT to deal with arrays of data. We shall look at SAVE first.

	Stack notation	Description
SAVE	val pos	A value and the array position reside on the stack before SAVE is executed.
2 *	val 2 ✕ pos	Since addressing is byte-oriented, two times the position (an offset)
POINTS	val offset add	will be added to the address of the array
+	val newadd	to compute the new address of the referenced entry
!	(empty)	before execution of ! .

These shenanigans (tabulated above) are needed to compute the address of the individual cell into which the data will be stored. The process of doubling the position number and adding it to the address of the first entry is called computing the *offset* of an *element* of the array.

If we call the address pushed to the stack (on execution of POINTS) add, then the first value is stored at address add+2(1) = add+2, the second value will be stored at add+4, the third at add+6, and so on. All this is necessary because Forth (like most BASIC, Pascal, and FORTRAN systems) locates itself in memory using 8-bit bytes but mostly stores numbers in 16-bit cells.

Here is a representation of the portion of memory allocated to the dictionary entry for POINTS.

Address of cell	Position in array	Offset	Contents of cell
11584			Name of the variable
.			
.			
.			
11594			Code for variables
11596	0	0	Room for a 16-bit integer

Without ALLOT, this would be all there was to the POINTS dictionary entry. Through its use of the dictionary pointer, however, ALLOT adds the following to the memory allocated to POINTS:

82   The Forth Language

Address of cell	Position in array	Offset	Contents of cell
11598	1	2	Room for another 16-bit value
11600	2	4	Room for another 16-bit value
.			
.			
.			
11696	50	100	Room for the 50th 16-bit value

In all this, what is easy to overlook is that there is a location at `add+0` that corresponds to the "zeroth" entry in the array. That is the array position into which we would have stored a solitary value if the variable had been created without `ALLOT`. This zeroth array position can be very useful in providing a location for a data count or an array value to which we need to compare our individual values. But now we need to briefly look at the ways Forth *retrieves* array values.

Recall the definition of `GET`:

`: GET 2 * POINTS + ? ;`

This word contains the same Forth phrase

`2 * POINTS +`

for computing the offsets that we encountered in `SAVE`. Thus, execution of `GET` consists merely of calculating the offset address of the desired datum and fetching it.

`7 GET<ret> 16 ok`

We shall be using more elaborate words for "getting" data in Chap. 5, but first we need to consider 32-bit arrays.

4.8 Double-Integer and Floating-Point Arrays

As an example of the use of arrays devoted to handling 32-bit numbers, enter:

`0. 2VARIABLE WEIGHT 80 ALLOT<ret> ok`

Although we need the 32-bit version of `VARIABLE`, allocation of additional memory space for floating or double integers uses the same `ALLOT` that we have seen before. Each double or floating value requires 4 bytes, however, so we must be careful to `ALLOT` 4 times as many bytes as there are values to save. This array can hold 80/4 or 20 floating-point values. For practice, we shall use it to store the atomic weights of the first 20 elements. Rather than using a word to do the job for us, we shall enter the values into the array manually.

`1.008 WEIGHT 4 + 2!`	Hydrogen, element 1
`4.003 WEIGHT 8 + 2!`	Helium, element 2
`9.012 WEIGHT 12 + 2!`	Beryllium, element 3
.	
.	
.	
`40.08 WEIGHT 80 + 2!`	Calcium, element 20

For a 32-bit value, the offset is 4 times the position number for the element of interest. We can thus define a word, `?WEIGHT`, to retrieve atomic weights from the `WEIGHT` array as:

`: ?WEIGHT 4 * WEIGHT + 2@ F. ;`

This word expects to find the atomic number of the element of interest on the stack, computes the offset as 4 × the atomic number, adds the offset to the address of the base value in the array, fetches the value, and prints it.

`7 ?WEIGHT<ret> 14.0099 ok`   Nitrogen

If you wish, you can use exactly the same type of array to handle 32-bit integers on your Forth system as well.

4.9 Byte Arrays

Just as the Forth words `@` (fetch) and `!` (store) handle 16-bit values and the double-length words `2@` (two fetch) and `2!` (two store) deal with 32-bit storing and fetching operations, Forth also provides a pair of words to deal with transfers of data from and to 8-bit byte locations. These words are called `C@` (character fetch) and `C!` (character store), respectively. Their names imply their greatest usefulness, handling 8-bit character representations. Characters (letters, numerals, punctuation marks, and special characters) are usually stored two per cell (in 8-bit bytes) in computer systems. As you will see in Chap. 6, this system promotes efficient data storage, since the representation of a single character requires no more than 8 bits anyway.

Generation of a "byte" array is carried out in exactly the same way as a single- or double-integer array, but it is not necessary to double or quadruple the position number to compute the offset. In Chap. 7, where we shall look closely at the input-output (I/O) operations that Forth uses in handling both text and data, we shall also examine much more closely the uses of byte arrays and the words C@ (character fetch) and C! (character store).

4.10 Problems

1. Return to Chap. 3 and rewrite FALL, using BRITISH and METRIC, words you will also define to store the appropriate value of g in the variable GRAVCON. Then use GRAVCON in your definition of FALL.

2. Explain the following interaction between a Forth programmer and a Forth system: DECIMAL BASE ? 10 ok.

   OCTAL BASE ? 10 ok

   HEX BASE ? 10 ok

3. Charles Moore is a strong proponent of the use of integer arithmetic wherever such use is practical. Indeed, his initial uses of 2CONSTANT were in storing *pairs* of single-length integers for use with */ (star slash). Rewrite the conversion words in Prob. 5 of Chap. 3, this time defining the unit-factor conversion constants in a double-length constant, as in

   3937 1200 2CONSTANT M>F

   : .M>F M>F */ . ;

4. Write a word called !WEIGHT to store floating-point atomic weights in the floating-point array WEIGHT. The word should work like this:

   1.008 1 !WEIGHT<ret> ok (fweight at.no. .....)

   where the weight and atomic number are 32-bit floating-point and 16-bit integer values, respectively. The old word ?WEIGHT can retrieve the values for you.

Chapter 5
Decisions, Loops, and Logic

The preceding chapters have taught you to write Forth words that manipulate the stack and carry out arithmetic operations on both integer and floating-point numbers. In this chapter you will learn how to use a special set of Forth words to do such manipulations over and over again, branching back into a definition in such a way that a portion of that definition is executed repetitively. This type of programming is called a "loop." The control of the system as it loops through a definition is the responsibility of a set of Forth words that make logical decisions.

5.1 Decisions

In Chap. 4 we wrote a very simple application to store and fetch pollution data from an array of values designated for the storage of NO_x levels for a particular period. Suppose someone asked us to identify the particular days in that period during which the NO_x levels exceeded 20 ppm. We could use a word like GET, which we wrote in Chap. 4, to display each of these values and visually determine whether each exceeded the limit of 20 ppm. But such an approach is not only unsophisticated, it also does not make use of Forth's efficient decision-making capability.

Recreate the array of NO_x data that you used in Chap. 4. Then enter this new version of GET:

: GET 2 * POINTS + @ ;   Use of @ (fetch) rather than ? (question mark) leaves value on the stack rather than dotting it off.

and enter this new word as well:

: TEST GET 20 > IF ." Excessive Level of NOx " THEN ;

85

TEST, using GET to obtain a value from the POINTS array, compares the value on top of the stack with 20 and, if the value is the greater of the two, prints the ." (dot quote) message.

Try it:

```
1 TEST<ret> Excessive Level of NOx ok

2 TEST<ret> Excessive Level of NOx ok

3 TEST<ret>   ok

4 TEST<ret> Excessive Level of NOx ok
```

Again, the order of TESTing the variable's contents is irrelevant.

```
11 TEST<ret> Excessive Level of NOx ok

6  TEST<ret>   ok
```

The keys to the operation of TEST are the Forth words > (pronounced "greater than"), IF, and THEN. Let us consider > (greater than) first.

The Forth word > (greater than) is an example of Forth's comparison operators. These are words which examine values on the stack to determine whether or not a particular condition pertains. The results of the examination are left on the stack in the form of a *flag*. Enter this:

```
11 27 > .<ret> 0 ok

50 25 > .<ret> 1 ok
```

Forth's > (greater than) tested the top two 16-bit integers. In the first case 11 is not greater than 27, so > (greater than) left a 0 on the stack. The pair of values is gone, by the way, as you can demonstrate to yourself with .s. In the second case > (greater than) left a 1 on the stack, its response whenever the condition being tested is true. It is true that 50 is bigger than 25. The 1 is called a *true* flag. On the other hand, the 0 left by > (greater than) when it established that 11 was not bigger than 27 is called a *false* flag.

Comparison Operations

In the nineteenth century, the English mathematician George Boole developed algebraic techniques for dealing with the concepts of truth and falsehood. If 0 is used to represent false and a number other than 0 (usually 1) is used to represent truth, the veracity of a condition becomes representable in the form of an algebraic equation.

Table 5.1 16-Bit Comparison Operators

Operator	Name	Stack notation
=	Equal	(n n ... flag)
>	Greater than	(n n ... flag)
<	Less than	(n n ... flag)
0=	Zero equal	(n ... flag)
0<	Less than zero	(n ... flag)
0>	Greater than zero	(n ... flag)

In such equations, a term is said to have a *logical value* of zero when the expression is false and a nonzero logical value when the expression is true.

Boolean algebra is very compatible with binary arithmetic and digital electronics. As a consequence, boolean algebra and *truth tables* have become essential tools in the toolbox of computer programmers and electronic engineers alike. Later in this chapter we shall look more closely at Forth's use of boolean operations. Now we need to list the 16-bit comparison operators. Along with their stack notations, they are presented in Table 5.1.

The first three entries in Table 5.1—= (equals), > (greater than), and < (less than)—expect two values on the stack. The last three entries in the table compare the value on top of the stack with 0.

```
2 0= . <ret> 0 ok

- 5 0< . <ret> 1 ok

- 5 0> . <ret> 0 ok
```

These operators are introduced here because they provide Forth with the ability to "decide" whether or not to repeat or skip a portion of a definition. As indicated above, they do this in conjunction with IF.

Conditionals

Recall the definition of TEST.

```
: TEST GET 20 > IF ." Excessive.... " THEN ;
```

The stack effects of the words that constitute TEST are:

| TEST | n | Begin with a number representation of a position in an array on the stack. |
| GET | n | Convert to the corresponding value. |

88 The Forth Language

20	n 20	Push a 20 to the stack.
>	flag	Compare, drop values, and set flag.
IF		Decide, drop flag, and . . .
."		print message only if IF found a true flag.
	"	Remember, ." . . . " has no net stack effect.
	THEN	Terminates the portion of the definition to be executed if IF found a true flag.

Note the actions of IF.

1. If IF finds true, it executes the words that follow it all the way up to THEN.
2. If IF finds false, it skips the words between IF and THEN and proceeds with execution of the words following THEN.
3. IF destroys its flag. This keeps the stack uncluttered with old flags.

Actually, in TEST there were no words following THEN. Here is a better definition of TEST that prints a message regardless of the flag; the message differs in the case of tolerable levels of pollutant.

: TEST GET 20 > IF ." In " THEN ." tolerable levels " ;

If your NO_x array is still intact, you can try this definition.

1 TEST<ret> Intolerable levels ok

3 TEST<ret> tolerable levels ok

Forth has certain rules for use of IF . . . THEN constructions within other words. The most important are:

Rule 1 Every IF must have a corresponding THEN to terminate its action.

Rule 2 IF . . . THEN constructions *must* be contained within defined words [between : (colon) and ; (semicolon)]. They cannot be used interactively.

Rule 3 The Forth word ENDIF may be used as a synonym for THEN. Some programmers prefer this name. Forth will print an error message and refuse to EXECUTE words that do not have a matching THEN (or ENDIF) for every IF.

Rule 4 IF will accept *any* nonzero value as an indication of a logical true condition.

Alternate Execution

In defined Forth words like our TEST, the words following THEN are always executed, regardless of the value of the flag. Forth provides a procedure that allows us to define words that will EXECUTE one part of the definition or another, depending on the results of IF's examination of the flag. This procedure is called *alternate execution,* and the portions of the definition which may or may not be executed are called *alternative phrases.* The Forth word responsible for this action is ELSE. In general terms, Forth words that use alternative phrases look like this:

```
: WORD .. IF phrase1 ELSE phrase2 THEN phrase3 ;
```

The words preceding IF set the flag. If *true,* phrase1 is executed, but not phrase2. If *false,* phrase2 is executed, but not phrase1. Phrase3 will be executed regardless. As in our first version of TEST, phrase3 does not even have to be there, as in this further version of TEST:

```
: TEST GET 20 > IF ." Pollution Alert " ELSE ." Tolerable air " THEN ;
```

Now that we have access to the alternative phrase, we must add another rule to the above list of IF ... THEN rules.

Rule 5   Whatever happens between IF and ELSE, the changes that occur in the stack depth must be the same as the changes between ELSE and THEN.

(Novice Forth programmers occasionally forget to put the THEN into their definitions, particularly in words that contain ELSE. When that happens the INTERPRETer prints an error message, and you must redefine your word properly.)

Nested Conditionals

You can use IF ... THEN constructions within other IF ... THEN constructions. Each IF must be terminated by its own THEN, of course. Here is the longest definition we have written thus far, and our *last* version of TEST.

```
: TEST GET DUP 30 > IF ." Foul Air! Hide. "     ELSE
       DUP 20 > IF ." Stay Indoors. "            ELSE
       DUP 10 > IF ." Minor Eye Irritation. "    ELSE
              ." Have a Nice Day. "
       THEN THEN THEN DROP ;
```

Try it. The DUPs have been added so that > (greater than) in the alternative phrases has a value to test. Since it has been DUPed in each phrase, it is important to DROP it at the end of the definition.

5.2 Loops

The IF ... ELSE ... THEN construction allows the programmer to design words that selectively execute portions of the word based on the results of a decision. Another set of words allow the programmer to construct words that repeat portions of a definition more than once. This type of programming structure is called a *loop*. If the number of times the loop is to execute is known at the time the word is written, the resulting word is called a *definite loop*. Loops which begin and will only terminate after some condition is detected by Forth are called *indefinite loops*. We will develop several examples of each type of loop.

When does one use a loop? When it is convenient to do so. Suppose you wanted to print the squares of the integers from 1 to 3. As a confident Forth programmer you would enter

```
1 DUP * . 2 DUP * . 3 DUP * . <ret> 1 4 9 ok
```

Printing the squares of the integers from 1 to 10 would take more of your time, but you could do it. Following the same approach, however, the squares of the digits from 1 to 2000 would take too long to be worth the trouble. Better to use a definite loop.

Definite Loops

In Forth, a definite loop is executed by

1. Pushing onto the stack two numbers, one representing an initial value for the "loop counter" and another representing the maximum value of the loop counter. These 16-bit values are called the *index* and the *limit* of the loop, respectively.
2. Putting the words that are to execute repetitively between the Forth control words DO ... and ... LOOP.

For example, define and execute the word SQUARES.

```
: SQUARES 100 0 DO I DUP * . CR LOOP ;
SQUARES<ret>  0
1
4
9
16
.
```

. ok   Fast, wasn't it?

The words between DO and LOOP (I DUP * . CR) are repeated 100 times during the execution of SQUARES. To help you understand how this word works, here is an introduction to the workings of the *return stack*.

The Return Stack

Execution of a looping word in Forth requires that Forth keep track of

1. The number of times the loop has executed.
2. The number of times the loop is destined to execute.

These values, the index and the limit of the loop, are the first parameters that we have encountered in Forth that are stored and manipulated in an area of memory that is neither a constant, a variable, nor an array location, nor is it the "parameter stack" with which we have done so much. Rather, the loop index and limit are stored on Forth's other stack, the so-called return stack.

The effect of the Forth word DO is to pop the top two values from the parameter stack (index and limit) while pushing them to the return stack.

	Parameter stack	Return stack
	0	
Before DO	100	empty
		0
After DO	empty	100

LOOP tests the top two values on the return stack:

1. If index < (is less than) limit, the index is incremented and execution branches back to the word following DO.
2. If index = (equals) limit, execution passes to the word following LOOP, and the index and limit are dropped from the return stack. This is the *loop termination*.

Here is a closer look at SQUARES.

```
: SQUARES
    100         Limit on parameter stack.
    0           Index on parameter stack.
    DO          Begin loop. Push index and limit to return stack.
    I           Copy top of return stack to parameter stack.
```

DUP	DUP it.
*	Multiply.
.	Print the product.
LOOP	Increment index; compare limit and index. Go on if equal; if not equal, return to word following DO.
;	End of definition.

Now that you know how DO and LOOP function, the only unfamiliar words in our definition are I and CR. The definition of I follows.

I   Copy the top value of the return stack to the parameter stack. Increase the parameter stack depth by 1; no effect on the return stack.

I is one of the most useful of Forth words. Many words containing definite loops are created under conditions in which the "inner" words, those between DO and LOOP, need to know the value of the loop's index each time through. This is obviously the case with SQUARES. I copies the value of the index so that the DUP *. part of the definition can square and print the resultant value.

SQUARES also marks the debut of CR. One of Forth's I/O words, CR produces the same result in your output that a *carriage return* would produce on a typed page. Use CR whenever you want to start printing on a new line.

The index and limit do not have to be part of the definition. Consider this definition of SQUARES:

: SQUARES 0 DO I DUP * . LOOP ;

Remember, DO wants to find two values on the (parameter) stack. This version of SQUARES was written to allow the programmer to enter the limit at execution time, rather than incorporating it into the word.

4 SQUARES<ret> 0 1 4 9 ok

9 SQUARES<ret> 0 1 4 9 16 25 36 49 64 ok

If you attempt to execute this version without a limit value on the stack, you will either get an error message or an unpredictable result (depending on whether or not the stack had an old value remaining on it from a previous blunder).

Note that the last value printed by our version of SQUARES is *not* the value of the limit squared. LOOP increments the index, *then* compares it to the limit. As a consequence, I never gets to copy the index when it equals the limit. Although this may at first seem to be a strange feature of the language, it is actually a direct reflection of the simplicity and power of Forth. We shall use this feature to our advantage later.

Here is another example, this time using an external stack parameter as a value for the words inside the loop.

: TIMESTABLES 10 0 DO DUP I * . LOOP DROP ;

1 TIMESTABLES <ret> 0 1 2 3 4 5 6 7 8 9 ok

4 TIMESTABLES <ret> 0 4 8 12 16 20 24 28 32 36 ok

Again, the word presented a total of 10 values, as requested, beginning with 0. However, the top values were 9 and 36, not 10 and 40. To get the top values to be 10 times the outer stack parameter, we could define TIMESTABLES as:

: TIMESTABLES 11 1 DO DUP I * . LOOP DROP ;

The presence of DROP at the end of the definition cleans up the parameter stack after execution. If you have kept close tabs on the stack contents for this word, you will have noticed that DUP duplicates the top of the stack to give the index (copied from the return stack by I) something to multiply. DROP ensures a clean stack for whatever word follows.

Sometimes it is useful to have the ability to leave a loop earlier than would occur if we allowed the normal LOOP routines to terminate the loop for us. For such applications Forth includes the premature loop termination word LEAVE.

Early Loop Termination

Our definition of TIMESTABLES above will always give the same number of products, regardless of their contents. Suppose, for some peculiar reason, you wanted the definition of TIMESTABLES to write only the values that are less than 50. Rewrite your definition, including the underlined phrase.

: TIMESTABLES 11 1 DO DUP I * DUP . 50 > IF LEAVE THEN LOOP DROP ;

The additional DUP provides the 50 > portion of the definition with a value to compare and the IF LEAVE THEN portion brings about an early termination, provided > (greater than) leaves a true (1) on the stack.

5 TIMESTABLES<ret>   5 10 15 20 25 30 35 40 45 50 ok

6 TIMESTABLES<ret>   6 12 18 24 30 36 42 48 54 ok

7 TIMESTABLES<ret>   8 16 24 32 40 48 56 ok

Do not be surprised at the appearance of values greater than 50 in the output line. Remember, the test to determine whether or not to LEAVE the loop occurs *after* the value has been printed.

Although it looks complicated at first, LEAVE is trivially simple. All it does is alter the value of the limit on the return stack so that the limit equals the index, forcing termination at LOOP's next execution.

All the LOOPing that has been presented thus far has used integer arithmetic exclusively. But you can carry out 32-bit math within loops as easily as the 16-bit variety, as long as you keep careful track of the stack. In scientific applications particularly, double-integer and floating-point operations which can be performed within a loop can greatly assist in creating simple and effective programming applications.

5.3 Loops Containing 32-bit Arithmetic

Before we introduce floating-point and double-integer operations into our loops, it is important to recall that the loop's own bookkeeping parameters, the index and limit, are 16-bit integer values. As such, they cannot be used in either double-integer or floating-point math operations. Forth systems provide a set of conversion words that convert one type of number into another. Along with their stack effects, they are presented in Table 5.2.

Not all these words are defined in all Forth systems. If your system has floating point, for example, but lacks FIX and FLOAT, you will find their definitions in "Floating-Point Support" in App. B.

As an example of the uses of these conversion words, write a word to compute the square roots of the integers from 1 to 100. Call the word ROOTS.

```
: ROOTS 101 1 DO I DUP . FLOAT FSQRT F. CR LOOP ;
```

Try it:

```
ROOTS 1 1.0000E0

2 1.4142E0

3 1.7320E0

      .
      .
      .

100 10.0000E0   ok
```

Table 5.2 32- to 16-bit and 16- to 32-bit Conversion Operators

Operator	Name	Stack Notation
FIX	Floating to single integer	(d ... n)
FLOAT	Single integer to floating	(n ... f)
S>D	Single to double	(n ... d)
D>F	Double to floating	(d ... f)
F>D	Floating to double	(f ... d)

5.4 +LOOP

Sometimes it is useful to create a loop that increments the index by a value other than 1. For such applications you can use Forth's +LOOP (pronounced "ploop"), a word which works with FOR just as LOOP does, but for which the amount that the index increases (or decreases) is decided by the programmer. It works this way: Suppose you wanted to print squares of the even numbers from 2 to 100. You could write a word like the one below.

```
: EVEN-SQUARES 100 2 DO I DUP * CR . 2 +LOOP ;
```

+LOOP works just as LOOP does, except that the index is incremented by an amount that precedes the word +LOOP in the definition of the +LOOP-containing word. EVEN-SQUARES, for example, gives the values of the squares of even numbers only.

```
EVEN-SQUARES<ret> 4
16
36
 .
 .
```

One of the most useful features of +LOOP arises when the programmer takes advantage of the possibility that the value of the increment can be negative, allowing construction of loops that work downward.

```
: COUNTDOWN 0 10 DO I . ." Remaining " CR -1 +LOOP ;
```

```
COUNTDOWN<ret>  10 Remaining

9 Remaining

8 Remaining
```

96 The Forth Language

```
1 Remaining  ok
```

  In device-control applications, for example, where we might need Forth to control a voltage ramp which could either increase or decrease with time, +LOOP neatly fills the bill.

  Thus far, our loops have all been written with a predetermined number of executions. That is why they are definite loops. Forth uses the very same logic operators with which we began this chapter to establish whether or not to terminate the loop.

1. For a LOOP or a +LOOP with a *positive* increment, the loop will terminate when the index reaches or exceeds the limit.
2. For a *negative*-increment +LOOP, the loop will terminate when the index exceeds, not just equals, the limit.
3. No matter what the combination of index and limit, the loop will execute at least once. This occurs because the comparison of the index and limit values first occurs when execution first encounters LOOP, *after* execution of the words between DO and LOOP.

5.5 Indefinite Loops

Forth also provides for the construction of loops which terminate as a consequence of tests made within the phrases set forth by the programmer. Such structures are *indefinite loops*. The following examples will serve as an introduction to indefinite-loop structures as well as to some more of Forth's I/O words.

  Enter the following definite loop word:

```
: RIGHT 64 24 DO I SPACES ." >>>>> " CR 2 +LOOP ;
```

SPACES is a Forth word which inserts a number of blank spaces into the output character stream. Its stack notation is, simply, SPACES (n . . .).

  Try RIGHT:

```
>>>>>
 >>>>>
  >>>>>
   >>>>>
    >>>>>
```

Now enter this obviously complementary word:

`: LEFT 24 64 DO I SPACES ." <<<<< " -2 +LOOP ;`

and

`: WOBBLER BEGIN RIGHT LEFT ?TERMINAL UNTIL ;`

When you execute WOBBLER, a cute pattern of arrows BEGINs to wobble back and forth across the terminal screen. In the absence of your intervention, this pattern will repeat endlessly. To stop WOBBLER, you must touch a key on your terminal. Nearly any key will suffice. (Stay away from the "break" key, however; the "repeat" and "shift" keys are also useless for this purpose.)

The definition of WOBBLER contains five words, two of which were introduced above; the others, BEGIN, ?TERMINAL, and UNTIL are totally new. BEGIN and UNTIL are indefinite loop words. ?TERMINAL is an I/O word.

The function of ?TERMINAL is inspection of the incoming data line to establish whether the operator has pressed a key since the last execution of ?TERMINAL. The stack effects of ?TERMINAL are (... flag). If a key has been touched, a true(1) flag is left on the stack. If the operator has been idle, ?TERMINAL leaves a false(0) flag on the stack. We will look at all the Forth I/O words in Chap. 6. ?TERMINAL is introduced here only to provide a flag for the BEGIN ... UNTIL indefinite loop construction.

BEGIN ... UNTIL Loops

Just as DO and LOOP work together to control a looping process within a word, BEGIN and UNTIL set up a programming structure like this:

`BEGIN word₁ word₂ word₃ . . . wordₙ flag UNTIL`

Execution begins with word₁ and proceeds in the normal fashion. When execution reaches UNTIL, a test is made of the flag that UNTIL expects to find on the top of the stack. In the case of our silly word WOBBLER, the flag was provided by ?TERMINAL. If UNTIL finds false (0), execution branches back to the word following BEGIN, word, in this case. If UNTIL finds true (1), execution proceeds with the word following UNTIL. Such indefinite loop constructions are very useful in device control and real-time data acquisition applications, and we will use them over and over in Part II.

Here are the stack effects of BEGIN and UNTIL when they are executed:

BEGIN (...)   BEGIN has no net stack effect. It serves to mark the point to which execution will return when UNTIL finds a false flag.

UNTIL (f ...) UNTIL destroys its flag, just as IF does.

As the names of the words imply, a BEGIN ... UNTIL indefinite loop continues *until* something becomes true. There is another indefinite loop construction that repeats endlessly *as long as* a specified condition remains true. It is called the BEGIN ... WHILE ... REPEAT loop.

BEGIN ... WHILE ... REPEAT **Loops**

In this type of indefinite loop the test for loop termination is made in the middle of the loop. The form of the loop's construction follows this pattern:

BEGIN word$_1$ word$_2$ ... flag WHILE word$_i$ word$_i$+1 ... REPEAT ...

In the first pass through the loop the words between BEGIN and WHILE are executed. WHILE looks at the flag left on the stack and, if it is a true, executes the words between WHILE and REPEAT, then branches back to the words following BEGIN.

If a false flag is found, WHILE sends execution to the words following repeat, and the loop is terminated. Like the BEGIN ... UNTIL loops, BEGIN ... WHILE ... REPEAT loops are particularly useful for real-time applications, the focus of Part II. We will use both types of indefinite loops to advantage in our interfacing examples. But before we move on to such practical applications, you must learn a little more about Forth's ability to deal with logical operations.

5.6   More Logic

Frequently we will need an application to execute a particular part of a definition based on the results of more than one test. For instance, it would be inadvisable for a computer-controlled mass spectrometer to allow the high voltage to be applied to the electron multiplier detector unless the analyzer was under a high vacuum *and* the display electronics was switched on. Without actually defining them, suppose the mass spectrometer application included a pair of words that each examined the respective hardware and set a "device ready" flag on the stack.

CHECK/PRESSURE (... f)

CHECK/DISPLAY (... f)

As before, a true(1) flag will be interpreted as a ready indication, whereas a false will imply that the requisite condition has not yet been attained.

We can now write a simple word, READY, that checks both the pressure *and* the display and leaves a single flag on the stack. This flag will be true(1) only if both conditions are met.

: READY CHECK/PRESSURE CHECK/DISPLAY AND ;

The overall stack effects of READY are the same as those of our CHECK ... words.

READY (... f)

The key to its operation is obviously the Forth word AND.

Boolean Operations

The boolean operations are AND, OR, and NOT. AND and OR combine the truth values of two separate expressions in much the same way that we all do in our spoken language. For example, (1) we will go to the beach if it is sunny *and* if there is gas in the car, or (2) we will go to the movies if it is raining *or* if there is nothing good on television.

The best way to portray boolean operations is through "truth tables."

AND	0	1
0	0	0
1	0	1

If both states are true, the AND result is true. If either is false, the result of the AND operation is false, just as the AND operation between two false states is also false.

The truth table for OR is:

OR	0	1
0	0	1
1	1	1

The OR result is true if either state is true, or if both are true.

Actually, the proper name for this OR operation is the "inclusive OR." There is another boolean operator which is called the "exclusive OR." We will use the symbol XOR to represent the exclusive OR, for which the truth table is:

XOR	0	1
0	0	1
1	1	0

Obviously the exclusive OR gives a true result only when one or the other state is true but not both.

The last boolean operation for which we need a truth table is NOT. This operation simply reverses the value of an expression.

NOT	1	0
	0	1

Now we can more clearly understand our word READY. Let us assume that both the vacuum system and the display electronics are "ready" for the operation of the instrument.

```
READY
CHECK/PRESSURE    1        It is true that pressure is low enough.
CHECK/DISPLAY  1  1        It is true that the display is turned on.
AND               1        It is true that the instrument is ready.
```

Indeed, the functions of the boolean operations AND, NOT, OR, and XOR are exactly duplicated in the Forth words with the same respective names. Table 5.3 illustrates the "Forthian" truth tables, based on the stack effects of these boolean Forth words.

As you can clearly see from the truth tables, NOT has the effect of reversing the boolean value of a flag on the stack. This is also the exact effect of the comparison operator 0=. Some Forth systems do not even have NOT included in their basic vocabularies, assuming that the programmer will use 0= whenever it is necessary to reverse the logical value of a parameter.

Up to this point we have used the boolean AND, OR, and XOR operators as though they were suited only for manipulations of logical values corresponding to true(1) and false(0) flags. In fact, these operators are far more powerful than these simple applications suggest. These logical oper-

Table 5.3 Truth Tables for Boolean Operators

Before	Operation	After
0 0	AND	0
0 1	AND	0
1 0	AND	0
1 1	AND	1
0 0	OR	0
0 1	OR	1
1 0	OR	1
1 1	OR	1
0 0	XOR	0
0 1	XOR	1
1 0	XOR	1
1 1	XOR	0
1	NOT	0
0	NOT	1
1	0=	0
0	0=	1

ators are actually designed to operate on the full complement of bits in 16-bit cells, bit by bit. The applicability of such a feature of Forth's design at first seems obscure. But later, when we begin the task of interfacing our computers to real-time devices, we shall use these operations to make decisions based on the contents of individual bits in the actual address locations corresponding to the interface to our real-time devices.

Here are some introductory illustrations of the use of boolean logic operations at the bit level. In Part II, we will recall these examples as you learn how hardware uses specific bits in a designated location to alert the computer to the status of various aspects of the device's condition.

Logic, Bit by Bit

In order to best illustrate the logical operations on a bit level, set your Forth system to binary.

BINARY ok

Now enter the following phrases:

11100 1010 AND U.<ret> 1000 ok

11100 1010 OR U.<ret> 11110 ok

11100 1010 XOR U.<ret> 10110 ok

The operations of the logical operators AND, OR, and XOR operate on *all* the bits in the relevant cells. Perhaps the best way to illustrate this is with the following sort of notation:

```
           11100            11100             11100
    AND     1010     OR      1010     XOR      1010
           -----            -----             -----
            1000            11110             10110
```

The values are right-justified and each bit is AND ed with its partner on a bit-by-bit basis. There are no carrys or borrows involved, and the processes are neither addition nor subtraction. Rather, they are called AND ing and OR ing.

One of the most potent features of these operations appears when we need to detect the value of a particular bit in a designated cell. Suppose that the status of the interface between the computer and its disk drive is available at octal address 177400, and that we need to write a word to determine whether the drive is ready for a read or write operation. The design of disk drives and other I/O hardware interfaces traditionally includes implementation of a "ready bit" which we will assume in this application to be set to a true(1) in bit 7 of address 177400_8 when the ready state is attained. To be certain that any data sent to the disk would not be lost, we should include a word that suspends any transfer of data to the device until the ready signal is obtained. Assuming that the system is set to OCTAL when this definition is entered, here is such a word.

: WAIT BEGIN 177400 # 200 AND UNTIL ;

WAIT contains an indefinite BEGIN . . . UNTIL loop which can only terminate when UNTIL finds a true(1) flag. That flag can only be provided by the 177400 @ 200 AND phrase.

Here is how that comes about:

```
         - - - - - x - - - - - - -       Bit 7 is ready bit.
    AND            1 0 0 0 0 0 0 0       To be AND ed with $200_8$.
    gives          1 0 0 0 0 0 0 0 = true    If ready.
    or             0 0 0 0 0 0 0 0 = false   If not yet ready.
```

Remember, *any* nonzero value will be acceptable to IF and words that use IF (such as UNTIL) as an indication of true. That is why 200_8 suffices to terminate the wait state set up in our demonstration WAIT word.

You will find that words like WAIT are indispensable in helping you learn simple ways to understand the hardware applications of your computer system.

5.7 Problems

1. a. Define a Forth word, PARA, to draw a sideward-facing parabola on the screen. Your output should resemble this:

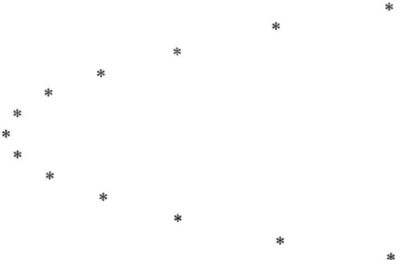

   b. Rewrite PARA to display a parabola with the open end facing upward.

2. a. Define a word, EVEN, that prints Even or Odd depending on the value on top of the stack when the word is executed.

   b. Define another such word, EITHER-EVEN, that prints a message if either of the top two stack values is even.

3. Write a Forth loop routine which examines all the elements of an array (like the POINTS array) to compare each entry with the contents of a variable called LIMIT. Call the highest-level word in your routine EXAMINE. The stack notation for EXAMINE must be (count address ...) and should function thus:

   20 LIMIT ! 30 POINTS EXAMINE<ret>

   Limit Exceeded in Entry: Value:

2	27
7	31
15	22
21	23
22	26 ok

4. Write a Forth word, ZERO-OUT, that "fills" a specified number of locations in a specified array with zeroes. Stack effect must be (count addr ...), where addr is the *starting* address for the operation and count represents the number of *bytes* to be affected. Be very careful writing and testing this word, since you can very easily "zero-out" all your computer's RAM memory, including Forth's dictionary, if you are not careful.

5. Examining a large array point by point can be tedious. Write a word called DUMP (count addr ...) that displays the contents of a specified number of *cells* in a particular array. The display should show 10 entries per row, as in

```
20 POINTS DUMP<ret>
```

```
 0   0   0   0  17   0   0  14   0   0
19 176 189 189 176 135 133 111 121 191
```

<u>ok</u>

Chapter 6

Input-Output, Editor, and Disk

Now that you have mastered the first five chapters of this book, you are probably anxious to learn the techniques necessary to access the system's disk drives and line printers. In this chapter, you will learn the methods with which Forth uses peripheral devices to save applications programs and data as well as the programming skills necessary to create your own text editor.

6.1 Character Representations

Until now, you have not had to concern yourself much with the inner workings of the input-output operations that allow you to communicate with the computer. Therefore it may come as a surprise to you that Forth transfers information to your terminal and receives information from you in return as coded characters in a stream of 8-bit bytes. These bytes contain numerically coded representations of the data that you have induced the computer either to accept from your terminal or to send to you. This coding process includes letters, punctuation marks, and other special-purpose symbols, as well as numeric information.

The ASCII Code

The high-level Forth word that bears the responsibility for sending characters to terminals is called `EMIT`. Enter this:

```
65 EMIT<ret> A ok
```

The definition of `EMIT` is essentially this: "Send to the terminal the single character for which the 'code' value appears on the stack." The stack effects of EMIT are (n ...), where n is the code value of the particular character desired. Try this:

```
66 EMIT<ret> B ok
```

```
67 EMIT<ret> C ok
```

and so on. The particular code in which uppercase letters A, B, and C are represented by the values 65, 66, and 67, respectively, is called the ASCII code (for American Standard Code for Information Interchange), and it comes as close to a *standard* code for character representation among the many computer designers and manufacturers as we are likely to find. It is certainly the standard code in use among micro- and minicomputer manufacturers.

Originally designed for use with teletypewriters, the ASCII code consists of

Character types	Decimal codes
33 special nonprinting characters	0–31 and 127
26 uppercase letters	65–90
26 lowercase letters	97–122
10 numerals	48–57
1 blank space	32
32 punctuation marks	33–47, 58–64, 91–96, and 123–126

Nonprinting Characters

The special nonprinting characters were originally intended for machine-to-machine communications when teletypewriters were used for sending telegrams. Today some of these characters are used to control certain terminal features, whereas others are ignored by both the terminal and the sending computer system. Regardless of their use, these special characters are called "control" characters. Among the control characters which are of utmost importance in Forth applications, as well as applications written in virtually any other language, are those tabulated below.

Code (decimal)	Name	Action or definition
7	BEL	Rings the terminal bell.
8	BS	Backspaces the terminal.
9	HT	Horizontal tab.
10	LF	Linefeed; advances the paper or moves cursor to next line.
11	VT	Vertical tab.
12	FF	Formfeed; moves paper to next page.
13	CR	Carriage return; moves the write mechanism back to the beginning of the line.
27	ESC	Escape; sends the computer a special "lead-in" character to alert it to take special action.

The way in which these control characters operate depends on the design of the particular system. For instance, the older teletypewriters can neither back up nor perform horizontal or vertical tab functions. Those old devices simply ignore decimal codes 8, 9, and 11. Other control characters work in exactly the defined fashion, even if a bit unexpectedly. Enter this:

`: DEMO 50 0 DO 13 EMIT I SPACES ." *" LOOP ;`

Execute it. If you have a "hard-copy" terminal, one that prints on paper, you can watch the action as DEMO spaces over an ever-increasing amount before printing an asterisk, then returns to print again, *but always on the same line.* On a video terminal the effect is similar, but the asterisk is obliterated with each pass of the cursor, effectively simulating a star moving across the screen (depending on the transmission rate of your system). Indeed, all 13 EMIT does is send the cursor or printhead to the farthest-left position in the current line.

Most novice programmers would expect the special character CR (ASCII 13) to return the carriage in the same way that a typewriter does, moving the printhead to the leftmost position and advancing the paper by one line. To actually accomplish that, you need to arrange for the following *pair* of ASCII characters to be sent to your terminal, as in this definition:

`: CR 13 EMIT 10 EMIT ; ( .. )`

Try CR, but do not bother to enter it, since it is already a part of your system, as previously indicated in Chap. 2.

Note that the Forth word CR has the effect of ASCII 13 (ASCII CR) *plus* ASCII 10 (ASCII LF). Unfortunately, this obviously confusing choice of names is too entrenched in both the ASCII and Forth jargons to eliminate now; you just have to remember whether you need CR or CR and use the appropriate form.

Fortunately, CR is the only control code name that is also a common predefined Forth word. Hence the confusion ends there, unless you feel inclined to enjoy teasing yourself with a few of your own exploratory definitions, like this one:

`: BEL 7 EMIT ; ( .. )`

Try it. Or better yet, put BEL into an indefinite loop like this:

`: NOISE BEGIN BEL ?TERMINAL UNTIL ;`

Table 6.1 ASCII Character Codes

Ch	Hex	Dec	Ch	Hex	Dec	Ch	Hex	Dec	Ch	Hex	Dec
NUL	00	0	SP	20	32	@	40	64	`	60	96
SOH	01	1	!	21	33	A	41	65	a	61	97
STX	02	2	"	22	34	B	42	66	b	62	98
ETX	03	3	#	23	35	C	43	67	c	63	99
EOT	04	4	$	24	36	D	44	68	d	64	100
ENQ	05	5	%	25	37	E	45	69	e	65	101
ACK	06	6	&	26	38	F	46	70	f	66	102
BEL	07	7	'	27	39	G	47	71	g	67	103
BS	08	8	(	28	40	H	48	72	h	68	104
HT	09	9	)	29	41	I	49	73	i	69	105
LF	0A	10	*	2A	42	J	4A	74	j	6A	106
VT	0B	11	+	2B	43	K	4B	75	k	6B	107
FF	0C	12	,	2C	44	L	4C	76	l	6C	108
CR	0D	13	-	2D	45	M	4D	77	m	6D	109
SM	0E	14	.	2E	46	N	4E	78	n	6E	110
SI	0F	15	/	2F	47	O	4F	79	o	6F	111
DLE	10	16	0	30	48	P	50	80	p	70	112
DC1	11	17	1	31	49	Q	51	81	q	71	113
DC2	12	18	2	32	50	R	52	82	r	72	114
DC3	13	19	3	33	51	S	53	83	s	73	115
DC4	14	20	4	34	52	T	54	84	t	74	116
NAK	15	21	5	35	53	U	55	85	u	75	117
SYN	16	22	6	36	54	V	56	86	v	76	118
ETB	17	23	7	37	55	W	57	87	w	77	119
CAN	18	24	8	38	56	X	58	88	x	78	120
EM	19	25	9	39	57	Y	59	89	y	79	121
SUB	1A	26	:	3A	58	Z	5A	90	z	7A	122
ESC	1B	27	;	3B	59	[	5B	91	{	7B	123
FS	1C	28	<	3C	60	\	5C	92			7C	124
GS	1D	29	=	3D	61	]	5D	93	}	7D	125
RS	1E	30	>	3E	62	^	5E	94	~	7E	126
US	1F	31	?	3F	63	_	5F	95	DEL	7F	127

Just be sure to remember to include ?TERMINAL in your definition, or you will be stuck with a noisy, unstoppable monster.

Table 6.1 lists the entire ASCII code set, along with the decimal and hexadecimal values for all the characters. You may find it handy to keep a copy of this table near your computer. (If your system has a printer, you will find it simple to print a copy of the table after you have finished Chap. 7.)

Printing Characters

The organization of the table as presented here gives a clearer picture of the design of the ASCII codes. Consider the codes for both lowercase letters a and b and uppercase letters A and B, for example. The hex values for A and B are 41 and 42, respectively, corresponding to the binary values 1000001 and 1000010, while a and b have respective hex codes 61 (1100001), and 62 (1100010), values differing from the corresponding uppercase symbols only in the value of bit 5. On a normal terminal keyboard, pressing a key causes the terminal to send the computer a character representation consisting of a string of bits, each of which is either 0 or 1 depending on the character being sent. On most keyboards, bit 5 is automatically set (its value is 1), unless the shift key is pressed simultaneously, or unless the shift lock key is locked in place.

Indeed, the function of the shift key on the keyboard is to set bit 5 to 0 for characters having hex codes above 5F. Likewise, the binary representations of the control characters (00 through 1F) can be sent to the computer by holding down the "control" key while depressing another key.

BEL, for instance, is 07, while uppercase G is hex 47. The binary equivalents of these codes are 111 and 1000111, a difference in only bit 6. The control key, when pressed, forces bits 6 and 7 to 0, regardless of the other key pressed. While the control key is down, only hex codes 00 through 1F (binary 0000000 through 0011111) can be sent, values corresponding to the control characters in the first column of Table 6.1. Hold down the control key and press "G." You should hear the terminal bell if yours is an ASCII terminal. Later you will learn how many of these nonprinting control characters are used in the "hand-shaking" operations that computers use in sending data back and forth. Now we will continue our investigations into the inner workings of Forth's input-output operations.

ASCII is a word that prints the ASCII characters from hex codes 20 through 7F, or 32 to 127 in decimal. Try it:

: ASCII 127 32 DO I EMIT LOOP ;

110 The Forth Language

```
ASCII<ret> !"#$%&'()*+,-./0123456789:;<=>?ABCDEFGHIJKLMNOPQRSTUV
WXYZ[ ]©_abcdefghijklmnopqrstuvwxyz ok
```

Every one of the printing characters that the ASCII codes include was printed by this word, in "ASCII order." This list of sequential numbers and letters constitutes a "string" of characters. Although the order of appearance differs, any text, even a list of Forth definitions, is merely a string of characters.

Forth can "output" strings of characters (. " ... ", for example) and Forth can "input" strings of characters (as happens every time you enter a definition or execute a predefined word). Now, you need to learn how Forth can "save" a string of characters in a useful (retrievable) fashion. A pair of the key words needed for this task are KEY and PAD.

6.2 Single-Character Input

Enter this sequence:

```
KEY<ret>
```

No ok will appear, nor will Forth appear to produce any response. In fact, Forth is waiting for you to enter a character, any character.

The definition of KEY calls for suspension of other computer operations and entry into a mode called an "I/O wait state," a particular computer routine in which the system enters an indefinite loop waiting for terminal input. Once a key is pressed, however, the I/O wait state is terminated, and the system proceeds to process whatever commands remain in the command sequence. In the case of KEY, the remaining words in KEY's definition call for the word to leave on the stack the ASCII code equivalent of the character which was entered.

```
KEY<ret> E ok

.<ret> 69 ok
```

One convenient feature of KEY, although not its principal use, is its ability to reveal the ASCII equivalent for any character. Suppose you needed to use EMIT to print a string of pound signs, # but you had no copy of Table 6.1 handy. The ASCII representation for the # character can be easily obtained by

```
KEY<ret> # ok

.<ret> 35 ok
```

The greatest usefulness of KEY arises when it is used with other character-oriented words such as PAD, or when it is used in the definition of multiple-character words such as EXPECT and WORD, words that we shall be coming to shortly. But first we need to examine the means Forth employs to put these characters someplace once they have been received by the system. As you might expect, Forth has provisions for several ways of dealing with incoming information. One of the simplest involves use of the "pad."

Forth's Scratchpad

When your Forth applications become sufficiently complex that you must save them for later use without reentering them each time, you will need to learn how to save character strings. Much of the work of saving your labors will fall upon a set of Forth words which, taken together, are called an *Editor*. In most cases you will not have to be fully aware of the inner working of your Editor, but if you ever need to save *data,* or if you should ever want to improve or rewrite your Editor, sooner or later you will need to use the pad.

The pad is an area of the computer's memory where character strings are stored and manipulated. Like a child's magic slate, Forth's pad gives no assurance of permanence. Rather, it is used as a scratchpad area for composing strings of characters as they are either entered by the programmer or emitted as output by Forth. (In the latter case, for instance, the pad is the area in which character string representations of values are assembled before being dotted off by the output routines.)

Buffers

In computer jargon the term "buffer" is used to describe an area of memory that is set aside as a temporary holding area for data, programs, or just about anything that will later be used someplace else. For example, the characters that you type on your terminal are stored in a memory region called the *terminal input buffer*. That is where the INTERPRETer finds the words and numbers you have been typing. Forth's disk operations involve rather large buffers called *block buffers,* which we will be using shortly.

Some buffers are assigned a fixed region in memory. Such buffers are usually associated with information that may have to remain in memory for a relatively long period before it is referred to or used. Disk block buffers fall into this category. Other buffers are allowed to "float" about in memory, above the dictionary or elsewhere. Such buffers are transient storage locations from which information must be accessed shortly after it is composed if there is to be any guarantee that it has remained intact, or "uncorrupted." The pad is one such buffer.

To ascertain the location of the `PAD`, enter

`PAD .<ret>` <u>10160 ok</u>

Like a variable, `PAD` returns an address, the *current* address of the pad. Your value will differ.

`PAD ( ... addr )`

Unlike the usual variables, however, the pad's address changes constantly. This is due to Forth's clever use of memory. Pad's address is defined in terms of the top of the dictionary. Whenever a new word is defined, or a variable or constant is created, the address of the pad moves to give the dictionary a clean area in which to work.

Before actually writing information into the pad, we first need to clear it. `FILL` is a handy (but dangerous) word that allows us to write as many of a particular character as we want into as many locations of the computer's memory as we wish.

`FILL ( addr count code ... )`

`FILL` expects to find a starting address, a number of *bytes,* and an ASCII code value on the stack. On execution, `FILL` fills the region of memory starting at "addr" with "count" bytes of code characters.

▶ *The programmer must be careful with FILL. Too large a value for count or a wrong starting address can easily wipe out Forth, dictionary, stack, pad, and all.*

It is safest to imbed `FILL` in another word like `CLEAR`, a word that you should now define on your system. Be sure your system is expecting `DECIMAL` numbers for this exercise.

`: CLEAR PAD 64 32 FILL ;` <u>ok</u>

`CLEAR` will put 64 bytes of ASCII 32 (blank spaces, see Table 6.1), starting at the address of the pad. There is no set limit for the pad's size, incidentally. We use 64 locations here for the convenience of the words to follow.

Writing on the Pad

Later, when your application requires that you erase or clear large regions of memory for data storage or other numeric applications, you will want to precede FILL with 0 rather than 32 on the top of the stack. This ensures that binary zeros are written to the desired locations, rather than "space" characters.

Now you are ready to write your first real I/O application. You are going to compose the words that will allow you to write a simple text editor. This editor will allow you to create organized pages of Forth words that can be saved on the computer's disk drives or magnetic tape. You will use the pad as a composing area, and your first task will be to write a pair of Forth words that allow you to write to the pad, and then to display the pad's contents.

Initially, you need to define a variable that will store the location of any particular character within the pad. We call such use of an address to store another address a "pointer" to the specific location of interest. This use of a pointer to an address will be used again when you learn the techniques of storing data as it is acquired from various instruments and devices.

```
0 VARIABLE CHRADD<ret> ok
```

Next you will need a word to accept characters from the terminal, one by one, and store them in the pad. This word will have to clear the pad first, so that a string of characters of any size will always have blanks at the end, instead of ending with whatever trash was left over from the last use of the pad.

Enter this definition:

```
: INPUT CLEAR PAD CHRADD ! BEGIN KEY DUP CHRADD @ C! 1 CHRADD +! 13 = UNTIL ;
```

INPUT consists of:

1. Clearing the pad (CLEAR)
2. Initialization of the contents of the variable CHRADD with the address of the pad (PAD CHRADD !)
3. An indeterminate loop (BEGIN ... UNTIL) which:
   a. Awaits a character (KEY)
   b. DUP's it for later (DUP)
   c. Fetches the address to send the character (CHRADD @)
   d. Stores it [C! (character store)] and increments the address of the destination address (1 CHRADD +!)
   e. Tests the DUPed copy of the character to see if it was a carriage return (13 =)
   f. Terminates the indefinite loop if it was, or returns for more characters if it was not

114 The Forth Language

Input will accept any characters entered at the keyboard and store them in a character string in the pad. Before you use `INPUT`, however, you need to compose a word to let you see what you have accomplished. We will call this word `.PAD`.

Reading the Contents of the Pad

Enter this word:

```
: .PAD PAD 64 TYPE CR ;<ret> ok
```

The definition of `.PAD` contains only one unfamiliar word, `TYPE`. As its name implies, `TYPE` types characters. The origin of the characters can be anywhere in memory, since the operational definition of `TYPE` is:

`TYPE ( addr n ... )`   Send n characters, beginning at address `addr`, to the output device.

In our definition of `.PAD`, `PAD` supplies the address and 64 provides a count.

Now that you have entered your pair of input and output words, along with the support word `CLEAR`, you are ready to do some I/O operations. First be sure that you have entered the requisite words with a `VLIST`.

```
VLIST<ret> .PAD INPUT CLEAR CHRADD . . . ok
```

Remember, `INPUT` has `KEY` within an indefinite loop. When you execute `INPUT`, the system will enter a `WAIT` state, awaiting characters. You must follow `INPUT` with a carriage return to get the process started.

```
INPUT<ret>
```

If your definition was correct, you should now be able to enter a line of text.

```
Forth is a river in the south of Scotland.<ret> ok
```

Since Forth will not return the cursor after `INPUT`, the entire transaction will actually look like this:

```
INPUT<ret> Forth is a river in the south of Scotland.<ret> ok
```

To get it back, use `.PAD`:

```
.PAD<ret> Forth is a river in the south of Scotland.            ok
```

Input-Output, Editor, and Disk 115

`.PAD` is nondestructive.

```
.PAD<ret> Forth is a river in the south of Scotland.         ok
.PAD<ret> Forth is a river in the south of Scotland.         ok
.PAD<ret> Forth is a river in the south of Scotland.         ok
```

To clear the pad, use `CLEAR`.

```
CLEAR .PAD <ret>                                             ok
```

Notice that each ok in the lines above lies far to the right of the last character in the string. And in the last example, a clear pad still appears to have something in it. That's because it does contain 64 blank characters, (ASCII 32). `TYPE`'s definition calls for it to send a number of characters to the terminal, regardless of their nature.

`FORGET` your old `.PAD`. Here is a better definition that has only one additional word and produces a much more attractive output.

```
: .PAD PAD 64 -TRAILING TYPE CR ;
```

This new definition has the Forth word `-TRAILING` inserted between the character count and `TYPE`. The task of `-TRAILING` is inspection of the character string that `TYPE` is to transmit, and if there are so-called trailing blanks in the character stream, it merely adjusts the value of the count so that `TYPE` does not have to bother printing meaningless spaces. The stack designation for `-TRAILING` is:

```
-TRAILING ( add count₁ ... add count₂ )
```

Use this version of `.PAD` to print the contents of the pad:

```
.PAD<ret> Forth is a river in the south of Scotland. ok
```

Now you can experiment, entering and retrieving lines of text, including various symbols and punctuation marks. You can even include `BEL` (`control G`) in the text stream, if you wish, but beware of incautious experimentation with the other control characters. Some hardware relies on control characters to assist in the communications protocol between terminal and computer, and you can disrupt communication by sending the wrong character. (Digital Equipment Corporation systems and some others, for example, will halt character transmission to a terminal on receipt of a `control S`, and the only way to resume communication is to send a `control Q` to the system.)

Now that you have become proficient with KEY and PAD, we can introduce the Forth words that handle *groups* of characters. These words are defined by using KEY, as you might have predicted, and provide much more efficient means to compose your Editor.

6.3 Multiple-Character Input

Taken with our word CLEAR, our previously defined INPUT actually bears a strong operational resemblance to the predefined Forth word EXPECT. Enter this new definition of INPUT:

```
: INPUT CLEAR PAD 64 EXPECT ; ok
```

Obviously a lot simpler than our earlier definition, this new version of INPUT can accept as many as 64 characters from the keyboard, storing them in the pad. The keyword to the simplicity of this version of INPUT is, of course, EXPECT.

```
EXPECT     ( addr count ... )
```

EXPECT, like KEY, suspends processing and enters a WAIT state, anticipating "count" characters from the terminal or a carriage return, whichever occurs first. As the characters arrive, EXPECT stores them in memory, starting at address addr. In the present case, the phrase PAD 64 EXPECT will accomplish the sequential transfer of as many as 64 incoming characters to the pad. Try it.

```
INPUT<ret> No, I don't want to go to the pad<ret> ok
```

```
.PAD<ret> No, I don't want to go to the pad<ret> ok
```

Of course, EXPECT can send the incoming characters to *any* address, not just the pad, and in Part II we will use EXPECT to accept data from an external device, storing the values in an array.

One of the annoying features of our word INPUT is the need to enter a carriage return to initiate the WAIT state, and another carriage return to terminate the incoming character string. There is a way around the problem, of course, and as might be expected, it involves an even higher-level word than EXPECT. The word is WORD.

WORD

```
WORD     ( code ... )
```

WORD reads the incoming terminal character stream until it encounters *either* a carriage return *or* the character whose ASCII "code" was on the stack when WORD was executed. This character is called the *string delimiter,* and you choose whatever character you want WORD to watch for as it carries out its task. For example, when you are entering a new definition, the INTERPRETer uses WORD to scan the incoming characters which constitute the Forth words in your definition. Since each Forth word is separated from its neighbors by at least one blank space, INTERPRET splits out each Forth word with the phrase 32 WORD, since 32 is the ASCII code for a blank space.

In writing an Editor, however, you want WORD to accept any and all characters up to the carriage return. The way to accomplish that is to precede WORD with a delimiter that will not normally appear in the incoming character stream. Customarily, Forth programmers use the phrase 1 WORD for this purpose. (Actually, ASCII 1 is <control>A, a character which can possibly be sent from a terminal, but would not be sent in the normal course of events.)

Unlike the case with EXPECT, you do not have to specify an address to which WORD is to send your characters. WORD always sends them to its own buffer, a region of memory that moves about in much the same way as the pad. Furthermore, WORD is much more sophisticated than EXPECT, in that it actually keeps track of the number of characters that it has encountered during its scan of the input character stream. That count is stored in the first byte of WORD's buffer. Later, when the string has to be moved elsewhere, the contents of that first byte can be accessed to tell the system exactly how many bytes to move.

Now we can look more closely at WORD's buffer. One of your Forth system's variables is dedicated to storage of the location of the next available 16-bit cell in the dictionary. That variable is called DP (or, on some systems, H). The name is an acronym for "*dictionary pointer.*" WORD uses the location pointed by DP as the first cell in its buffer. This obviously means that WORD's buffer suffers from the same transient existence as does the pad, but that is OK, since we shall be quickly moving our strings out of that buffer as soon as they have been collected.

To determine the contents of the dictionary pointer, you can use the predefined Forth word HERE. The definition of HERE is simply:

: HERE DP @ ;

> Let us digress to look at a useful application of HERE. You can execute HERE . on your system, then define a new word and execute the phrase again to determine just how many cells a particular definition requires.

HERE . 10030 ok

: .SQUARE DUP * . ; ok

HERE . 10050 ok

Using HERE, we find that a short word to simply print the square of the 16-bit number on top of the stack occupies only 20 bytes. Remember the Forth word ROOM from Chap. 2 and App. A? ROOM uses HERE to determine the amount of space left in memory between the stack and the dictionary pointer. Since that is the area of RAM allocated for new definitions, ROOM is a handy tool for checking availability of memory for large applications. Now, back to the task at hand, looking into WORD's buffer.

COUNT

As indicated above, WORD not only deposits the designated text string in the buffer pointed to by the contents of DP, but it begins that string of characters with a character count. Whenever you encounter a predefined Forth word that goes to all that trouble, you can count on the existence of another Forth word that will use the designated information. In this case the appropriate word is COUNT.

COUNT (addr ... addr+1 n)

COUNT looks at a character string beginning at the address on the top of the stack, offsets the address by 1 (to bypass the count byte for the benefit of subsequent words), and extracts the count byte, converting it to a 16-bit number. Obviously, COUNT was tailor-made for use *following* WORD. Not as obvious, but just as important, is that COUNT is just the right kind of word to *precede* the character-moving instructions.

Moving Characters in Memory

Our earlier versions of INPUT accepted characters (using either KEY or EXPECT) from the keyboard and moved them directly to the pad. WORD, using its own buffer, leaves us with a string *n* characters long starting at a particular address which is *not* the pad. Before we can use .PAD or TYPE, we need to move our characters to the pad. In fact, in other, non-editing applications as well, numerous occasions will arise when we need to move characters and data about in memory.

To accomplish this, Forth provides character-moving instructions that can move the contents of any number of bytes anywhere in memory. This word is called CMOVE.

In addition, some Forth systems also include a cell-moving instruction MOVE and a special instruction for copying bytes from one location to another starting at the high end of the byte string. This word is <CMOVE. MOVE executes faster than CMOVE on 16-bit processor-based Forth systems, and <CMOVE is useful when moving strings over very short distances in memory. Both these words are discussed in App. C, "Forth Dialects," and applications employing both also appear in Part II. Our present needs will be served nicely by CMOVE.

CMOVE (addr$_{from}$ addr$_{to}$ n ...)

As the stack notation implies, CMOVE expects three values on the stack. On execution CMOVE copies n bytes, one at a time, starting at addr$_{from}$, to the memory locations starting at addr$_{to}$. Although the name implies otherwise, CMOVE actually *copies* the region of memory starting at the first address to the region starting at the second. The original character string is not affected. We can now use CMOVE in our definition of a very efficient input word. To be consistent with existing words on some Forth systems, this word will be TEXT.

TEXT

Enter the following definition. It expects that you have already defined CLEAR. (Your system may already have TEXT.)

: TEXT CLEAR WORD HERE COUNT PAD SWAP CMOVE ; ok

TEXT has a very simple stack designation:

TEXT (c ...)

Using the character whose ASCII code appears on the stack at execution time, TEXT clears the first 64 bytes of the pad. Then, using WORD, COUNT, and CMOVE, it moves all the input characters to the pad. From there, we can use .PAD or some other words to access the characters from the pad.

Look closely at the definition of TEXT. You will find SWAP just preceding CMOVE. The phrase COUNT PAD puts into place the addresses and count needed by CMOVE, but in the wrong order (addr n addr). SWAP quickly takes care of that (addr addr n).

You are ready to try TEXT, but, by now you have probably lost your definition of .PAD. So enter it again, just in case, and proceed with this exercise.

The Forth Language

```
: .PAD PAD 64 -TRAILING TYPE ; ok

1 TEXT This is a line of text to go to the pad.<ret> ok

.PAD<ret> This is a line of text to go to the pad. ok
```

Although it may not seem like a big deal now, this new word, TEXT, will be invaluable in creating your Editor. Without any fuss, TEXT quickly and easily copies to the pad whatever is typed after it is executed.

If there were a way to copy the pad onto a magnetic disk, we could save all our definitions, 64-character line by 64-character line, just by composing them on the pad and then sending them to the disk. Of course, there is a way to do just that, but first we need to look at the ways in which Forth uses the computer's magnetic media, specifically the disk.

6.4 Disk Storage and Virtual Memory

In Part II we will look more closely at the details of the hardware in the various kinds of disk devices which are used in Forth systems. In this chapter we will focus on the programming aspects associated with saving and editing Forth applications.

Most computers do not possess sufficient memory locations to store all the applications programs that a programmer, or group of programmers, may compose over a long period of time. Furthermore, the design of current computer memory chips requires that power must be constantly applied to the memory chip to ensure retention of data. Finally, the exchange of information between computers requires some sort of medium upon which programs and data can be permanently stored in a mailable form. For these reasons, almost all computer systems have some sort of memory-storage device in the form of either magnetic tape or disk.

At the present time, the magnetic disk system is the medium of choice for storing information on the typical Forth computer, although slower and considerably less expensive magnetic tape devices which use audio-type cassette tapes also provide reasonably efficient storage on some microcomputer-based Forth systems.

Under control of a fairly sophisticated set of disk-controlling functions, such memory devices can appear to the programmer as though they were virtually extensions of the computer's dynamic memory. Consequently, disk memory systems are frequently referred to as *virtual memory*.

Forth organizes the allocation of storage areas on a magnetic disk into units called *blocks*. Each Forth block has 1024_{10} bytes of storage capacity. Since 1024 is just over 1000, it is common in computer parlance to approximate 1024 as 1K (after the Latin metric prefix kilo which is usually symbolized by k). Thus, a Forth system may have as few as 16 such 1K blocks of disk storage, or it may possibly have many hundreds of blocks for saving programs and data.

Regardless of the computer system in use, and even though many other computer operating systems use blocks which are 512_{10} or even 256_{10} bytes in size, a Forth block can be assumed to contain 1024 bytes. The choice of 1024-byte block size was not arbitrary. Rather, it reflects another of the impressively practical aspects of Forth's design.

A typical video computer terminal has a screen display consisting of 24 lines, each of which has as many as 80 characters. Some less expensive or special-purpose terminals have 20-line, 64-character displays. Forth's 1024 character blocks, when divided into 16 lines of 64 characters each, fit nicely into either type of screen. Indeed, some Forth systems actually call each Forth block a screen for exactly this reason. One of the first things you need to learn to do is to inspect the contents of the blocks on your system.

Listing Forth Blocks

The preexisting Forth word that allows us to display the contents of a block (or screen) is LIST. LIST expects to find a 16-bit block number on the stack. Without explaining, we LISTed a Forth block in Chap. 4 when we wrote the gas law application. Since that particular application was saved in block 104, we can list it by simply executing LIST with 104 on the stack, i.e. with 104 LIST<ret>. The results appear in Fig. 6.1. There are several important things to notice about this listing.

1. The lines are numbered from 0 through 15 rather than 1 through 16. Line 0 contains information surrounded by parentheses. Such infor-

```
Block  # 104
    0 ( Ideal Gas Law, Integer Version, Forth Applications )
    1
    2 0 VARIABLE OXYGEN           0 VARIABLE VOLUME ( Liters )
    3 0 VARIABLE NITROGEN         0 VARIABLE TEMP   ( Degrees Kelvin )
    4 0 VARIABLE HELIUM           0 VARIABLE TOTAL  ( Total moles )
    5
    6 : MOLES OVER TOTAL +! ! ;   ( Calc's n[i], accumulates in TOTAL)
    7 : LITERS VOLUME ! ;         ( Stores volume in variable VOLUME )
    8 : DEGREES TEMP ! ;          ( Stores the temperature )
    9
   10
   11 : PRESSURE    @ TEMP @ VOLUME @ */ 624 10 */ . ." Torr " ;
   12
   13 : CLEAR    0 OXYGEN ! 0 NITROGEN ! 0 HELIUM ! 0 TOTAL ! ;
   14
   15
```

Figure 6.1 A typical Forth block listing

mation constitutes a label or heading for the block, and will be ignored by the INTERPRETer when the block is loaded later. This use of line 0 as a label is optional, but advisable.

2. The line numbers are actually not part of the block's contents. They are provided by LIST for our convenience.

3. The block number that appears on the top of the listing is also not saved within the 1K of characters that occupy the block. It too is put there by LIST.

And there is at least one important thing that is not obvious from this listing. When executed, LIST stores in one of Forth's predefined user variables the value of the disk block most recently listed. The first part of the LIST definition is the phrase DUP SCR !. In this way the variable SCR is always available so that the programmer can access the block number of the most recently listed disk block. We will use this variable to great advantage in writing our Editor.

As is the case with all nonprimitive Forth words, LIST is itself defined in terms of other, lower-level Forth words. Indeed, we can easily write our own simple listing procedure and in the process learn a lot about Forth's disk- and buffer-manipulation techniques. Since Forth provides LIST to list a block with labeled lines and a block number header, it would be a waste of time to simply recreate an already useful word. Rather, we will write a word to list a block without any extraneous information. Enter these definitions:

```
: LTYPE 64 -TRAILING TYPE ; ok    ( addr ... )
: VIZ BLOCK DUP 1024 + SWAP CR DO I LTYPE 64 +LOOP ;
```

LTYPE is just like .PAD except that it needs to find an address on the stack at execution time. That allows it to be used anywhere text is to be TYPEd. Indeed, if we had been aware earlier that such a word would be useful now, we would have defined it at that time and then defined .PAD as

```
: .PAD PAD LTYPE ;
```

illustrating again the importance of keeping it simple. As simple as it looked at the time when we defined it, .PAD was actually too complex. Oh well, such is Forth!

In this application, however, the key word is VIZ, and the key word in VIZ is BLOCK. Let us try it, and then we will dissect VIZ to see how it works. Like LIST, VIZ expects to find a block number on the stack. We will VIZ block 108 by entering 108 VIZ<ret>. The results appear in Fig.

6.2. Of course, your results will differ, with your screen showing something else entirely, possibly garbage.

In this listing you will find two old friends, CLEAR and TEXT. Also in this listing are three new words: P, L, and SAVE. Taken together, these five words constitute the sought-after Skeleton Editor, so called because it provides a tiny but efficient bare-bones editing application, which we will use to save our work in virtual memory. Do not enter it yet, however, because you still need to learn how to use some of the fundamental disk-control words.

Note that the definition of VIZ includes CR within the DO ... LOOP construction. The 1024 bytes of information stored in the disk block do not contain any CR or LF control characters.

Forth assumes that words that access the disk blocks will provide their own carriage control characters. In fact, the contents of an empty disk block are a continuous 1024-character-long string of ASCII 32 (blank spaces) uninterrupted by any other characters. This practice saves valuable disk space, since imbedding ASCII carriage return codes would waste at least 1 out of every 64 characters.

Now that we have composed a Forth word that allows access to every line within a given Forth block, we can compose a similar word to access a given line in every available Forth block. While it may not seem useful at first, such a word will enable us to keep tabs on the content of all the blocks in our Forth applications library. To maintain conformity with Forth systems in which such a word is predefined, we will call our word INDEX.

Indexing Forth Blocks

It is traditional in Forth virtual memory operations to designate the first line of a block which contains definitions or other ASCII coded informa-

```
( The Skeleton Editor, Forth Applications        May 83 )

: Clear    pad 64 32 fill ;            ( Clear the Pad )

: Text     clear word here count pad swap cmove ;
           ( Get a line of text and move it to the pad )

: P        1 text 64 * scr @ block + pad swap 64 cmove ;
                       ( Move the line into the buffer )

: L        scr @ list ;   ( List the last block listed )

: Save     update flush ; ( Save the block on the disk )
```

Figure 6.2 A list without linenumbers

tion a label for that particular block. Since parentheses can be used to bypass the INTERPRETer process as a block is loaded, their presence surrounding the text in the zeroth line has no effect on the interpretation of the block's contents and clearly identifies a block as having been written by a Forth programmer following this tradition. INDEX can be defined thus:

```
: LTYPE 64 -TRAILING TYPE ; ( Same LTYPE as above )
: INDEX CR 1 + SWAP DO I 3 .R SPACE I BLOCK LTYPE
?TERMINAL IF LEAVE THEN CR LOOP ;
```

Your system may already have INDEX. If not, you can enter it now. INDEX expects to find a starting block number and an ending block number on the stack.

```
INDEX ( n_start n_end ... )
```

The phrase 1 + SWAP increments the limit and reverses the order of the block numbers to get them into the proper order for DO.

The crux of INDEX lies in the I BLOCK LTYPE phrase within the DO ... LOOP. As we will see shortly, BLOCK provides the address where a memory copy of a disk block can be found. LTYPE merely prints the first 64 characters. Try INDEX. Your screen will quickly fill with an index of your disk. Note the use of the phrase ?TERMINAL IF LEAVE THEN to allow a premature termination of the INDEX if you get bored with it. When you enter INDEX be sure to precede it with two block numbers. You should get results like those in Fig. 6.3.

```
1 9 INDEX<ret>
```

As we have observed, the keyword in disk operations is BLOCK. This word is responsible for the transfer of information from the disk into

```
1 ( Introduction to the load blocks in the CSUN-forth library )
2 ( Terminal Personality Block....H19-A VT52 emulation..       )
3 ( Terminal Personality Block....Intecolor VT52 emulation...  )
4 ( Error, Warning, and other messages - blocks 1 of 2 )
5 ( Error Mesages,        block 2 of 2  )
6 ( EDITOR - SET-UP )
7 ( EDITOR, BLOCK 3 )
8 ( EDITOR, BLOCK 3 )
9 ( EDITOR, BLOCK 4 )
```

Figure 6.3 Index of blocks 1 through 9

memory and, as such, is actually the word that qualifies the disk as a virtual-memory device.

To understand the operations of *any* Forth words that use the disk, including INDEX, LIST, VIZ, and any data-storage words you may write later, you need to thoroughly understand the effects and operations of this deceptively powerful word.

BLOCK

Character transfers like CMOVE and FILL operations and fetching and storing processes are all operations that take place in the computer's dynamic, or random access memory (RAM). As fast as virtual devices are, they are nowhere as fast as RAM in transferring and/or altering the contents of individual bytes or cells. For that reason Forth systems carry out the modification of a disk block's contents by first copying the contents of the block into a 1K buffer in RAM, making any desired modifications there, and then copying the contents of the buffer back to the disk, even if only one cell is to be modified. This technique is not unique to Forth, by the way, but is almost universally used in computer disk-operating systems.

The task of moving blocks about falls on BLOCK. Here is BLOCK's stack designation:

BLOCK (n ... addr)

Like LIST, BLOCK expects to find a block number on the stack. When BLOCK is executed, it does the following:

1. BLOCK checks to determine whether the contents of the specified disk block are already in memory in one of the disk buffers.

2. If the block is in memory in a block buffer, BLOCK returns the address of the buffer in which the block was found.

3. If the block is not in RAM, BLOCK copies the block into the least most recently used block buffer and then returns the address of that buffer.

4. Before copying a disk block into a buffer, BLOCK checks on whether the contents of the buffer have been designated as modified or updated. If so, the contents of the buffer are copied to the disk into the appropriate disk block *before* the incoming disk block is copied into the RAM block buffer.

Remember, a disk block is a region of a magnetic disk. A block buffer is a region of RAM. BLOCK copies the *contents* of a disk block into a block buffer in RAM and vice versa. Forth programmers, like all others, tend to become very sloppy in discriminating between buffers and their contents. They tend to use the word BLOCK for everything. Guard your terminology in this area until you are comfortable with these concepts. Now you have enough information to enter the definitions for the Skeleton Editor.

6.5 The Skeleton Editor

Figure 6.2 lists the five definitions which constitute the Skeleton Editor. Enter them in the order in which they appear in that listing, and confirm with VLIST.

```
VLIST<ret> SAVE L P TEXT CLEAR . . . . . .
```

This application will not need INPUT or .PAD. Indeed, we only defined them as pedagogical tools to get to the current level of sophistication.

▶ *In some Forth systems, notably Forth-79, the function of the word* FLUSH *which appears in the definition of* SAVE *is taken by a synonym,* SAVE-BUFFERS. *If you encounter a problem in defining* SAVE *because your system does not recognize* FLUSH *just substitute* SAVE-BUFFERS *in its place.*

Now for the trial run! First, find an empty disk block by one of the following techniques, listed in increasing order of sophistication:

1. Ask someone which disk block(s) you can use.
2. Enter 1 LIST, 2 LIST, and so on, until you find an empty block.
3. Define and use a word with a DO ... LOOP containing within the loop:
   I LIST ?TERMINAL IF LEAVE THEN

Once you have located an empty block, LIST the block again to be sure it is empty. Assuming that the empty block is number 109, your resulting display should resemble Fig. 6.4, the screen display of a totally empty Forth block.

Verify that user variable SCR contains the proper block number.

```
SCR ? 109 ok
```

Now you can use the Forth word P to *put* a line of text into the block buffer corresponding to disk block 109. P expects to find the number of the line at which you want the string put on the stack, and it will store the line in the block buffer associated with the last screen listed, i.e., in the block whose value is stored in SCR. The stack notation for P is

```
P     ( n_line ... )
```

```
Block  # 109
   0
   1
   2
   3
   4
   5
   6
   7
   8
   9
  10
  11
  12
  13
  14
  15
```

Figure 6.4 An empty block

After you have created your first disk block, we will look closely at the inner workings of each of the words in the Skeleton Editor.

Using the Editor to Edit the Editor

Follow Forth tradition and put a documentary comment string in line 0 of the buffer first.

```
0 P ( The Skeleton Editor )<ret> ok
```

You are going to use the Skeleton Editor to enter the Skeleton Editor itself onto a disk block. From now on, even after the computer has been turned off, you will be able to retrieve the Skeleton Editor from the disk with only one word. Although the terminology has a slightly different meaning, since you are using the Editor to edit itself, you can think of this as a bootstrap editor operation. Later you may wish to use this bootstrap process to enter a more sophisticated editor which may then be used in the creation of an even more sophisticated editor which can.... . A very Forthish process indeed.

The Editor's word L is defined as:

```
: L SCR @ LIST ;
```

Obviously, L LISTs the last block LISTed. To use it you need not enter a block number, since LISTing 109 earlier has stored the proper value in SCR.

Verify that the comment line entered to line 0 is now in the block buffer. Again, your display should resemble Fig. 6.4, but with a title appearing in the first line.

128 The Forth Language

```
Block  # 109
   0 ( The Skeleton Editor, Forth Applications       May 83 )
   1
   2 : CLEAR    PAD 64 32 FILL ;  ( Clear the Pad )
   3
   4 : TEXT     CLEAR WORD HERE COUNT PAD SWAP CMOVE ;
   5
   6
   7 : P        1 TEXT 64 * SCR @ BLOCK + PAD SWAP 64 CMOVE ;
   8                       ( Move the line into the buffer )
   9
  10
  11 : L        SCR @ LIST ;   ( List the last block listed )
  12
  13 : SAVE     UPDATE FLUSH ; ( Save the block on the disk )
  14
  15
```

Figure 6.5 The Skeleton Editor

Remember, the Editor's word P sends the text to a region of the block buffer corresponding to a specific line number, but not to the disk—not yet.

Now enter the definitions. Since there is so little to enter, use every other line to enhance later readability (see Fig. 6.2). You should also enter the comment line associated with each definition.

```
2 P : CLEAR    PAD 64 32 FILL ; ( Clear the pad )<ret> ok

4 P : TEXT     CLEAR WORD HERE COUNT PAD SWAP CMOVE ;<ret> ok

6 P : P        1 TEXT 64 * SCR @ BLOCK + PAD SWAP 64 CMOVE ;<ret>ok

7 P            ( Save line in the block buffer )<ret> ok

8 P : L        SCR @ LIST ; ( List the last block listed)<ret> ok

10 P : SAVE    UPDATE FLUSH ; ( Save the block on disk )<ret> ok
```

If you make an error and you do not notice it until after you have entered the return key, simply retype the line.

Now verify your work with L. You should obtain a listing like Fig. 6.5. If the block looks OK to you, send it to the disk. To accomplish that, you will need to use SAVE, the final word in the Skeleton Editor.

```
SAVE <ret> ok
```

If your terminal is near the disk drive, you should be able to hear the drive whirring as your very first application is written into the disk. In the next section you will learn how to retrieve this disk block, entering CLEAR and `TEXT` and the rest of the editor into the dictionary. For now, though, you need to learn how your Editor works, starting with `P`.

Saving Blocks on the Disk

First we need to closely examine the inner workings of our Editor's `P`, the word that puts lines into the selected block buffer. The best way to do that is through an exhaustive stack analysis. As you develop your own Forth applications, such analyses, of both your own and Forth's predefined words, will greatly enhance your understanding not only of Forth but of other computer languages as well. Use the horizontal stack format.

`: P`	n	`P` expects a line number.
`1 TEXT`	n	`TEXT` moves the incoming text to the pad. The number 1 is actually the string delimiter for `WORD`.
`64 *`	offset	Calculate the character offset into the buffer, 64 characters per line times the line number.
`SCR @`	offset block	Last block listed.
`BLOCK`	offset addr	Convert the block number to the address of the buffer in RAM. Copy the block from the disk if necessary.
`+`	$addr_b$	Calculate the address of the selected line in the buffer, `addr+offset`.
`PAD`	$addr_b$ $addr_{pad}$	Put the address of the pad.
`SWAP`	$addr_{pad}$ $addr_b$	`SWAP` for the upcoming ...
`64 CMOVE`	(empty)	64-byte move.
`;`		End of definition.

Remember, `TEXT` uses `WORD` to intercept lines of text from the incoming stream of keyboard information. `P` uses `TEXT` to move the text lines to the pad from whence they are assembled in the block buffer.

Again, `P` sends information only to the block buffer. The job of sending the resulting 1024-byte block falls to `SAVE`. Here again is the definition of `SAVE`:

`: SAVE UPDATE FLUSH ;`

The responsibility of `UPDATE` is to label the most recently referenced block buffer as modified. Recall that `BLOCK`, before copying a disk block to a block buffer, checks the status of the buffer to determine whether or not the buffer has been updated. The word that updates the buffer by so labeling it is UPDATE.

FLUSH (or SAVE-BUFFERS) has the task of actually sending any (and all) UPDATEd block buffers to their respective areas on the disk. We will discuss the details of its operations in Part II.

The stack descriptions of these two words belie their usefulness and the underlying complexity of their accomplishments.

UPDATE (...)

FLUSH (...)

Novice Forth programmers are sometimes confused by the actions of FLUSH. Perhaps its name was a bad choice, and the selection of SAVE-BUFFERS for the same word in the Forth-79 Standard helps to alleviate confusion for programmers using that system. To keep it straight, remember, FLUSH *preserves UPDATEd blocks on the disk.*

Along with FLUSH, Forth provides another word that affects the block buffers, but this one does its job *without* sending the contents of the buffer to the disk. Indeed, no information is sent anywhere. This word is called EMPTY-BUFFERS.

Suppose you have spent an hour or two experimenting with a routine to save data in disk blocks. You have made an awful mess of the buffer, filling it with garbage, and you cannot remember whether or not you have used UPDATE to mark the block as updated. Worse, you need to LIST some other block. If you use a word that calls BLOCK, an updated block already in the buffer that BLOCK will use for your incoming block will be automatically sent to the disk, where it may obliterate some other important information. To circumvent this, you can bamboozle BLOCK by emptying the block buffers before BLOCK has a chance to FLUSH them to the disk.

EMPTY-BUFFERS ok

As far as the system is concerned, your buffers are empty and there is no need to send anything to disk. The stack description of EMPTY-BUFFERS is identical to that of UPDATE and FLUSH:

EMPTY-BUFFERS (...)

Now that you know how to avoid inadvertently saving the wrong block on the disk, we need to consider again how to deliberately SAVE a particular block.

Novice programmers frequently forget to SAVE their applications after entering them. It is an easy error to make since LISTing a particular block will display it if it is in a buffer without looking for the application on the disk. For instance, suppose you fill a block buffer with text and then forget to SAVE it. When you turn off the system, the buffer's contents, residing only in volatile RAM memory, are all lost. To avoid this calamity, be careful to save your applications after creating them. Even the most sophisticated editors require that you deliberately execute some special word like SAVE to render your labors permanent.

You will have more to learn about sophisticated editors later. Now you need to learn how Forth allows you to reuse the information you have so laboriously saved on the disk.

6.6 Loading Forth Definitions from the Disk

Some Forth words are so elegant in their simplicity that it is difficult to fully appreciate how they work. FLUSH is such a word. So is LOAD. Restart your Forth system and enter this:

`109 LOAD<ret>` ok

(If you put your Skeleton Editor on some other disk block, LOAD that one rather than 109.)

Like LIST and BLOCK, LOAD expects a block number on the stack. On execution, LOAD does the following:

1. LOAD checks to determine whether the designated disk block has been copied to a block buffer.
2. If the block is found in a buffer, the text in the buffer is sent to the INTERPRETer *exactly* as it would have been had it been entered by hand at a terminal.
3. If the block is not found, the text is copied to a block buffer first, then sent to INTERPRET, just as above.

You can check the effects of the loading process on your system with a VLIST.

`VLIST<ret>` SAVE L P TEXT CLEAR ... ok

The Skeleton Editor definitions are now in your dictionary, ready for use.

If you load the same block more than once, the effect is the same as if you had reentered the definitions by hand.

109 LOAD<ret> CLEAR has already been defined. TEXT has already been defined. P has already been defined. L has already been defined. SAVE has already been defined. ok

VLIST will show

SAVE L P TEXT CLEAR SAVE L P TEXT CLEAR ...

This can constitute a problem. Suppose you have entered a series of definitions only to discover that you have left out a crucial Forth word someplace. You can repair the disk block with whatever Editor you are using, but what about the dictionary? Indeed, the problem can become acute on one of those inevitable bad days when everything goes wrong and you wind up updating your disk block time after time after time.

Remember FORGET? Just FORGET back to the earliest definition in your application *before* reLOADing. The dictionary will remain concise and unambiguous and you will maintain tight control of your system.

As your applications become more and more complex, it will soon happen that more than one block will be needed to accommodate the necessary text. When that occurs you can use one designated block to load the other blocks in the system. In some ways *load blocks* are like Forth words, but on a larger scale. Just as you can use a series of words to build a definition to accomplish a particular task, you can also address a particular application for your Forth system by creating a special block with a particular configuration that sequentially loads other blocks of Forth definitions. Such a block is called a load block.

Like any other executable Forth word, LOAD can appear in a block that

```
Block    # 75
   0 ( Text Development load block: CSUN Chemistry Net-Forth )
   1    decimal    2 load page    1 warning !
   2 cr ." CSUN Chemistry Department Net-Forth.. "
   3         revvid ." Text Development  configuration  " vid  cr
   4 cr ." loading assembler.. " 10 load 11 load 12 load
   5         13 load 14 load 15 load
   6 cr ." loading tools.." 90 load 91 load 92 load
   7
   8 cr ." loading video editor.. " 20 load 21 load 22 load 23 load
   9         24 load
  10
  11 cr ." loading clock & printer routines.. " 95 load 97 load
  12 cr ." loading Net-Forth support routines.. " 93 load
  13 cr ." loading floating point support.. " 94 load
  14
  15 cr room
```

Figure 6.6 A textbook-development load block

is itself destined to be loaded. A programmer who dedicates a block to such a purpose has created a load block. Figure 6.6 illustrates a load block for a general-purpose Forth system used to write this textbook.

To load all the definitions on all the Forth blocks referred to by the entries in this block, all the programmer needs to do is type:

```
75 LOAD<ret> ok
```

Many of the blocks loaded by this block are also potentially useful in many other applications, but others are not. For example, a telescope-control application, designed to be used by technicians and astronomers other than the original programmer, would not need a video editor, but would undoubtedly need a stellar tracking routine. When the observatory's Forth system is to be used for data acquisition, the telescope load block will be used. When new Forth words are being created, the Editor containing load block will be used.

The load block shown in Fig. 6.6 is ordinarily used to configure a Forth system with a dictionary containing special tools (such as .S), an efficient video editor which acts like a word processor, and the Forth words necessary to enable Forth to control a printer. This is a minimum configuration useful to the author of a book on Forth. Other load screens on the same disk can load different combinations of disk blocks to configure Forth to acquire data from various instruments, maintain an equipment inventory, or generate video graphics.

6.7 Numeric Output

By this point you have become proficient in dealing with the input and output of strings of ASCII characters, but, other than dot, you have not yet learned to use any of the tools which Forth provides to enable the output of actual numbers. Remember, a number on the stack is a *binary* value, not an ASCII representation. To send that value to an ASCII device such as a terminal or printer requires that the binary value somehow get converted to an ASCII representation.

Consider for a moment an arbitrary decimal value, say 1791. The binary representation of this value is 11011111111 and if we were to enter it to a running Forth system, NUMBER would duly push it to the stack where it would occupy one 16-bit cell.

```
0000110111111111
```

Binary representation of 1791

On the other hand, if we were to include 1791 within a definition and save it in a disk block, the number would be saved in two cells (four separate 8-bit bytes), each byte holding the ASCII representation of an individual digit.

0 0 1 1 0 0 0 1	Binary representation of 49, ASCII 1
0 0 1 1 0 1 1 1	Binary representation of 55, ASCII 7
0 0 1 1 1 0 0 1	Binary representation of 57, ASCII 9
0 0 1 1 0 0 0 1	Binary representation of 49, ASCII 1

Storing numbers in binary format is always more economical in terms of memory usage than storing them in ASCII. The decimal number 32000, for instance, requires only one 16-bit cell in binary but five 8-bit bytes in ASCII format.

Suppose you wanted to send the number 1791 to the terminal *without using each individual decimal digit:*

: 1791.PRINT 49 EMIT 55 EMIT 57 EMIT 49 EMIT ;

1791.PRINT<ret> 1791 ok

In this example 49 EMIT sends the ASCII character 1, 55 EMIT sends the character 7, and 57 EMIT outputs the 9 character. We have created a word that is useful only for outputting one specific value, but it does illustrate an important feature that must be part of whatever general-purpose word we ultimately write to output binary values. The word must contain provisions to sequentially convert to ASCII and then EMIT each digit individually. Such a word could then be used to output 16-bit, unsigned values in the same fashion as dot.

Enter these Forth words:

0 VARIABLE CNT<ret> ok

: DECOUT   0 CNT ! BEGIN 1 CNT +! 10 /MOD DUP 0= UNTIL
           DROP CNT @ 0 DO 48 + EMIT LOOP ;<ret> ok

Push a value onto the stack and try outputting it with DECOUT.

1791 DECOUT<ret> 1791 ok

427 DECOUT<ret> 427 ok

This word appears to behave a lot like our old friend dot; let us see how it works.

DECOUT	n	Begin with a value on the stack.
0 CNT !	n	Initialize the character counter.
BEGIN	n	Begin character-by-character conversion.
1 CNT +!	n	Increment the counter.
10 /MOD	r q	Divide by 10, leaving the remainder and the quotient.
DUP	r q q	Duplicate the quotient.
0=	r q f	Is it 0 yet?
UNTIL	r q	If not, branch back to /MOD the quotient again.
DROP	r . .	After the last pass, drop the 0 quotient. There will be as many remainders left on the stack as there were digits in the decimal number.
CNT @ 0 DO	r . .	Begin a definite loop to do count digit conversions.
48 +	r . r+48	Convert binary value to ASCII code. And send it off.
EMIT	r .	Go back for another.
LOOP	r .	Finished.
;		

A stack analysis of a word containing an indefinite loop can sometimes be confusing. In this case the key to DECOUT lies in the phrase:

BEGIN 1 CNT +! 10 /MOD DUP 0= UNTIL

The termination of the indefinite loop will occur when there are no more digits in the original value to be converted. The number of values left on the stack after UNTIL will depend on the magnitude of the original decimal value being converted. The best way to visualize this is through the exercise of monitoring the behavior of the stack as the word executes a sample number like 1791.

Contents of stack	Contents of CNT	Comments
1791	0	Initially.
1 179	1	After first pass.
1 9 17	2	After second pass.
1 9 7 1	3	After third pass.
1 9 7 1 0	4	After fourth and last pass. Now control passes on to DROP.
1 9 7 1	4	After DROP.

Next the definite `DO-LOOP` takes over, adding 48 to each value and `EMIT`ing one digit in each pass. Why 48? The ASCII codes for the *characters* 0 through 9 are decimal 48 through 57 respectively. Adding 48 to the binary value on the stack converts each digit to its ASCII character equivalent. Note that the digits are in exactly the proper order to be sent to the output device; the first digit to go is on the top of the stack.

This conversion method is not unique to Forth, by the way. FORTRAN, BASIC, and Pascal, as well as most assemblers, use virtually the same divide-and-conquer technique.

It is not necessary to enter this word permanently into your system. Not yet, anyway. The standard . (dot), that came with your system does all this and more. For instance, as written, `DECOUT` outputs only base-ten character representations.

1791 OCTAL DECOUT<ret> <u>1791 ok</u>

That is why we call it `DECOUT`. The standard . (dot) is converted by using whatever base you desire. If that sounds like a very complicated feat, by the way, consider that all that is required to add such capability to `DECOUT` is (1) replacement of the 10 in the definition with `BASE @`, and (2) for bases greater than tens, adjusting the ASCII offset accordingly. By the way, our version of `DECOUT` executes faster than Forth's . (dot), since it has less to do.

More serious is `DECOUT`'s inability to deal with two's-complement values.

−1 DECOUT<ret><u>/ ok</u>

Note that / (slash) is the ASCII character corresponding to code 47, or 48 − 1. Likewise, `DECOUT` converts −2 and −3 to the punctuation marks . (dot) and − (minus), respectively. These are ASCII 46 and 45. If you are fascinated by character conversions, and if you are eager to fix your `DECOUT` to cover the range of possible 16-bit values, take an early look at Prob. 5 at the end of this chapter.

Another, more easily remedied flaw in our definition becomes apparent when we attempt to output more than one number. Compare

1791 8844 DECOUT DECOUT<ret> <u>88441791 ok</u>

with

1791 8844 . .<ret> <u>8844 1791 ok</u>

As you might have foreseen, `DECOUT` sends no spaces after outputting the last character. To alleviate this, simply add `32 EMIT` to the definition just after `LOOP`.

It would not be unreasonable for you to wonder why we have spent this much time on a word that has no apparent advantages over other previously defined Forth structures such as dot. Justification follows two lines of argument. First, this analysis obviously helps in understanding the inner workings of numeric output. It is always better to understand what your system is doing than to use it blindly. It is much more important, however, that the standard Forth output operations—dot and the rest— are tied to the primitive `EMIT`, which, in turn, is coupled to the systems output terminal device and, usually, to that device only.

Suppose you wanted to use your Forth system to print paychecks for your firm, which specializes in design and fabrication of rubber baby-buggy bumpers. You want Forth to allow you to enter the data at your video terminal, and then you want it to print the paychecks on the high-speed lineprinter. Meanwhile, you need to have the system occasionally check the factory's supply of rubber stock and print the daily inventory on another printer in the supervisor's office. Forth can do all this, even on a single-user system, but not with the standard `EMIT`, and not with the standard dot either.

On some Forth systems `EMIT` can be fairly easily modified to send its output to any device you desire, but on other Forth systems such modification is beyond the skills of the average user. In the former case, you can easily use the standard output words for all applications. In the latter, the programmer occasionally needs to use words like `DECOUT`, as you will see in Part II, Chap. 7, when you learn how to divert Forth's output to an alternate output device in your first lesson in device-control applications.

`DECOUT` has provided you with an introduction to the inner workings of Forth's numeric output words, and you have used . (dot) since the beginning of your exposure to the language. But there are many more features to Forth's number routines, including the concept of *formatted output*.

6.8 Formatted Output

When a 16-bit value residing on the stack needs to be outputted, we have routinely used . (dot) as the output word. Further, as you learned in Chap. 3, 32-bit integers can be outputted with the predefined word `D.`, another member of the Forth I/O family, and we have used `F.` to send floating-point values to our terminals as well.

At first glance, it appears that this set of numeric output words can handle virtually all contingencies, but there are occasions when this simple collection of I/O tools is simply not enough.

Go back to the listings of various blocks made earlier in this chapter, and notice that the linenumbers are positioned with their right edges aligned.

Right-Justified Output

Right-margin alignment is called *right justification*. The individual lines of characters in this book (and most other high-quality publications) are right-justified as well. When you write a Forth word that outputs characters on sequential lines, however, unless you use special precautions, the data will be *left-justified*. Consider the following phrase:

```
1 . CR 10 . CR 100 . CR 1000 . CR 10000 . <ret>
```

```
1

10

100

1000

10000  ok
```

To output the same values in a right-justified manner, you need to use a new Forth word, .R, for "print, right-justified." Enter this phrase:

```
1 5 .R CR 10 5 .R CR 100 5 .R CR 1000 5 .R CR 10000 5
.R<ret>
```

```
    1

   10

  100

 1000

10000 ok
```

This time the data appear right-justified, just as they do at the left edge of the block lists discussed earlier.

The stack notation for the output word .R indicates its greater complexity compared to plain old dot. Compare

.R (n width ...)

with

. (n ...)

In the previous phrase, the 5 s in the n 5 .R parts of the phrase were included to dictate the width of the field in which the number was to be right-justified.

The series of output words which are included in traditional Forth systems are summarized in Table 6.2.

Formatting Output with .WITH

In addition to the traditional Forth I/O words, innovative programmers have invented powerful and flexible extensions of the language to assist in the display of numeric values. One such set of new words written in the course of preparing this book is represented by the Forth word .WITH (pronounced "dot with"). Here is how it is used. (Your system probably does not have .WITH, but the definitions that constitute it are found in App. D, "Number Formatting." You can enter them any time, but it is practical to use a load block).

Suppose you wish to use Forth in financial calculations that require printing amounts of money, such as account balances or invoices. A special word that prints monetary amounts can easily be created by using .WITH. Enter this phrase:

: .$ .WITH $? ###. ##" ;<ret> ok

The new word just compiled, .$, has been created to print values with a

Table 6.2 Numeric Output Words

Type of number on stack	Output words	
	Left-justified	Right-justified
8-bit signed	. (n ...)	.R (n width ...)
16-bit unsigned	U. (u ...)	U.R (u width ...)
32-bit signed integer	D. (d ...)	D.R (d width ...)
32-bit unsigned integer	UD. (ud ...)	UD.R (ud width ...)
32-bit floating point	F. (f ...)	

preceding dollar sign, a minus sign if necessary, and a decimal point separating dollars from cents. Try it.

12312 .$ $ 123.12 ok

−10000 .$ $ −100.00 ok

The key to .$ is the collection of symbols which follow .WITH in the definition of .$, $ ‾###. ##. In this context, .WITH is called a "format generator," and $ ‾###. ## is called a "format specifier." .WITH is an immediate word, and its definition includes WORD. When you use .WITH in a definition, it incorporates the string of ASCII characters following into the definition of the new word, up to the first quotation mark encountered. In this respect .WITH behaves like ." (dot quote).

The definition of a formatted output word like .$ must have *both* the word .WITH *and* its accompanying format specifier. Otherwise an error condition will develop.

When the new word is *executed,* the format specifier is used to selectively print individual digits from the value on top of the stack, interspersing them with the symbols contained in the specifier. This is accomplished with a special version of DECOUT.

In a format specifier certain symbols have special significance. Specifically, ASCII 35 (#) and ASCII 63 (?) indicate exactly where Forth should emit individual digits and the sign of the value (minus sign for negative, blank for positive). Try these:

: .ANIMALS .WITH ### Gorillas and" .WITH ### Gnus" ;<ret> ok

177 14 .ANIMALS<ret> 14 Gorillas and 177 Gnus ok

As in any Forth output operation, words containing .WITH will print the value on top of the stack first. If you are creating an application which will be used by the uninitiated, you can include Forth stack-manipulation words within the definition of the word containing .WITH to reorder the stack before outputting values.

: .BUGS SWAP .WITH ### Ants and" .WITH ### Flies" ;<ret> ok

19 38 .BUGS<ret> 19 Ants and 38 Flies ok

If you provide a format specified that has fewer # symbols than there are digits in your value, Forth will not output your number. Rather, the digits are dropped from the stack and a string of asterisks is displayed. This is called an "overflow condition." As far as Forth is concerned, an overflow is OK, and other than the asterisks, no error message will appear.

```
12345 .WITH ####"<ret> ****ok
```

The characters in the format specifier and the digits can be intimately mixed, as in

```
: .TIME .WITH ##:##:00" ;<ret> ok
1314 .TIME<ret> 13:14:00 ok
```

or

```
: .MASH .WITH #*#*#*#" ;<ret> ok
4077 .MASH<ret> 4 *0 *7 *7 ok
```

If your value is negative and you have neglected to provide a minus sign in the format specifier, an erroneous value will be sent to your terminal. So, whenever there is even a remote possibility that the value may be less than zero, include a ? (question mark) in the specifier.

```
0 VARIABLE INSTOCK 0 VARIABLE SOLD<ret> ok
: .INVENTORY INSTOCK @ SOLD @ - .WITH ?### Available ";<ret> ok
23 INSTOCK ! 77 SOLD !<ret> ok
.INVENTORY<ret> - 54 Available ok
```

Whatever they are, somebody had better get some more soon.

32-bit Integer Formatted Output

If you need to format the output of a double-length integer, you will have to use D.WITH, .WITH's 32-bit relative. The definition of D.WITH is also given in App. D, "Number Formatting." (Indeed, .WITH uses D.WITH as well.) Here is a 32-bit version of .$, the money formatter.

```
: D.$ D.WITH $#,###,###.##" ;<ret> ok
1234567.00 D.$<ret> $1,234,567.00 ok
```

The choice of the question mark as the place marker for the sign of the value (rather than a minus sign, ASCII 45) was made to allow hyphenated values, like telephone numbers, to be outputted with D.WITH as in:

: .PHONE D.WITH ###-###-####" ;

2135551212 .PHONE<ret> 213-555-1212 ok

In some accounting applications it is appropriate to have the sign appear *after* the value. This poses no problem for words using .WITH. Redefine .INVENTORY with ###? as the format specifier, for instance, and the result will be

.INVENTORY 54- Available ok

As we have seen, .WITH can be used interactively, as in the example using 12345 .WITH ####" above. It can appear in the definition of an output word in a disk block or entered from the terminal, or it can appear within a DO -loop.

: .SQ CR 10 0 DO I DUP .WITH ## Squared is "DUP * .WITH #### " CR LOOP ;

.SQ<ret>
0 Squared is 0
1 Squared is 1
2 Squared is 4
.
.
9 Squared is 81
  ok

BASIC programmers will recognize the influence of BASIC's PRINTUS-ING -type format specifiers in the operations of .WITH words. Not only is Forth a relatively new language, it is flexible enough to adapt the finer features of other languages to its own advantage. As your programming skills develop, you will find occasions where the ability to extend the language to suit your own purposes is a welcome and powerful feature of Forth.

6.9 Problems

1. Write a version of VIZ that does exactly what LIST does, displaying every 64-character line with a leading linenumber and a block number heading.

2. Write another version of VIZ which displays 21 lines of 48 characters each. The last 16 characters in the block should appear in the 22d line.

3. Assume that you are the author of a text on Forth and that you need to compose a Forth word that will (*a*) LIST a block and (*b*) accept from the terminal

a title character string that will then be printed *centered* just below the listing. Call the word DISPLAY. Call the word that calculates how many spaces to insert CENTER.

4. Carry out a stack analysis for INPUT similar to the one we used for PRICE in Chap. 2. Show that there is no net stack effect.

5. Write a word like DECOUT that can also accommodate negative values. You might want to first test for negative, EMIT the code for − (minus), then use ABS, and finally DECOUT itself.

6. Write and test HEXOUT.

7. What negative value would have to be on the stack to cause execution of the original DECOUT to result in the clanging of the terminal's bell?

Part

II

Hardware Control with Forth

Introduction

As you have seen, the origins of Forth are deeply rooted in applications of computer interfacing techniques to scientific instrumentation. So it is not surprising that Forth excels in programming computers to control instruments and devices, to gather data, and to assist in the subsequent analysis of the collected information.

To become adept at exploiting Forth's unique abilities in these areas, Forth programmers must become skilled in more than just the intricacies of the language. They must also become at least passingly familiar with the relevant features of the instruments and devices, as well as with some of the inner workings of the computer itself.

The level of requisite familiarization depends upon the complexities of the task at hand, of course, and in many cases, all you really need to know to get by is where the cables plug into the computer and how to turn it all on. In all cases, however, a good foundation in the "hardware" aspects of the facility is important in developing an efficient relationship with the equipment and its applications.

In a book like this, it is important to provide enough information to materially assist an earnest interfacer without discouraging the novice programmer by giving a plethora of technical detail. But it is still important to include enough useful, working descriptions of the computer's hardware to allow a beginner to tackle a device-control or real-time data-acquisition application without having to hire a consulting engineer and systems analyst to finish the job. The author's task in this area would be materially aided if there were available a real computer system that could serve as a model for all other computers. Unfortunately, no such universal machine exists, nor will it ever, in all likelihood. But there is one computer which, by virtue of the elegance of the design of its instruction set, and because it is present in nearly every academic, industrial, and large business installation, comes closer than any other to qualifying as a universal computer. It is the Digital Equipment Corporation's PDP-11.

The specific details of computer interfacing will be presented first, using descriptions of the PDP-11. Where relevant, comparisons will be made with other systems, such as the Z-80 or 6502. Most of the time, however, the similarity in design between other computer systems and the PDP-11 will render comments or comparisons unnecessary.

When specific device-interfacing techniques are being considered, examples and applications will be drawn from uses of typical instruments used in engineering, computer, chemistry, physics, and medical laboratories. There are no radio-telescope applications in this book.

As pointed out in the introduction to Part I, the best way to learn Forth is to use it. This is specially true when dealing with Forth in a real-time I/O environment. The very best way to learn to interact with your Forth system is to connect it to a display device (such as an oscilloscope) and a signal source (such as a spectrophotometer, a sine-wave generator, or even a simple variable-voltage power supply) and to practice data gathering and device controlling. But even if you are restricted to just your terminal for all input and output to Forth, the chapters in Part II include many useful exercises and practice opportunities. So go to your terminal and begin Part II.

Chapter

7

Introduction to Hardware: Input-Output

The first six chapters of this book were directed at the application of Forth to problems and exercises which were too general to be affected by the particular computer in use, and were independent of the external devices to which the computer may have been connected. That approach allowed us to focus on the underlying principles of Forth itself, saving us from the distractions associated with specific details of this or that particular kind of hardware. By now, though, a new Forth programmer should be ready to address some of the "hardware-specific" aspects of programming, the area in which Forth really excels.

In this chapter you will learn some of the fundamentals of computer design, including the means by which the central processor communicates with both its memory and some of its external, or peripheral, devices. You will also create your first device-control application as you write Forth words that allow a running system to access the computer's printer, and you will gain control of some of the special hardware features of your terminal.

7.1 Computer Organization

In many ways, modern computer design was pioneered by the English scholar Charles Babbage. In the mid-nineteenth century Babbage proposed the construction of an "analytic engine" which would possess (1) a processing unit (Babbage called it the "mill"), (2) input and output devices (he proposed using punched cards), (3) a device for saving data (he called it the "store,") and (4) the means to connect all these components together. Frustrated by the inadequacies of devices of his time, Babbage spent an entire lifetime trying to fabricate a machine for which then-current technology was not even remotely prepared.

Present-day jargon uses the abbreviations CPU (central processing unit), for Babbage's "mill," RAM (random-access memory) and ROM (read-only memory), for his "store," and the computer's bus for his interconnections. Technical detail aside, there is actually very little new in modern computers that Babbage had not already foreseen. The design of the Digital Equipment Corporation PDP-11/23 computer is clearly Babbage's dream come true more than a century later (Fig. 7.1).

In exactly the same way that satellite links and wires strung across the face of the planet provide the foundation of the intercontinental telephone network, the computer *bus* is the sine qua non of the modern computer. All data transfers between I/O devices, the CPU, and the computer memory take place along the bus. For instance, in the PDP-11, the bus consists of a parallel array of 16 lines along which both data and address information travel, with numerous additional control and power lines which are necessary for the operation of the computer. Transfer of information between devices attached to the bus involves a fairly complex sequence of events.

1. The CPU sends a signal through one of the bus control lines indicating that it wishes to take control of the bus, or to gain "bus mastership."

2. The CPU then places onto the 16 address-data lines the *bus address* of the device (the destination device) with which it wishes to communicate. It uses additional bus control lines to indicate whether the upcoming operation will be a fetch or a store operation.

3. If the intended operation is a store, the CPU indicates that *data* are to appear next on the bus, and then puts the data bits onto the data-address lines. The destination device reads the 16 bits of data from the data-address lines and signals when the process is complete.

4. If the operation is a fetch, the CPU waits for the device to indicate (using a control line dedicated to this purpose) that the 16 bits of data

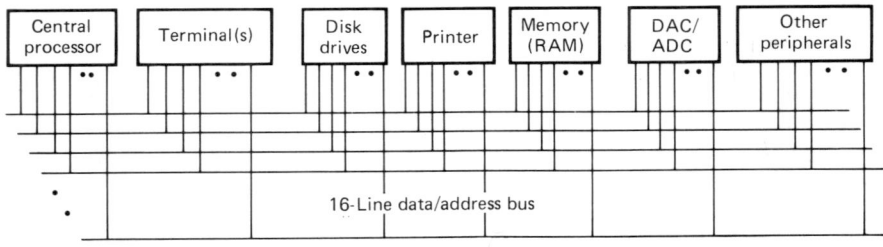

Figure 7.1 Architecture of the PDP-11 computer

are available on the data-address lines, reads the data into a register, and proceeds to whatever process follows.

The bus control and data-address lines are accessible to all connected devices. Whether or not they respond to an instruction from the bus master depends upon whether or not they have just been "addressed" by the bus master. The one-room schoolhouse provides a useful analogy. Though all pupils in the room hear everything the teacher says in interrogating various students, for a student to respond out of turn is considered inappropriate behavior.

When a program requests transfer of information from memory to the printer, for example, the CPU, as "master of the bus," queries memory, a cell at a time, and then sends each byte (half the contents of each cell) to the printer as it appears on the bus. Just as passenger and freight trains both use the same tracks, data *and* address references flow along the same set of lines under control of the bus *multiplexor*. This duplication of function simplifies the hardware at the expense of complicating the data-flow process.

The PDP-11 is a 16-bit computer, meaning that the aforementioned data transfers take place in 16-bit increments (hence the 16-line data-address bus), and that computer arithmetic is done in registers that can accommodate 16 bits at one time. In recent years 8-bit computers have become very popular. These microcomputers have only 8-bit registers, but through cunning use of "register pairs," they can handle 16- and even 32-bit values when necessary. Their advantage (low cost) frequently outweighs their principal shortcoming (low speeds associated with complex internal processing of 16- and 32-bit values). Led by microprocessors designed by Rockwell (6502), Zilog (Z-80), and INTEL (8080A), these 8-

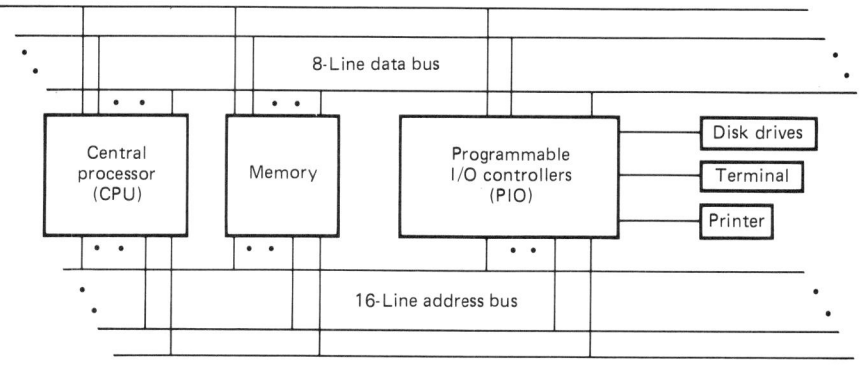

Figure 7.2 An S-100 bus-based computer design

bit computers provide a low-cost, convenient approach to effective computing.

Many of these 8-bit systems use the S-100 bus, originally designed by MITS Inc. This is an approximately 100-line bus which uses separate lines for memory addressing, data input, and data output (Fig. 7.2).

Regardless of the bus architecture in your system, flow of data between devices and memory remains under control of the bus master. Until recently, the mastership of the bus in microcomputers had always remained with the CPU. But the widespread use of inexpensive microprocessors like the 6502, 8080, and Z-80 systems has led to the emergence of direct-memory access (DMA) peripherals. These "intelligent" devices have the capability of controlling the flow of information to and from memory without the intervention of the CPU.

Here is a description of essentially how such devices work: Suppose you need to transfer a Forth block from memory to disk (remember FLUSH or SAVE-BUFFERS). In an ordinary system the CPU would control the entire process, fetching and storing, fetching and storing, byte by byte. But in a DMA device, usually a peripheral equipped with its own microprocessor, the device itself takes over the mastership of the bus, informing the CPU that its services are not needed for a while, and sending its data *directly* to the destination device. Obviously a DMA device must be sophisticated enough to handle both the addressing and the data aspects of the fetching and storing operations. Once the transfer has been completed, the DMA device relinquishes control to the CPU (or to another DMA device that needs the bus).

But as far as the Forth programmer is usually concerned, the exact details of bus transfers are less important than the ways in which Forth allocates the system's memory for such things as the dictionary and the block buffers.

7.2 Memory Organization

There are two aspects of the system's memory which the programmer needs to view: the *hardware* aspects, especially the actual layout of the accessible cells and the manner of addressing them, and the *software* aspects, the ways in which the language exploits the system's physical memory for its own internal purposes. Just as an operatic director is limited in set design by the architect's design of the theater, the designer of a computer language is limited by the features of the available hardware. To fully understand these constraints, you need to look closely at the ways in which the language uses the system's allocation of RAM. We will call this a lesson in computer geography.

PDP-11 Memory Geography

With 16 address lines available, it is possible for a computer to physically point to, or address 2^{16} individual locations in the computer's memory. This corresponds to 65536_{10}, or 200000_8 locations; in the design of the PDP-11, each of those locations is an 8-bit byte. Since the PDP-11 is a 16-bit device, this means that the absolute maximum of addressable memory that can be accessed is 65536/2, or 32,768 cells. We will assume for the present that the PDP-11 under consideration has a full complement of random-access memory, from all of which the system can fetch information and to all of which data can be sent for storage.

(The other type of memory—nonvolatile, *read-only memory* or ROM—can also be installed in PDP-11 computers, but we are not concerned with such memory here. In addition, larger PDP-11s can have as many as 24 address lines, allowing them to access far greater amounts of memory. Since most Forth applications are run on the smaller systems, we will focus on them in this chapter.)

In Fig. 7.3, physical memory in the PDP-11 is illustrated on the left,

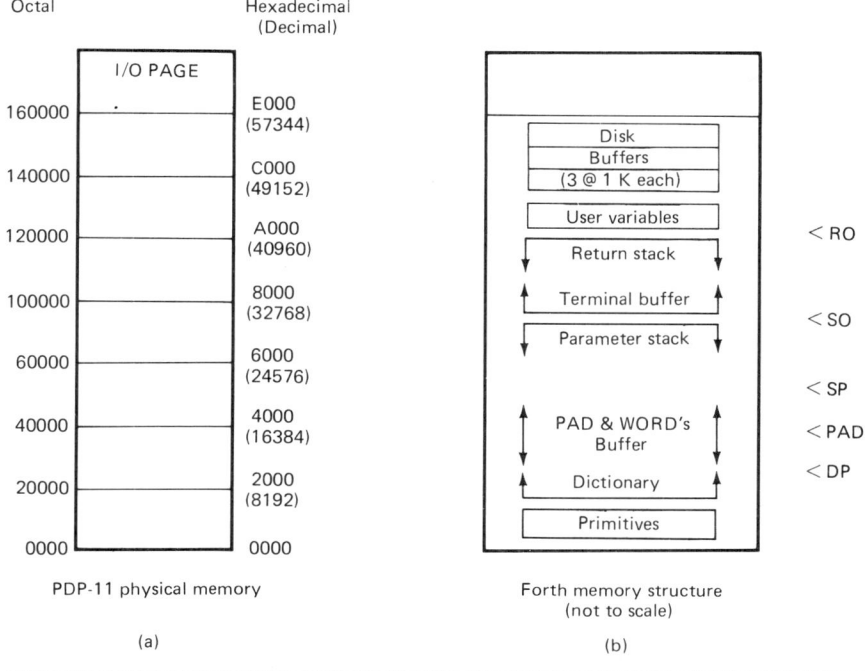

Figure 7.3 Forth's use of memory in the PDP-11

and the allocation of this memory to specific purposes in a typical PDP-11 Forth system is shown on the right.

For organizational purposes PDP-11 memory is divided into eight "pages," numbered 0 through 7. The lowest page holds addresses 0 through 8191_{10}, the second from 8192 through 16383, and so forth. Since each page holds just over 8000 bytes, the pages are called 8K pages.

The octal addressing traditions of Digital Equipment Corporation are evident along the left edge of Fig. 7.3, where the addresses of the lowest byte in each page are displayed. On the right side of the physical memory map appear the corresponding decimal and hex addresses. By convention, the lowest 1000 bytes of a PDP-11 are reserved for use by the computer's operating system, the set of controlling programs that oversee the operations of the computer. Even in those Forth systems that run without support of an external operating system, it is advisable to leave those bytes reserved.

The uppermost memory, page 7, is called the I/O page. Rather than the random access memory that populates the lower pages, the I/O page consists of locations that *act* like memory but are, in fact, the PDP-11's connections to the outside world. Thus, the process of printing a page of text involves sending a stream of characters, one by one, byte by byte, to the address associated with the printer. As far as the PDP-11 is concerned, all that data is being stored in that one location—and, in fact, it is ... on paper. Similarly, the disk drives and terminals occupy locations in the I/O page. Unlike early computers which required elaborate procedures to communicate with their own devices, no special set of commands is required to use these locations. This use of a portion of the computer's memory as a "user-transparent" window to the system's peripherals is not unique to the PDP-11. It is called *memory-mapped I/O*.

Forth Geography

Forth accesses the I/O page in exactly the same fashion as it would any other memory location; fetching operations bring data to the stack from some external device, and storing operations send data away. Later in this chapter you will be writing high-level Forth words that directly access the I/O page.

The right side of Fig. 7.3 depicts Forth's use of the PDP-11's memory. The primitives begin just above the reserved area, surmounted by the open-topped dictionary. The variable DP points to the top of the dictionary, allowing the system (and the user, if need arises) to know exactly which cells will house the next definition.

Floating just above the top of the dictionary are the PAD and WORD's buffer.

Extending *down* from a location pointed to by the variable S0, on a collision course with the PAD, dictionary, and WORD's buffer, comes the parameter stack. Despite our analogies that depict the stack as a deck of cards, in actual fact the "top" of the stack lies at the bottom of the stack's allocated portion of memory. Forth deals from the bottom of the stack.

Consider the definition

```
: Zap-the-Dictionary 20000 0 DO I LOOP ;
```

which does nothing more than copy a loop index onto the stack over and over. The stack depth will increase by one cell after each loop execution. Now that you can see just where (and what) the stack is, it should be clear why a word like Zap-the-Dictionary is aptly named.

The terminal input buffer (TIB) resides just above the parameter stack, growing upward toward the return stack. The TIB is where the incoming character stream is collected as you type on the terminal's keyboard. Because the return stack is rarely very deep and the TIB is never very full, collisions in this area of memory are uncommon.

Above the return stack is a region of high memory allocated for storage of the *user variables*. These are the variables, such as S0 and SCR, that the entire system needs and uses constantly. (Remember, although S0 and DP point to their respective memory regions, their *values* are stored with all the other user variables.)

Finally, near the top of memory, just beneath the I/O page, reside the three 1K-byte disk buffers. BLOCK transfers 1K Forth blocks into these buffers, the editors manipulate the contents of these same buffers, and SAVE-BUFFERS transfers their contents onto the disk.

7.3 Peripheral Devices and Communication Protocol

The uppermost page of PDP-11 memory, as mentioned above, is not memory at all. Rather, octal addresses 160000 through 177776 represent the actual "memorylike" locations of the interfaces between the computer system and its peripheral devices. In Sec. 7.5 we will look more closely at the anatomy of the I/O page. In this section we will merely look at the means by which those devices which are addressed through the I/O page communicate with the outside world.

Parallel versus Serial I/O

With only few exceptions (among them the PDP-11's infamous ancestor, the PDP-8/S), the *internal* transfer of information in a computer is carried out by *parallel* data transmission. In this method, as the name implies, the individual bits composing a byte or cell are transferred simultaneously along 8 or 16 parallel wires. The bus itself is a parallel transmission medium, for example. Since a given conductor carries only a fraction of the entire information package, parallel I/O methodology is used whenever large amounts of data need to be transferred over short distances at high transmission rates. But this advantage of speed is gained at the expense of hardware simplicity, particularly when the signals have to be sent more than a few meters. Beyond that limit the sheer amount of wire involved, coupled with the electrical constraints on data transmission in many closely spaced parallel lines, leads to the use of *serial* data techniques.

In serial transmission the individual bits are sent sequentially through one wire rather than simultaneously through many. Transmission over considerably longer distances is feasible, at the expense of transmission speeds. Generally, a computer communicates with its terminals in serial format, with disk drives in parallel, and with printers in either, depending on the speed and location of the printer involved.

Since the computer's internal protocols are parallel, external use of the serial technique must also involve translation of the parallel bus signals into serial format, and vice versa. The device that carries out this conversion is *universal asynchronous receiver-transmitter* (UART). A *serial interface* used to couple a terminal or other serial device to the bus must contain some sort of UART, today a single chip. This conversion, and a general view of the differing characteristics of parallel versus serial transmission are presented in Fig. 7.4, where the ASCII codes for "Aba" are converted to a serial format and sent off to a terminal.

Whereas parallel transmission resembles the start of a horse race, with all the animals moving forward simultaneously, serial transmission meth-

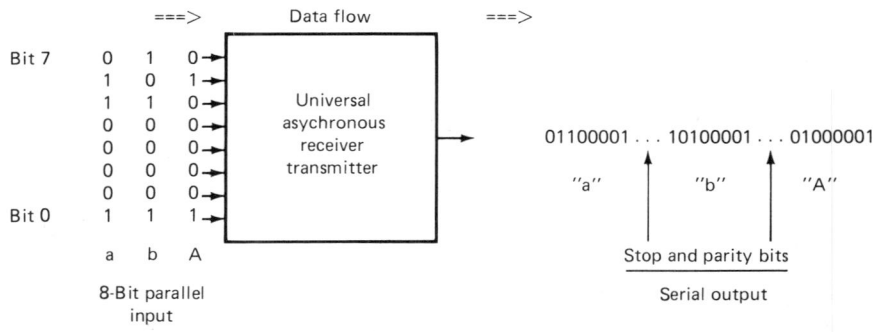

Figure 7.4 Parallel and serial transmission

odology evokes an image of a revolving door, through which each person passes in turn. The order of the passing is significant, however, the subject of a standard protocol in the electronics industry.

The Electronics Industry Association Standard: RS232C

Since various manufacturers' computer systems need to communicate with numerous types of terminals and other serial devices, the need for an industry standard for serial transmission protocol became obvious very early in the history of computer manufacturing. The most common format for serial data transmission is the Electronics Industry Association standard EIA-RS232C. In this standard a computer or "computerlike" device is called "data-communication equipment" or a DCE device. Terminals and other peripherals are called "data-terminal equipment" or DTE devices. This distinction becomes important when it is necessary to interconnect such devices. Under normal circumstances, DTE equipment can communicate with DCE devices but not with other DTE devices. Likewise, DCE devices are set up to communicate with DTEs only.

The standard also specifies a set of voltage levels for the digital communication signals and the significance of each and every pin on the connector. Today, some of the signals that are called for in the RS232C standard are no longer used, improved hardware reliability having made them unnecessary. In addition, it has become traditional to use a particular connector, the DPB-25, for RS232 applications, although this was not called

Table 7.1 EIA-RS232 Serial Communications Signal Standards

Pin no.	Signal description
1	Earth ground
2	Received data*
3	Transmitted data*
4	Request to send
5	Clear to send
6	Data set ready
7	Signal ground
8	Carrier detect
20	Data terminal ready

*The use of pins 2 and 3 for received and transmitted data is the convention of the RS232 standard for the computer ("Data Computer Equipment," DCE) end of the communications link. The functions of these pins must be reversed for "Data Terminal Equipment," DTE.

for in the original standard. Indeed, the nine different signals specified in Table 7.1 are sufficient for nearly all applications, and it is frequently sufficient to know that a computer with an RS232 serial interface (a DCE device) *transmits* its bits on pin 3 of the standard connector and *receives* on pin 2, while terminals and printers (DTE devices) *receive* on pin 3 and *transmit* on pin 2.

Baud Rate

The *rate* of transmission is another crucial aspect of serial computer communications. Receiving and sending devices must have matched communication speeds or the results will be unintelligible. Rates are measured in units of bits per second, called the device's *baud rate* (after M. Baudot, originator of a now obsolete 5-bit character code). For years, the standard teletype, operating at 110 baud (using an 11-bit representation for each 8-bit ASCII byte), set the communications standard at 10 characters per second. As UART technology improved and video terminals became increasingly available, the transmission speeds of new hardware increased accordingly. Not so long ago, 1200 baud (just over 100 characters per second) seemed phenomonal. Today, terminals capable of 19,200 baud are commonplace, and tomorrow's transmission rates will doubtless be much greater.

Now, with this introductory material at last out of the way, we are ready to write a set of high-level Forth words that will actually do something. In this case, we are about to write an application to send data to our computer's printer.

7.4 Accessing the Printer

Your Forth system may have come with the printer routines already written for you, in which case you may be tempted to skip this section. Please don't! The principles of interfacing presented here cover almost all devices, from robot arms and milling machines to spectrophotometers and chromatographs. The simple printer provides a useful starting point that will serve as an example for many later applications. And you will learn how to modify and perhaps improve the I/O routines that are part of your system at the same time.

I/O Interface

As you have seen, the link between the computer and the printer is the piece of hardware called the interface. The purpose of the interface is to act as a buffer between the CPU and the printer itself. There are several reasons why an interface is necessary.

First, even the fastest modern printer cannot print incoming characters as fast as the CPU can send them. The CPU communicates with the interface at bus speeds after all. Remember, as far as the CPU is concerned, the interface is just another cell in the system's complement of RAM.

Hence, one of the interface's responsibilities is to provide the running program with information on the status of the data-receiving and printing processes. One of the programmer's responsibilities, by the way, is to write the program carefully, so that it recognizes and uses the information made available to it by the interface.

For example, suppose you are "printing" a string of characters and at a particular instant the interface indicates that the printer's printhead is still in the process of moving into position to print the character. It would be inappropriate to require the printer to print a new character at such a time. Rather, the program must wait until the head is in the proper position, as indicated by some form of "ready" indicator on the interface, before sending another character. Although this whole process appears dreadfully complicated at first reading, rest assured that it is not. Forth was invented to handle just this sort of job.

Another reason for existence of the interface results from the differences in bus designs from one computer to the next. Without the intervention of a suitable interface, printer manufacturers would have to market different versions of their devices for every computer. It is considerably less expensive to employ an interface.

Finally, all modern computer systems use a parallel bus, while many printers expect their incoming data in serial format. Therefore, another of the interface's tasks, as we saw earlier, is conversion of the data from parallel to serial format.

How do we get our data to the printer? As we develop the Forth words that will ultimately answer this question, we will use a rather informal but effective "top-down" approach. Top-down programming is based on the premise that a programmer programs most efficiently by focusing on the larger aspects of the problem before attempting the definitions of the lower-level words. This is best illustrated by example.

A Top-Down Approach to Creating a Printer Application

In theory, given a memory-mapped system and a peripheral device with an infinitely rapid speed of response, all a programmer would have to do to print a string of characters would be to write a word that

1. Has access to the memory address of the beginning of the character string that is to be sent
2. Has access to the number of characters to be sent

158 Hardware Control with Forth

3. Has access to the address to which they are to be sent
4. Has the appropriate programming features to send them

The first two features obviously describe our old friend TYPE from Chapter 6. It will not come as a surprise that the first new word we are going to write will be a lot like TYPE operationally. However, the destination of the transmitted characters will be the printer rather than the terminal.

Let us call our word OUTPUT, for want of a better name. Even before writing any of its definition at all, we will determine what its stack effects must be.

```
OUTPUT ( addr,n ... )
```

Good Forth programming *demands* that the programmer remain constantly in touch with the stack effects of the words to be used, even before they have been defined.

Like TYPE, our new word will expect to find an address and a count on the stack. Unlike TYPE, however, our word cannot use the traditional EMIT, since that word is tied to the system's terminal, at least in most Forth systems.

As we have seen before, one of the best ways to learn any computer language is to closely examine the ways in which others have used the language to accomplish certain tasks. With our present needs in mind, consider this definition of TYPE:

```
: TYPE OVER + SWAP DO I C@ EMIT LOOP ;
```

The OVER + SWAP part of the definition sets up the limit and index for the DO ... LOOP, and the I C@ EMIT part of the definition copies the index value (the address). C@ fetches the character, and EMIT sends it off to the terminal. We can steal the relevant features of this word for our own use, then modify the rest of the purpose at hand. Actually, most of TYPE is perfect for us. Only the EMIT part is inappropriate, for obvious reasons.

The solution is to define a more general word that does what EMIT does, but does so without being tied to a specific device, and then to use the new word in the definition of OUTPUT. We will name our new word >DEV (pronounced "to device").

Before writing >DEV, though, we must give some thought to what it is intended to accomplish. >DEV is going to send characters to a device which appears to the computer to be a memory location. Therefore >DEV needs access to an address to which to send the characters. The easiest way to handle this is through use of a CONSTANT.

Introduction to Hardware: Input-Output 159

    xxxxxx CONSTANT XBUF

In this context we will use xxxxxx to represent the actual physical address of the interface, which we will call XBUF. As yet we do not know what its value is, but rather than be distracted by this, we will forge ahead with our definition, remembering that we must provide the real address later.

Remember, whenever XBUF is executed, as is always the case with constants, the *value* xxxxxx will be automatically pushed to the stack. Now we can define >DEV.

    : >DEV WAIT XBUF C! ;

Simple. We needed a word that can force the computer to wait for the device to be ready before allowing us to send characters to it. Therefore we included in our definition the word WAIT. Never mind that we have not the foggiest idea how to make a computer wait for anything; we will write that part later. (Top-down program design is a procrastinator's delight.)

The stack notation for >DEV will be the same as that for EMIT,

    >DEV (c ...)

but the character is sent to the address stored as the constant XBUF rather than to the address of the terminal.

Now we can define OUTPUT, an easy task with TYPE serving as a paradigm.

    : OUTPUT OVER + SWAP DO I C@ >DEV LOOP ;

Our entire application, at this stage of its evolution, looks like this:

    xxxxxx CONSTANT XBUF
    : >DEV WAIT XBUF C! ;
    : OUTPUT OVER + SWAP DO I C@ >DEV LOOP ;

It would be nice if we could use OUTPUT now, either in the definition of a printer application or in some other useful way, and we almost could, were it not for the two clear shortcomings.

First, we do not have a value for xxxxxx, obviously a hardware-specific parameter that we must know for our particular machine. Second, we have made no provision for our word WAIT to "wait" for the interface to inform the program that it's OK to send another character. This too is a hardware-specific function. Because of these two shortcomings, we must digress temporarily so that we can get these hardware details out of the way.

7.5 Hardware Input and Output

As you have seen earlier in this chapter, the upper 4K cells of a PDP-11's memory are reserved for the use of interfaces to the outside world. Most of these will be serial (terminal and printer) or parallel (disk and/or tape drive) interfaces. In addition, analog-to-digital converters, digital-to-analog converters, and incremental plotter interfaces are sometimes found residing in specific cells of the I/O page. By tradition of convenience, DEC systems reserve certain sites in the upper 4K cells for particular devices which are commonly found on all computers, such as the operator's terminal. Other computer manufacturers have similar sets of regularly used addresses for their operations as well.

The standard set of addresses reserved for PDP-11 interfaces is given in Table 7.2.

Remember, Digital Equipment Corporation systems use octal arithmetic in allocating memory locations for devices in the I/O page. The octal system, although not exactly unique in the computer industry, certainly runs counter to the prevalent trend to employ hexadecimal numbering of memory locations. Forth is about as "unpicky" as a language can be in this area, fortunately, and therefore decimal and hex memory references are also included in Table 7.2. You can use whatever suits you.

Table 7.2   PDP-11 I/O Page Interface Addresses

	Address		
Octal	Hex	Decimal	Device
177560	FF70	65392	Console terminal
177546	FF66	65382	Line-time clock
177514	FF4C	65356	LA180 printer
177400	FF00	65280	RK05 hard disk
177170	FE78	65144	RX02 floppy disk
176670	FDB8	64952	General-purpose serial interfaces
	through		
176500	FD40	64832	
174400	F900	63744	RL01 hard disk
170440	F120	61728	Digital-to-analog converter
170420	F110	61712	Real-time clock
170400	F100	61696	Analog-to-digital converter
167770	EFF8	61432	General-purpose parallel interfaces
	through		
167750	EFE8	61416	

Introduction to Hardware: Input-Output 161

Since most printers communicate with the computer by using an RS-232 standard serial interface, which is similar to a terminal but lacks a keyboard, we will deal with the techniques for interfacing both keyboards and screens or printing devices in this section.

On a small, single-user PDP-11 like the low-end PDP-11/03, the programmer's terminal occupies I/O page locations 177560 through 177566 (octal), and the printer, if the system has one installed, resides at 176500 through 176506. Surprisingly, the interface for as simple a device as a terminal or printer requires dedication of four of the 16-bit cells in the I/O page. Why?

A terminal is obviously a bidirectional device. In actuality it is a *pair* of bidirectional devices, one transmitting information to the host computer (the keyboard) and the other displaying information as it arrives from the computer. The two usually function independently of one another.

In a PDP-11, the share of the I/O page that is allocated to a particular terminal must provide for communication in *both* directions. That requires two cells, one for each direction of communication. (Actually, half a cell, or 1 byte, is enough to contain the representation of an ASCII character, but the PDP-11 is a 16-bit machine, and it is operationally much easier to use an entire cell for a character than to split a cell in the I/O page.) These cells are called *data buffers* or *data registers*.

In addition, there must be some provision for providing the running program with information on the status of both the keyboard and the screen (or printhead). To accomplish this, two additional cells, called *sta-*

```
Receiver Status
Register, RCSR            _ _ _ _ _ _ _ _ R _ _ _ _ _ _ _
add = 175600₈
Receiver Buffer
Register, RBUF            _ _ _ _ _ _ _ _ P D D D D D D D
add = 176502₈
Transmitter Status
Register, XCSR            _ _ _ _ _ _ _ _ R _ _ _ _ _ _ _
add = 176504₈
Transmitter Buffer
Register, XBUF            _ _ _ _ _ _ _ _ P D D D D D D D
add = 176506₈
Bit position:             15 14 13 12 11 10 9 8 7 6 5 4 3 2 1 0
 _ ... unused bit position     R ... a ready bit indicating the interface
                                     is ready to send or receive another
                                     character (bit 7, read only).
 D ... one data bit            P ... a parity bit, frequently ignored.
```

Figure 7.5 DLV11 registers

162 Hardware Control with Forth

tus registers, are appropriated for the uses of the interface. The four cells associated with a particular serial device such as a terminal are portrayed in Fig. 7.5.

Input Operations

The first, or lowest, address is associated with the status of the *receiver,* and the second with the data (a character) to be *received.* In this context, the definition of receiver is made from the point of view of the computer. It is through the keyboard that the computer receives its character input, and another name for the receiver status register is *keyboard status register.* We will call this hardware address the RCSR (for *r*eceiver *c*ontrol *s*tatus *r*egister) to be consistent with the Digital Equipment Corporation nomenclature for their product. When the value of the contents of bit 7 of the RCSR is set to 1 by the interface, the running program can assume that the character available at the address RCSR+2, or RBUF, is valid and OK to be read into memory.

Is all this really necessary?

No matter how fast you can type, your computer can read the contents of the keyboard buffer more quickly than you can clobber the keys. What follows is not the exact definition of the character-input routines that your Forth system uses (KEY is a primitive, written in machine code). However, functionally, the character input routine works something like this:

```
BINARY : ?READY BEGIN RCSR @ 10000000 AND UNTIL ; DECIMAL

: KEY ?READY RBUF C@ ;
```

The crux of this definition of KEY is the indefinite loop that constitutes most of the definition of ?READY. When you press a key, the interface holds the RCSR's bit 7 at 0 until the character is set in RBUF, ready to be read. Only when the data are settled in the buffer register, when the character is truly available to be read, will the interface set a 1 in bit 7 of the RCSR. Meanwhile, ?READY constantly monitors the RCSR, waiting for RCSR @ 10000000$_2$ AND to become true (1), thus forcing the system into a WAIT state that can terminate only when the interface indicates that the character is available. The ... RBUF C@ ... part of the definition then "reads" the character by copying it from the register and pushing it to the stack.

What if you try to quickly read the character again, before pressing the next key? Will you get the old character again? No.

The computer's interface is pretty smart. When RBUF is read, the interface immediately sets bit 7 of RCSR to 0 again, preventing KEY from

Introduction to Hardware: Input-Output

C@ing the same character to the stack more than once. This is why bit 7 is called the *ready bit*.

Here is another way to look at character input. Suppose the definition of KEY was simply

    : KEY RBUF @ ;

(Remember, KEY is the primitive that lies at the core of EXPECT and WORD.)

Next suppose this version of KEY was incorporated into the definition of WORD. Remember, WORD just keeps on inputting characters until it encounters its specified delimiter (see Chap. 6). Without provision for consulting the status register for the keyboard, this version of WORD would push a repetitious stream of characters, each a copy of the last character typed, onto the stack, wiping out Forth in seconds. To avoid this, we used ?READY to incorporate into KEY a provision to delay reading RBUF until the ready bit is set. Here again is the definition of ?READY.

    BINARY : ?READY BEGIN RCSR @ 10000000 AND UNTIL ; DECIMAL

This word is an example of a *tight loop,* a programming construction that results in a virtually functionless loop that does nothing but waste time waiting for something to happen. In this case ?READY waits for bit 7 of the RSCR to go high, allowing the 10000000 AND portion of the definition to leave a true flag for UNTIL.

The BINARY and DECIMAL words surrounding the definition are solely for convenience in portraying the definition of ?READY, by the way. We could dispense with them, as in

    : ?READY BEGIN RCSR @ 128 AND UNTIL ; (assuming base-10)

where the value 128 is the decimal representation of binary 10000000.

Although there are more sophisticated interrupt I/O techniques that avoid wasting CPU time in tight loops as ?READY does, you will find that these loop tricks are very useful tools in interfacing your system with outside devices.

Output Operations

The third cell associated with the PDP-11's serial interface is aligned with the status of the *transmitter,* and the fourth cell provides an address "through" which data (characters) can be sent to the device (printer or screen) attached to the interface. Digital Equipment Corporation calls the cell associated with the transmitter status XCSR, and the cell associated with the outgoing character is XBUF.

There is an exact correspondence between the functions of the bits in XCSR and RCSR, and between XBUF and RBUF, respectively. Just as bit 7 of RCSR goes high when a new character is available at the interface, bit 7 of XCSR goes high when the output device is ready to accept another character for display. Likewise, bits 0 to 7 of RBUF are read-only input bits, whereas bits 0 to 7 of XBUF are write-only bits associated with the outgoing data stream.

It follows that there must be some tight-looping techniques associated with sending a stream of characters to a terminal or printer. As implied above, the interfacing trick here is to avoid sending characters to the printer before it is ready for them. To handle this we need another version of ?READY, one that will let us monitor bit 7 of the XCSR and send a character only after the ready bit goes high.

It is time for you to enter some definitions. If you are using a system other than a PDP-11, or if your PDP-11 is part of a large time-sharing system that will not allow you to have direct access to the I/O page, consult your system's manual (for a small system) or a systems analyst (for a large system) to find out the necessary addresses to which to send your characters.

Now enter these definitions:

```
OCTAL     176504 CONSTANT XCSR  ( printer's status register )
          XCSR 2 + CONSTANT XBUF ( printer's output buffer )

DECIMAL

: WAIT    BEGIN XCSR @ 128 AND UNTIL ;              ( ... )

: >DEV    WAIT XBUF C! ;                            ( c ... )

: OUTPUT  OVER + SWAP DO I C@ >DEV LOOP ;           ( add,n . . )

: LPRINT  64 -TRAILING OUTPUT 13 >DEV 10 >DEV ;     ( add ... add,n )

: PRINT   BLOCK 16 0 DO DUP I 64 * + LPRINT LOOP DROP ;   ( n ... )
```

Entirely home-brew, this set of simple definitions can be used to print the contents of a block on the printer. Try it on one of your disk blocks, carefully. Be sure that your printer is turned on and set on-line, put a block number on the stack, and try PRINT.

Our sample output is shown in Fig. 7.6, a particular Forth block to which we will return. Of course, our primitive set of printer words has the shortcomings we would expect of a first attempt at such an application.

Introduction to Hardware: Input-Output

For instance, the listing is more like our earlier VIZ than a LIST, lacking linenumbers and block headings. Less obvious, but just as unsophisticated, our character output word >DEV has been specifically tied to whatever address we stored in XCSR. Indeed, >DEV is just as restrictive a word as EMIT, for it is certainly no more reusable. We can do better than this.

W!, a Hardware-Specific Interface Word

Look again at Fig. 7.6, the block we just listed, paying special attention to the words W! and XDECOUT.

The first of these words, W!, is a general-purpose word that is especially useful with Digital Equipment Corporation machines, wherein interfaces often use bit 7 as a ready bit, and the device buffer is almost always 2 bytes higher in memory than the corresponding status register. Corresponding versions can easily be written for any computer.

Now look for a moment at the definition of W!.

: W! BEGIN DUP @ 200$_8$ AND UNTIL 2+ C! ; (n add ...)

The BEGIN ... UNTIL portion of the word is, of course, our old friend WAIT without a built-in address to monitor (W! expects the address on the stack). The 2+ appears in the definition to offset the address on top of the stack so that it points to the data buffer rather than the status register.

The stack effects of W! are identical to those of C!, as you can see, but operationally the word "waits" until the interface informs the running program that it is ok to send the character along.

Also look at XDECOUT. Do you remember DECOUT from Chap. 6? One of the reasons given for the introduction of DECOUT then was the inability

```
( W! and Auxiliary Output Device support   ...Aug 83 )
          octal 176504 Constant xcsr 0 variable cnt
: W!      begin dup @ 200 and until 2+ C! ; decimal
: xdecout 0 cnt ! begin 1 cnt +! 10 /mod dup 0= until drop
          cnt @ 0 do 48 + xcsr w! loop ;
: xtype   over + swap do i c@ xcsr w! loop ;
: lprint  32 xcsr w! 64 -trailing xtype 13 xcsr w! 10 xcsr w! ;
: viz     block 16 0 do dup i 64 * + lprint loop drop ;
: print   block 16 0 do dup i dup xdecout 64 * + lprint
          loop drop ;
```

Figure 7.6 A printed block without header or linenumbers

of `EMIT` to send digits to any device other than the console. `XDECOUT` takes care of that. Its definition is identical to that of `DECOUT` except that the output phrase `XCSR W!` replaces `EMIT`. We will use `W!` in several applications.

Printing Blocks on the Printer

The highest-level definition in this one-block application is obviously `PRINT`. (Funny how the highest-level definitions are always in the lowest lines in a block.) Working in the same manner as `LIST`, `PRINT` has an identical stack notation:

```
PRINT ( n ... )
```

To the new Forth programmer, this new word was earned at the cost of an entire lesson in hardware interfacing. Although the lesson may have been unwanted, this simple lineprinter project is so typical of so many other types of hardware-specific problems that results easily justify the investment in development time.

Words like `W!` represent a class of machine-specific words that you can define to make your Forth system useful in ways which could not have been foreseen by the original implementers of Forth software. Creating, testing, and incorporating these kinds of words into your hardware-software environment can be a challenging process, and no one book can cover all the details of the equipment that you have at hand. But your satisfaction when you can at last sit back and watch *your* successfully interfaced device hard at work will be easily worth the investment in time and frustration. This will be especially true once the programming time you are investing returns to you in the form of time you save by the application.

However, the responsibility for learning the details of your hardware falls upon you. Delivered with your printers, terminals, disk drives, and other hardware there should have been technical manuals that describe the operations and design of your components, and you may have even read beyond the initial "set-up" pages. If you did, you probably encountered a section or chapter on "escape codes," for nearly all peripheral I/O devices (except virtual memory) sold for or with modern computer equipment use this kind of control lingo.

7.6 Escape Sequences

One of the Forth words that comes with some systems is `PAGE`, the word that can be used to clear the screen on a CRT-type terminal, moving the cursor to the upper left at the same time. Try it on your system. (If you are using a *hard-copy* terminal, such as a thermal printer or printing terminal, you obviously cannot use `PAGE` as described. But read on, there will be more for you shortly.)

```
PAGE<ret> PAGE ?
```

If it did not work, do not be disappointed. You have just been presented with an opportunity to write your first *escape sequence,* or *escape code.*

Go to the manual for your terminal. Somewhere, usually in a table or appendix, you will find a list of strange symbols called escape sequences, along with a terse description of what each sequence is supposed to do. (If you have had trouble understanding just what this table is for, that does not reflect on you. With few exceptions, peripheral manufacturers have been abysmally inept at finding competent writers to describe the inner workings of their products.)

Look for the entry that gives the escape sequence or code for any of these functions:

`Cursor Home`	Move cursor to upper left.
`Erase to End of Page`	Erase from current position to the bottom of the page.
and: `Clear display`	Clear entire screen, *and* move cursor to upper left.

For example, if you have a Zenith-19 terminal, you will find these escape sequences at the back of your "Operations Manual":

Cursor Home	ESC H
Erase to End of Page	ESC J
Clear Display	ESC E

For other, similar terminals, you may find

Cursor Home	ESC H
Erase to End of Page	ESC J
Clear Display	(No entry)

while for an Intecolor 2400, you will find

Cursor Home	ESC [f
Erase to End of Page	ESC [0 J
Clear Display	(No entry)

Your terminal may use yet another set of escape sequences.

What do these sequences do? First, in the escape sequence tables, `ESC` is the representation of ASCII 27, a nonprinting character that is now used by many devices as a "lead-in" control character. When the stream

168 Hardware Control with Forth

of incoming characters contains an ASCII 27, the device will not only not print the ESC (it is nonprinting anyway), it will also not print the next character or characters, even if it normally could. Rather, the designers of the device have programmed it to exhibit some predetermined response which depends on the characters following ESC.

Video Hardware Escape Sequences

If you have a Zenith-19, a VISUAL terminal, a DEC VT-52, or some other device that uses Digital Equipment Corporation's VT-52 escape codes, enter this:

```
27 EMIT 72 EMIT 27 EMIT 74 EMIT<ret>
```

The screen should be clear, and Forth's little ok should now appear in the upper left of your screen. (If it did not work, your terminal is probably in some "non-DEC" mode. Check the manual.)

Right now you could define PAGE as

```
: PAGE 27 EMIT 72 EMIT 27 EMIT 74 EMIT ;
```

but it would be more efficient use of dictionary space to define a special word to send the lead-in escape and its follow-up character:

```
: PESC 27 EMIT EMIT ; ( c ... )
: PAGE 72 PESC 74 PESC ; ( ... )
```

If you have worked your way this far into this chapter, you have clearly demonstrated the persistence that is the hallmark of a successful interfacer. Consequently, you will be using a lot of escape sequences. PESC makes the job easier.

A useful trick is to include the definition of PAGE in a load or tools block that you load at the beginning of each Forth session. Here is another useful definition that can be included in that block.

```
: LIST PAGE LIST ;
```

You will get a LIST has already been defined message at load time, but that is OK, for now your new version of LIST looks a lot nicer when the screen is automatically cleared before each block is listed.

What if you have a terminal that does not use these escape codes? Define PAGE in terms of the sequences that your terminal does use. If you have an Intecolor 2400, for example, the definition of PAGE could be written as

: PAGE 27 EMIT 91 EMIT 102 EMIT 27 EMIT 91 EMIT 48 EMIT 74 EMIT ;

but that would be foolish. Better to use a word like `PESC` for this hardware too. But first let us see why this version of `PAGE` is so long.

When escape sequences first became a desirable feature that peripheral manufacturers were adding to their terminals, there was no official set of escape sequences that were then sanctioned as an industry standard. The ASCII standards did not cover such things, and there was no agreement on what codes should accomplish what. The largest peripheral-manufacturing firms, such as Digital Equipment Corporation, Hazeltine, and Lear-Siegler, simply used whatever codes seemed reasonable to them, hoping that, by capturing a large share of the market, *their* system would become the standard. We have all seen this philosophy at work in the communications and entertainment industries.

Smaller manufacturers hitched their wagons to their favorite star, hoping to make the right choice as they built their devices to emulate the instruction set of one of the big guys' terminals. That is why all kinds of terminals which emulate the DEC VT-52 are available, even though Digital Equipment Corporation phased out that particular model years ago.

Other manufacturers, more skillful or more cautious, overloaded their hardware with features that let their system emulate many different versions of their competitors' stuff, *just by sending the terminal the correct escape sequence.* Enter the schizophrenic terminal.

The irony here, of course, is that the programmer needs to know what kind of terminal the particular piece of hardware thinks it is before telling it to think it is something else. Unless the programmer is very careful, this can lead to disastrous results. The classic tale in this regard is that of the unnamed manufacturer's Wonderterminal. It thought it should behave like a brand-X color-graphics device, but it was sent the brand-Y code that told it to act like a VT-52. What the programmer did not know was that brand Y's "Imagine you are a VT-52" escape sequence is the same as brand X's command to clear the screen and lock the keyboard. Instant catatonia resulted.

Of course, some manufacturers are much too careful to let a little problem of mistaken identity get in their way. For that reason the VT-52, and some others, can actually identify themselves in response to an escape-sequence query from the host computer: "Who are we today, Sybil?" Hence the need for a standard.

The ANSI Standard

The need for standardizing escape sequences became obvious very quickly, and the organization that accepted responsibility for this task was the American National Standards Institute (ANSI). Communication between devices will still use the ASCII codes for printing and nonprinting characters, but what those escape codes will do is the subject of a useful standard, ANSI Standard 3.64.

The Intecolor 2400 uses the ANSI 3.64 escape sequences (or some of them, anyhow). Look again at the definition of **PAGE** with ANSI 3.64 codes:

```
: PAGE 27 EMIT 91 EMIT 102 EMIT 27 EMIT 91 EMIT 48 EMIT 74 EMIT ;
```

This definition includes a lot more than the previous definition of **PAGE**, because the ANSI standard needs to be all things to all applications—a common limitation of standards. Fortunately, Forth is very good at handling these kinds of situations, as demonstrated by Fig. 7.7, the display of three different Forth blocks. In the listing of block 128, for example, we find a "terminal personality block" for a terminal which adheres to the ANSI 3.64 standard. Block 127, when loaded, initializes a Forth system to use a Zenith Z-19, and the third block in Fig. 7.7 illustrates the codes for an Intecolor 2400, in VT-52 emulation mode.

If you have a terminal that you wish to use with your Forth system, and you want to take advantage of its graphics or other characteristics without having to rewrite all the words that use other escape sequences, you should write a terminal personality block for it (and for each type of terminal that you might ever use). In the application itself, use only the high-level words, such as **PAGE**. When you are going to use the application, just load the appropriate personality block before loading the application's load block. For an operational example of this principle in action, see App. E, "The Universal Screen Editor." Later, when we explore the other capabilities of our terminals and printers, we will look much more closely at the words in these personality blocks.

Why is the ANSI version of **PAGE** so much longer than the VT-52 version, by the way? Standard 3.64 is a *postfix* standard. This means that the initiation of an escape-sequence response will not necessarily be terminated after a fixed number of characters has been received. Rather, the receipt of a *Command String Introducer Pair,* or **ESC [** in the standard, sets the terminal in a COMMAND mode which will accept an indeterminate number of characters. (This jargon prompts the use of the chosen name for the Forth word **CSI** in block 128.) The termination of the COMMAND mode occurs upon receipt of a "termination" character, whose identity varies from sequence to sequence.

If all languages were as flexible as Forth in the way in which it can cope with the vagaries of its associated hardware, the pressure to adopt a standard such as ANSI 3.64 would have been less intense. And Forth's skills

Introduction to Hardware: Input-Output 171

do not end at the video terminal. They can be applied wherever device-control applications require the flexibility to adapt to the available hardware.

Now we are ready to examine the uses of escape sequences by printers and other such hard-copy devices.

```
Block  # 127
   0 ( Terminal Personality Block....Z19 in  VT52 emulation..          )
   1 : pesc 27 emit emit ;            ( Send an escape sequence )
   2 : home 72 pesc ;                 ( Cursor to upper left )
   3 : page home 74 pesc ;                     ( clear screen )
   4 : putcur 89 pesc 31 + emit 31 + emit ;  ( home is 1,1 not 0,0 )
   5 : revvid 112 pesc ;              ( terminal to reverse video )
   6 : vid     113 pesc ;             ( terminal to normal video )
   7 : graph  70 pesc ;               ( enter graphics mode )
   8 : nograph 71 pesc ;              ( exit graphics mode )
   9 : nocur 120 pesc 53 emit ;                ( Cursor off )
  10 : cur  121 pesc 53 emit ;                 ( Cursor on )
  11 : getchr drop key ;       ( disregard chr following <esc> )
  12
  13
  14 : list page list ; ( video terminal can clear screen to list )
  15

Block  # 128
   0 ( ANSI Personality Block: For terminals using 3.64 standard   )
   1 : Csi   27 emit 91 emit ;        ( ANSI Leadin characters )
   2 : Home csi 72 emit ;             ( Cursor to upper left )
   3 : page home csi 50 emit 74 emit ;         ( Clear the screen )
   4
   5 0 variable cnt     ( ANSI cursor addressing needs digits.......)
   6 : decout 0 cnt ! begin 1 cnt +! 10 /mod dup 0= ( Calc's val )
   7         until drop cnt @ 0 do 48 + emit loop ; ( for putcur )
   8
   9 : putcur csi decout 59 emit decout 102 emit ; ( ANSI cur add )
  10
  11 : cur ; : nocur ; ( Some ANSI terminals cannot suppress cursor)
  12
  13 : getchr    drop key drop key ; ( drop unnec. chrs after <esc>)
  14
  15 : list page list ; ( good ter. can clear screen prior to list )

Block  # 129
   0 ( Terminal Personality Block....Intecolor VT52 emulation...    )
   1 : pesc 27 emit emit ;            ( send an escape code )
   2 : home 72 pesc ;                 ( cursor to upper left )
   3 : page home 74 pesc ;                     ( clear screen )
   4 : putcur 89 pesc 31 + emit 31 + emit ; ( home is 1,1 not 0,0 )
   5
   6
   7
   8
   9 : nocur ;  : cur ; ( Too bad! Intecolor can't do either one! )
  10
  11 : getchr drop key ;    ( to ignore the char. following <esc> )
  12 : revvid ;
  13 : vid ;           ( fill in later )
  14
  15
```

Figure 7.7 Terminal personality blocks

Hard-Copy Escape Sequences

There are many printers and plotters on the market, most of which are controllable through series of escape codes similar to those we have been using with our video devices. Some are incredibly sophisticated, offering word-processing and graphics features along with high-speed data printing, while others are more modest (and usually lower in cost).

One of the most versatile of such devices is the Mannesman-Talley (MT) printer, a hard-copy device which is capable of both high-speed, lineprinter-quality printing in its DATA-DISPLAY mode and "correspondence-quality" printing. Not surprisingly, all its features are controlled by escape codes. Figure 7.8 illustrates some of the more routine escape codes to which the MT printer responds. This figure presents a *printer personality block* for this particular piece of hardware. This block is loaded before a Forth application that uses the printer is run, essentially customizing the Forth system to the hardware available.

Figure 7.9 illustrates a few of the type styles that this particular printer uses under the control of these escape sequences. The first is a 17-character-per-inch, rapid-printing, compressed style that is invoked by the Forth word DATA17. This mode is great for displaying more than the usual 80 characters per line. Next is shown the CORRESPONDENCE mode, 12-characters-per-inch style (CORR12), followed by the bold, double-density, 10-characters-per-inch style (DATD10D).

Your printer probably has a similar but not identical set of codes. To use the capabilities of your system to its fullest, you must carefully examine the documentation that accompanied your hardware and then prepare a load block similar to the block shown in Fig. 7.8. The implementation of escape-sequence hardware programming into your system's environment will be a clearly visible demonstration of Forth's utility in device-control applications.

```
0 ( Direct access escape codes for the Mannesman Printer )
1 : >P     xcsr w! ;
2 : ec>pr    27 >P 91 >P swap >P >P ; ( n n ... )
3 : data             48  121 ec>pr ;
4 : corr             49  121 ec>pr ;
5 : corr10   corr 52  121 ec>pr ;
6 : corr12   corr 53  121 ec>pr ;
7 : data5    data 48  119 ec>pr ;
8 : data6    data 49  119 ec>pr ;
9 : data8    data 50  119 ec>pr ;
10 : data10D data 51  119 ec>pr ;
11 : data10  data 52  119 ec>pr ;
12 : data12  data 53  119 ec>pr ;
13 : data17  data 54  119 ec>pr ;
14 : uline           52  109 ec>pr ;
15 : nouline         48  109 ec>pr ;
```

Figure 7.8 Mannesman-Talley printer escape sequences

```
Once upon a midnight dreary, while I pondered, weak and weary,
Over many a quaint and curious volume of forgotten lore,-
While I nodded, nearly napping, suddenly there came a tapping,
As of some one gently rapping, rapping on my chamber door.
"Tis some visitor," I muttered, "tapping at my chamber door;
Only this, and nothing more."

                    Edgar Allen Poe
```

```
Once upon a midnight dreary, while I pondered, weak and weary,
Over many a quaint and curious volume of forgotten lore,-
While I nodded, nearly napping, suddenly there came a tapping,
As of some one gently rapping, rapping on my chamber door.
"Tis some visitor," I muttered, "tapping at my chamber door;
Only this, and nothing more."

                    Edgar Allen Poe
```

```
Once upon a midnight dreary, while I pondered, weak and weary,
Over many a quaint and curious volume of forgotten lore,-
While I nodded, nearly napping, suddenly there came a tapping,
As of some one gently rapping, rapping on my chamber door.
"Tis some visitor," I muttered, "tapping at my chamber door;
Only this, and nothing more."

                    Edgar Allen Poe
```

Figure 7.9 Various type styles selected with escape codes

In Chap. 8 you will learn how Forth can assist you in effectively using the computer to control nondigital devices such as spectrometers, electronic devices, and electromechanical devices such as XY recorders. Such applications rarely require escape codes, by the way, but they do require that the programmer thoroughly understand interface registers.

7.7 Problems

1. Write a word that waits for bit 7 of a particular 16-bit cell to indicate a ready condition before using C@ to fetch a character from the stack to the address. Call the word W@, and be sure that its stack notation is: W@ (add ... c).

2. One of the useful features of a word like W! is that it can be used with either a variable, a constant, or a literal to provide it with an address for the location of its destination. For example, if properly written, the phrase 7 XBUF W! should cause your printer to ring its bell (unless it is literally a dumb printer that has no bell). Use W! to rewrite PRINT so that it can easily be used for more than one printer on your system.

Chapter 8

Analog Signals: Data Acquisition and Device Control

This chapter will deal with the techniques by which Forth can be used to acquire data from external devices which produce analog rather than digital signals. You will also learn how to use Forth to control external devices which can accept computer-generated analog voltages. The techniques which involve computer interfaces to such real-world devices are called *analog-to-digital* and *digital-to-analog* conversions, respectively, and are usually abbreviated A/D and D/A, respectively.

8.1 Digital-to-Analog Conversion

Suppose you were given the job of designing an application that would allow you to use your computer to produce any desired voltage (within certain practical limits). Your computer has only a few dc voltages available inside (+5 and +12 usually), and handles all its data internally in a digital format. Obviously, to generate and control an infinitely variable voltage you would need to employ some additional hardware, devices which use the digital data-transfer facilities indigenous to your computer to create the desired voltage. Such devices are called *digital-to-analog converters* (DACs).

As you know, the computer business abounds with abbreviations and acronyms. In the absence of a firm traditional nomenclature, we will adopt the convention of using "D/A" to represent the *process* of digital-to-analog conversion, and "DAC" to represent the *device* that does the conversion. Analogously, "A/D" and "ADC" will refer to the respective processes and devices associated with analog-to-digital conversion.

Figure 8.1 illustrates the fundamental concepts underlying digital-to-analog conversion. A DAC consists of a set of binary inputs, a dc reference voltage input, and an analog output. An 8-bit DAC has 8 binary inputs, a 12-bit DAC has 12, and so on.

The output voltage of the DAC is expressed as $V_{ref} \times R$, where R is the magnitude of the binary input value relative to the maximum possible binary input value. That is, $R = n/(2^8)$ for an 8-bit DAC or $n/(2^{12})$ for a 12-bit DAC, where n is the binary value sent to the DAC by the computer.

For an 8-bit DAC there are 2^8 possible values (0 to 11111111_2, or 0 to 255_{10}) that can be sent to the DAC. This limits the capability of the DAC to a fixed set of 256 different values that it can produce over the range of its reference voltage. These restrictions are the cause of the limited *resolution* of a DAC. Thus, an 8-bit DAC has a resolution of 1 part in 256 (2^8) for instance, while a 12-bit DAC has a resolution of 1 part in 4096.

Table 8.1 lists output voltages for a representative sample of binary inputs to both 12- and 8-bit devices, assuming a 10.000-V reference voltage in both cases. Note that the finest voltage gradations possible are 39.1 mV and 2.44 mV for the 8- and 12-bit DACs, respectively.

Better resolution can be obtained, but at a higher price. A 16-bit DAC, for example, with 2^{16} possible voltages available over its voltage span, has a resolution of 1 part in 65536 (0.153 mV with a 10.000-V reference) but costs considerably more than 12- or 8-bit devices.

The examples of DAC utilization in this section will be based on the Andromeda Systems' DAC11 12-bit digital-to-analog converter. This device, designed for the Q-bus of the smaller PDP-11 computer systems, actually has four separate channels of analog output, each memory mapped as a 16-bit cell in the I/O page of the PDP-11. Other manufacturers offer very similar devices.

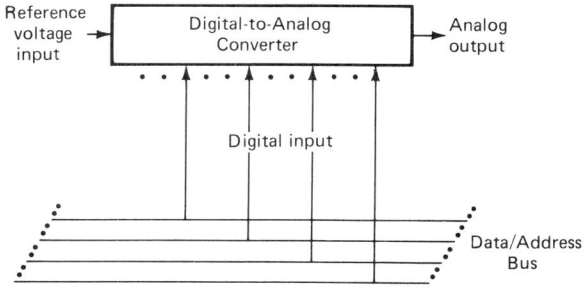

Figure 8.1 Diagram of a digital-to-analog converter

Table 8.1 Voltages Obtainable from 8- and 12-bit Digital-to-Analog Converters (0–10.00-V range)

Input (octal/decimal)	Output (8-bit dac)	Output (12-bit dac)
0000/0000	0.00 V	0.00 V
0077/0063	2.47	0.15
0377/0256	10.00	0.62
2000/1024	0.00*	2.50
7777/4095	10.00*	10.00

*Only the lowest 8-bits are significant to the converter.

Like most DAC hardware, the Andromeda system can be configured to generate voltages over a variety of output ranges. The output range is selected by means of switches or wire jumpers that are found on the device itself. The manual that accompanies the DAC should thoroughly explain the jumper configuration for your system.

Our initial examples will use only two of the DAC11's output channels, although the bus addresses of all four are tabulated below.

DAC	Bus address (octal)
0	170440
1	170442
2	170444
3	170446

Other manufacturers' DACs may or may not use these same addresses; consult your manual.

To communicate with the DAC, all you need do is store a value in the corresponding bus address. Of course we will use Forth's ! (store) for this purpose. A voltage proportional to the magnitude of the desired value will then appear at the relevant analog output. The appearance of the desired potential will not be instantaneous, however. The time required for the DAC's output voltage to stabilize (within predefined limits) after the digital equivalent has been sent to the DAC is called the *settling* time of the converter. For the DAC11, settling time is cited by the manufacturer as 3 μs. Thus we can reasonably expect that the desired voltage will truly be available (within 0.01 percent) at the output in that period of time. Since the typical processor cycle time for an individual PDP-11/03 machine-level instruction is also a few microseconds in duration, and a multitude of machine-level instructions underlie each Forth instruction, the settling time of the DAC is not usually a limiting factor in high-level Forth device-control applications.

Now that you have had an introduction to the principles underlying digital-to-analog conversion, you are ready to put Forth to work in a few D/A applications.

Forth and DAC

Let us assume that you have a small PDP-11 and a DAC11 with channels 1 and 2 attached to the respective horizontal and vertical inputs of an oscilloscope ('scope). By the way, an oscilloscope, with its rapid, two-dimensional display, is an ideal device for effective demonstration of D/A methods. If you do not have access to an oscilloscope, a voltmeter connected to the DAC's outputs can be used in its place.

Let us further assume that the DAC has been configured to display a range of voltages from 0 to +10.00 V (dc), and that your 'scope is set for horizontal and vertical deflections of 10.00 V full scale.

Enter the following constants (use a block if you wish; hex addresses are perfectly reasonable as well):

```
OCTAL CONSTANT 170442 DACY   ( Channel 1 D/A )
       CONSTANT 170444 DACX   ( Channel 2 D/A )   DECIMAL
```

Subsequent references to DACY and DACX will result in the appearance of the corresponding address on the stack. Now enter this definition:

```
: SCOPE DACY ! DACX ! ;  ( xpos ypos ... )
```

SCOPE stores the top two stack values in the addresses corresponding to the individual DAC channels. Try it.

```
0 0 SCOPE<ret> ok
```

An immobile dot will be displayed at the lower-left corner of the oscilloscope's cathode ray display. If it is not, you should adjust the horizontal and vertical position controls until it does. (Your 'scope should be configured to accept the DACX output as its horizontal input. You may need to use the external input feature of your 'scope to circumvent the customary time base used to drive the horizontal axis.)

Now enter:

```
4095 4095 SCOPE<ret> ok
```

The dot will move (within the settling time) to the upper right. If it does not, adjust the 'scope's horizontal and vertical span settings until it is clearly visible at the upper right.

Why 4095? The largest value that can be produced by a 12-bit DAC will be produced by the conversion of 111111111111_2, the octal, hex, and decimal equivalents of which are 7777, FFF, and 4095, respectively.

Having defined SCOPE and adjusted your oscilloscope, you can now access any point on the screen. Try these examples:

0 4095 SCOPE<ret> ok

puts the dot at the upper left, while

4095 0 SCOPE<ret> ok

accesses the lower right, and

2047 DUP SCOPE<ret> ok

will find a point near the center of your screen.

The same results would be obtained from

OCTAL 0 7777 SCOPE<ret>

7777 0 SCOPE<ret>

3777 0 SCOPE<ret>

or from a similar HEX routine, provided that the two values expected by SCOPE were on the stack in the correct order.

As far as order goes, SCOPE was obviously written to employ conventional cartesian coordinate notation (x, y) to point to screen positions, but any convention could be used, if done so consistently and carefully.

Note that the value of the desired voltage continues to appear at the DAC's output indefinitely. As long as the computer stays on and no other value is stored in the DAC's address, the converter will continue to produce that same voltage.

SCOPE represents your first analog control application. Easy to create, its usefulness is very limited. But if you install SCOPE in a LOOP, you can use your system to create all kinds of useful waveforms.

Waveforms

One of the most commonly used waveforms is the simple voltage ramp. For example, enter this definition:

: RAMP 4000 0 DO I I SCOPE LOOP ;

In this definition SCOPE is placed within a loop. SCOPE's requisite stack parameters are provided by using Forth's I to copy the loop counter to the stack twice.

When executed, RAMP will produce voltages which drive the 'scope's horizontal and vertical amplifiers at an equal rate. This will produce a single sweep with unit slope on the 'scope. Try it (Fig. 8.2a).

As you are aware, any ramp displayed in Figure 8.2 is the result of a digital-to-analog conversion and, as such, is subject to the resolution restrictions discussed above. In fact, it is not a true ramp at all. It is a staircase. The steps of the staircase result from the nonsimultaneous transfer of values to the two DACs. The so-called step size of the staircase is a direct consequence of the number of available bits, and hence the resolution of the converter.

The minimum step size occurs when the D/As are incremented by 1, as in the sample above. In this case the step size equals the resolution of the DAC. If we wish to produce a ramp with a slope either greater than or less than 1, we will have to increase the step size of the voltage increments to either the horizontal or the vertical DACs.

```
: STEEP-RAMP 2000 0 DO I I 2 *SCOPE LOOP ;<ret> ok
```

STEEP-RAMP (Fig. 8.2b) doubles the value of one of the copies of the loop counter before SCOPE gets to do the conversion.

```
: SHALLOW-RAMP 2000 0 DO I 2 *I SCOPE LOOP ;<ret> ok
```

Doubling the other copy of the counter produces the ramp depicted in Fig. 8.2c.

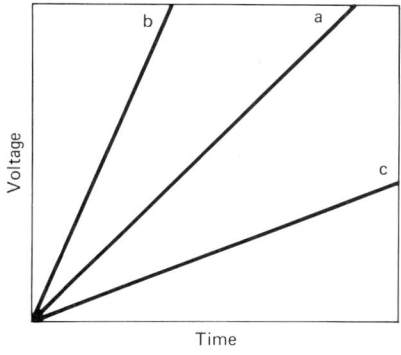

Figure 8.2 Voltage ramps

180 Hardware Control with Forth

Repeating Waveforms

Many real devices can be controlled by such a ramp, but others require a *repeating* waveform. To produce a ramp which repeats itself, use a word like RAMPS.

```
: RAMPS 0 DO RAMP LOOP ; ( n ... )
```

RAMPS expects to find a count on the stack. Its use is straightforward; just put a value on the stack and proceed.

```
10 RAMPS<ret> ok
```

In this case the ok appears only after the 10 ramps have been produced, so do not be surprised by the delay.

A defined waveform of indefinite duration can be created with an indefinite loop.

```
: RAMPS BEGIN RAMP ?TERMINAL UNTIL ;<ret> ok
```

This one could go on forever. Instead of ?TERMINAL, your application may use other Forth words to check device conditions and then provide the flag for UNTIL.

A Question of Time

If you are following these examples with an oscilloscope, you will by now have come to the realization that the ramps we have produced thus far are fairly slow on the electronics time scale. You can probably see the 'scope trace moving across the screen, sweeping from the lower left to the upper right. You may have applications that need a faster waveform than this version of RAMP can provide. On the other hand, you may need to create a very slowly varying waveform for some process-control application.

You need to learn how to gain control of the time dependence of your Forth applications. As you may have anticipated, there are several ways to do this.

Slowing Forth Down

Some Forth systems include a predefined word that does nothing more than mark time for a specified period. Usually the word is called MS, (n ...) and it does nothing more than stall for time for the number of milliseconds that was on the stack at execution time. If your system lacks

MS you can easily add it and learn a bit about the speed of your computer's operations at the same time.

Before we go farther, it is important to emphasize that MS gives an *approximate* time delay. If you need accurate timing you will need an internal quartz clock for your computer. Fortunately, we can easily calibrate MS, making it very useful for the majority of applications.

Here is a typical definition of MS:

`: MS 0 DO 32 0 DO LOOP LOOP ; ( n ... )`

This word consists of nested DO LOOPs. The inner loop, consisting of the phrase 32 0 DO LOOP, effectively does nothing but waste time. The value 32 was found by experiment to work nicely on the PDP-11/03 used in creating most of the Forth applications in this book. You will need to experiment to find the best value for your system. The outer loop relies on a stack value for its limit, allowing you to define words like

`: SEC 0 DO 1000 MS LOOP ;`

and

`: MINUTES 0 DO 60 SEC LOOP ;`

These are useful tools that you can keep on a tools block to be loaded by your load block at the beginning of a Forth session.

It is interesting to note that 32 "content-free" loops require about 1 ms on the smallest of the PDP-11 computers. This corresponds to about 31 μs per empty loop. This parameter can be used in *very* roughly estimating the relative speeds of various languages, if you feel the need to do so. On the same PDP-11, using the Digital Equipment Corporation BASIC-11 interpreter, the following program requires 55 s. It can be argued, of course, that comparison between times for empty loop execution is irrelevant and that what is truly important is a timing comparison for some useful task, but the fact remains that Forth is obviously much faster than BASIC in dealing with the decision-making and branching operations associated with looping.

```
10 FOR I = 1 to 1000
20 FOR J = 1 to 32
30 NEXT J
40 NEXT I
```

How, then, are these words used in timing operations? Simply plant them in your loops at critical points. Suppose you wanted to create a voltage ramp with a slope of 1.00 V/min, beginning at 2.50 V and increasing to 7.50 V. Such ramps are useful in many electrochemical applications, for example. Further assume that this slowly increasing voltage was to be output at DACY, and that your DAC is configured to span 0 to +10.00 V.

First, calculate the beginning and ending values for the limit and index of the word that will create the ramp. These are the decimal equivalents of the desired final and initial analog voltages.

```
4095 7500 10000 */ . <ret> 3071 ok

4095 2500 10000 */. <ret> 1024 ok
```

(In case you have forgotten, */ (star slash) was introduced in Chap. 3.) To avoid conversions between integer and floating-point numbers, we are using millivots rather than volts.

Next, calculate the time required for one ramp. This is easy: 5.00 min (from 2.50 to 7.50 V at a slope of 1.00 V/min).

The stepping interval is defined as time per step (the inverse of frequency), in this case 5.00 min/2047 steps. Again, however, it is easier to evaluate the interval in milliseconds to avoid using floating-point math. We will therefore express the stepping interval as 300000 ms/2047 steps, or 1476 ms/step.

Here is the desired word:

```
: SLOW-RAMP 3071 1024 DO I DACY ! 146 MS LOOP ;
```

As Forth executes, copying the loop's index to the DAC and creating an appropriate voltage, each operation of the loop is delayed 146 ms before the DAC output is incremented. The converter holds the output voltage fixed at the most recently requested level until Forth sends a new value to the DAC's address.

If you felt the calculation of the sample interval delay time was a bit unclear, you may prefer to use this predefined formula:

$$D = \frac{\text{range}}{\text{slope} \times M}$$

D represents the delay time in milliseconds, the desired slope is expressed in either millivolts per millisecond *or* volts per second and M represents 2^n, the maximum allowed input value to the converter (4095 for a 12-bit converter, 255 for an 8-bit device, and so on). Range, the conversion voltage range of the DAC, represents the configured output millivolt range for the DAC in use.

Analog Signals: Data Acquisition and Device Control

In this example, range = 10000 mV, slope = 0.016667 mV/ms and M = 4095, leading to a value of 146.5 ms for D.

You can incorporate MS, SEC, or MINUTES *anywhere* in a Forth application. These timing words allow Forth to throttle itself down to accommodate real-time interactions with relatively slow devices.

Now you need to learn the ways in which Forth can move more swiftly.

Fast Conversions

The crux of the first version of RAMP that we created earlier was the pair of phrases I DACY ! and I DACX ! which constitute the definition of SCOPE. The time required to execute either of these is a function of the computer hardware and the intrinsic characteristics of Forth's primitives CONSTANT, I, and !. As desirable as they would be, there are no Forth words like MS that can speed up the execution of SCOPE. But sometimes we need a very rapidly generated waveform, and frequently we need to acquire data from a very rapid source. Before Forth, programmers who needed to create applications using the utmost speed capability of their computers were forced to write their applications in the assembly language of their particular computer systems. This necessity required a great investment in both the time required to learn the machine-specific assembler and then to write the ultimate application. In some circumstances that investment is still necessary; contrary to the opinion of some experts, Forth is not the perfect or ultimate computer language, at least not yet.

Forth does provide a flexibility which is unequaled in contemporary languages, however, and this flexibility allows Forth at least two useful approaches to overcoming the difficulties associated with rapid conversions. The first, and most powerful, of these approaches uses the Forth *assembler*.

Consider the Forth words RAMP and RAMPS.

: RAMP 4095 0 DO I I SCOPE LOOP ; and

: RAMPS 0 DO RAMP LOOP ;

As far as speed is concerned, RAMPS is not problem at all. It is executed only once, and its internal loop is used only once for every 4095 executions for RAMP.

If you were to focus on the Forth words that are *speed-critical,* those words that act as the limiting factors in the application's performance, you would first address the limitations set by SCOPE and RAMP. This is where the Forth assembler comes into play. Suppose you were able to identify the speed-critical words in your application and rewrite them, *and them only*, in the assembly language native to your machine. Rather than creating an entire application in assembly language, you could create it in Forth, test it, and then rewrite only those one or two words that need to run at flank speed.

As good as this approach appears, there is a catch: Using the assembler is not that easy.

While a Forth assembler is easier than most machine-assembler programming, it is still harder to master than high-level Forth. This lesson is best taught by example. Here is the Forth assembler for the PDP-11 version of RAMP:

```
CODE    RAMP
            10000 # R1 MOV,
        BEGIN,
                R1 DEC,
                GT WHILE,
                R1 DACX MOV,
                R1 DACY MOV,
        REPEAT,
NEXT,
C;
```

Although there is more to this version of RAMP than the previous high-level definition, this code is not that hard to explain, and you can pretty well see how it works. For an assembler, CODE and C; serve the same purpose as : (colon) and ; (semicolon) in a normal definition. In this example, the PDP-11's Register 1 is used as an octal loop counter. The contents of that register are decremented and copied to the DACs as long as the counter's contents remain greater than 0. Once the counter reaches 0, the loop is terminated.

This version of RAMP executes about 8 times faster than the high-level Forth version. It uses slightly more dictionary space, but it can be called by RAMPS in exactly the same way as the previous version. Indeed, if *this* Forth assembler were as useful on other computers as it is on the PDP-11, it would be thoroughly treated in a separate chapter of this book. However, this version of RAMP is utter gibberish to the 8088-, Z-80-, 6502-, or 68000-based computer. It is specific to the PDP-11 device family. Furthermore, some Forth systems have no available assembler at all.

If you have access to Forth on a PDP-11, you are in luck. App. F, "A

Forth Assembler," describes Forth's PDP-11 assembler along with examples of its use. If you have another system, and if it has an assembler available, the documentation that came with Forth should describe its use for you. *But most of the time you will not need an assembler!*

Fortunately, regardless of the system available to you, there are other, high-level, Forth tricks that you can use to speed up the performance of your system. An example is this version of RAMP:

```
: RAMP 4095 0 DO I I SCOPE 8 +LOOP ;
```

Rather than incrementing the loop's counter by 1, as did the LOOP -using version written earlier, this version bumps the counter by 8. The results are that the word executes 8 times faster, with an 8 times greater step size, and has one-eighth the resolution of the previous version. Indeed, this reduction in resolution exactly corresponds to the replacement of a 12-bit DAC with a 9-bit model. Whereas the 12-bit DAC could display a total of 4096 discrete voltages, this software alteration has limited the display to 4096/8, or 512 discrete values. (Nine-bit DAC's are rare, by the way.)

Define RAMPS as you did earlier, and then execute it with this newer version of RAMP. Look at the screen of your scope as this new version operates. You should be able to see the individual steps clearly as the DACs jump from one value to the next. This clearly illustrates the speed-resolution tradeoff that characterizes both digital-to-analog and analog-to-digital conversion. The faster you want it to run, the fewer values you will be able to collect or generate.

Here is an even more sophisticated version that illustrates both Forth's flexibility and its simplicity.

```
1 VARIABLE SPEED

: SLOW      1 SPEED ! ;

: MEDIUM    3 SPEED ! ;

: FAST      9 SPEED ! ;

: RAMP      4095 0 DO I I SPEED @ +LOOP ;

: RAMPS     0 DO RAMP LOOP;
```

Try this version of RAMP. What other language allows you to control your system with commands like these?

```
150 FAST RAMPS<ret> ok
```

or

`2 MEDIUM RAMPS<ret> ok`

The elegant simplicity of Forth easily compensates its users for the time spent mastering it.

All the waveforms we have created thus far have been essentially linear functions. The generation of other sorts of waveforms is equally easy.

Nonlinear Waveforms

Suppose you wanted to display a catenary curve on your oscilloscope. The simplest equation for a parabola,

$$y = x^2$$

can be displayed on your oscilloscope using these simple Forth words:

`: PARA 4095 0 DO I DUP DUP 4095 */ SCOPE LOOP ;`

Try it. You will observe the 'scope's dot begin its travels at the lower left, hugging the bottom of the screen until it begins to rise more and more quickly, sweeping upward at last to its rendezvous with the upper-right corner of the screen. You can readily create an outer-looping word similar to RAMPS to have it repeat automatically.

Notice that the only difference between RAMP and PARA lies in the respective phrases I I SCOPE and I DUP DUP 4095 */ SCOPE.

Whereas RAMP's operation is obvious, PARA deserves a bit of explanation. The I DUP DUP portion of the word prepares a triplicate version of the counter on the stack. The lowest copy is destined for DACX. The phrase 4095 */ illustrates once more the usefulness of star slash. First, the top two copies of the index are multiplied together, resulting in the calculation of the square. (The 32-bit intermediate used by */ is crucial to this operation; otherwise any number larger than 256 on the stack would overflow the 16-bit cell.) Then the square is divided by 4095 to ensure that it will not overflow the 12-bit output capacity of the DAC.

If you do not yet understand all this fully, you will after you do a proper stack analysis.

Although we will later explore ways to transfer data from the computer's memory to the DACs, we are ready now to tackle the concept of analog-to-digital conversion.

8.2 Analog-to-Digital Conversion

As the name implies, an analog-to-digital converter (ADC) is the effective opposite of a digital-to-analog converter. From the computer's perspective, a DAC is an output device whereas an ADC is an input device. From the programmer's perspective, transfer of data to the DAC is a storing operation, while interaction with an ADC is done with fetches.

From a practical perspective, the DAC is an easier device to employ as an interfacing tool than an ADC because the programmer always remains in control of both the DAC's input (the digital signal sent to it) and its output (the proportional output voltage). The computer's input from the ADC (*its* output) is always subject to the nature of the analog input, an external, usually uncontrolled, source of voltage. Finally, the usual DAC applications do not have to be particularly concerned with the settling time of the converter, while conversions of analog signals to their respective digital representations more commonly involve constraints established by the conversion device itself.

Fortunately, much of the vocabulary that has been developed in our discussion of D/A processes applies to A/D ones as well. For instance, the block diagram of a typical analog-to-digital converter is presented in Fig. 8.3. One analog input produces a multitude of digital outputs. An 8-bit ADC produces the expected eight data lines alongside the mandatory control signals, while 12-bit or 16-bit ADCs output 12 or 16 data bits, respectively. Like the DAC, the resolution of an ADC is directly dependent upon the number of bits associated with the converter, and an ADC can be configured to accommodate a variety of input voltages. A 12-bit ADC, configured to span 0 to 10.00 V, has a resolution of 2.44 mV, just as the corresponding DAC does, while an 8-bit converter has a resolution of 39.1 mV.

Let us assume that you have a smoothly varying analog signal, like that shown in Fig. 8.4a. Further, let us assume that you have available a device which samples that analog signal 10 times during the signal's lifetime, creating a digital representation of whatever analog voltage it finds at its input, and holding that digital representation fixed at the device's output until the next sample is taken. (This process is the ADC's version of the DAC's technique of holding its output fixed until updated by the com-

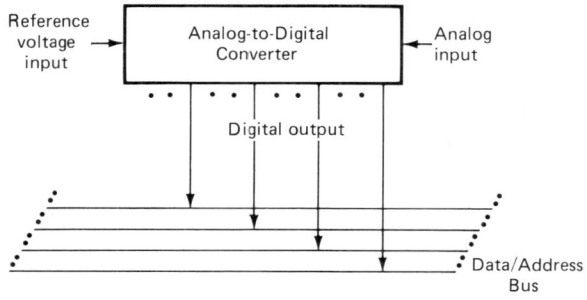

Figure 8.3 Analog-to-digital converter

puter. In A/D processes, this is called the *sample-and-hold* technique.) Finally, let us assume that the ADC available has 4-bit capacity, leading to a resolution of 1 part in 16.

How will the resulting digital representation appear? That depends directly on the resolution of the ADC and the number of samples taken. Consider Fig. 8.4b, the low-resolution digitized version of Fig. 8.4a.

This digitization of the signal in Fig. 8.4a has not created an accurate or useful representation of the original, by nearly anyone's definition. Although the low resolution of the converter has limited the replication of the original signal somewhat, the small sample size has had a very marked effect on the quality of the data representation.

Increasing the number of samples to 50 results in the data portrayed in Fig. 8.4c, while a higher resolution, 1 part in 256, results in the data seen in Fig. 8.4d. Obviously, the greater the number of samples and the higher the resolution of the converter, the better the representation of the original waveform. In the unobtainable limit of infinite resolution and unlimited samples, the representation of the data would be indistinguishable from the original. We will look more closely at these aspects of A/D conversions in Chap. 9. For now, however, we need to look closely at the role Forth plays in the digitization process.

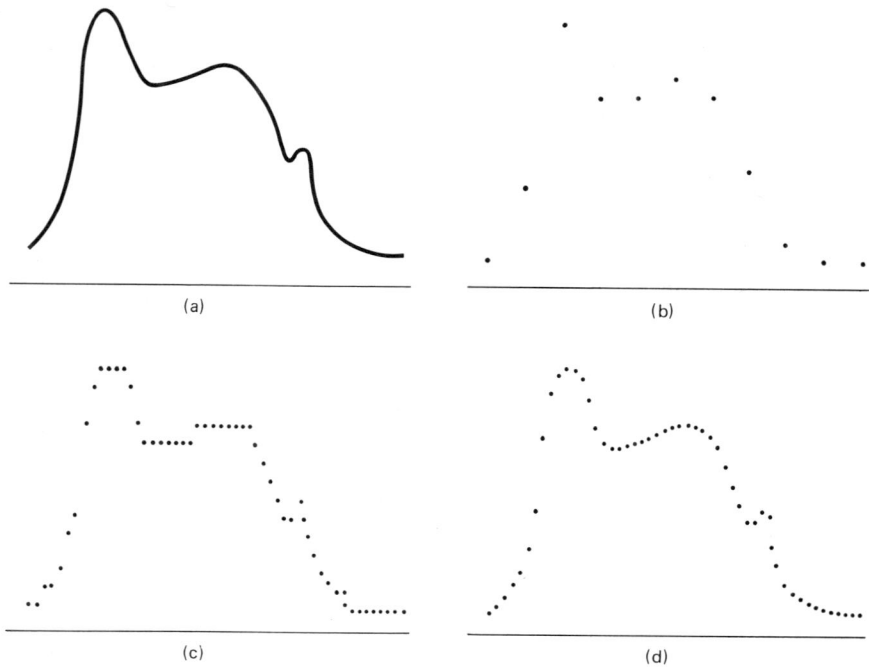

Figure 8.4 Digitization of an analog signal

Forth and the ADC

In this section you will learn about Forth's facility in the A/D process. This time the illustrations will use the Analogic MP6812 12-bit ADC coupled with a standard Digital Equipment Corporation DRV11 parallel bus interface. Unlike the Andromeda DAC11, the Analogic MP6812 is not specifically designed for use with a particular computer. Rather, its binary output needs to be coupled to the computer's bus with a suitable interface, in this case the DRV11. This combination is illustrated in Fig. 8.5.

The analog input to the Analogic converter is digitized and made available to the PDP-11 bus by way of the 12 parallel digital input lines of the DRV11 interface. In addition to the data lines, the cable between the Analogic converter and the DRV11 includes lines to allow the PDP-11 to initiate conversions and to interrogate the Analogic via the DRV11 to establish when the A/D process has been completed. The sampling frequency, or the rate at which the ADC samples the input signal, is selected by switches on the control panel of the ADC system.

The DRV11 is a bidirectional, 16-bit parallel interface for the PDP-11 Q-bus. It employs memory-mapped I/O by way of jumper-selectable addresses. It is shipped from the factory with the following addresses selected:

Description	Address (octal)
Status register	167770
Output register	167772
Input register	167774

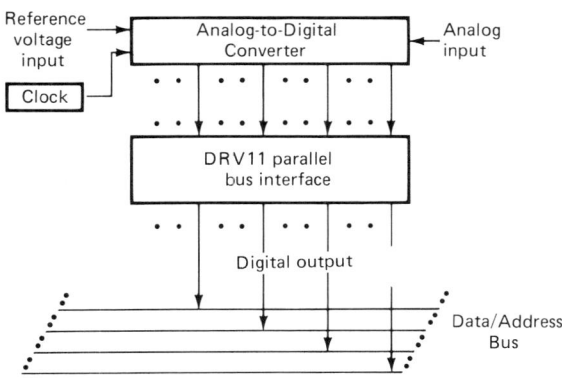

Figure 8.5 Analogic DRV11 12-bit ADC system block diagram

We will be using only its input capabilities in this example, letting Forth read the binary representation of the Analogic's output; thus address 167772 will not be used. In some ADC systems, the sampling rate is software-controllable. In such cases the interface's output buffer could be used to send sample-rate information to the converter.

Consider these Forth phrases:

```
OCTAL  167770 CONSTANT STATREG

       167774 CONSTANT DATA

: CWAIT BEGIN STATREG @ 100000 AND UNTIL ; DECIMAL

: CONVERT CWAIT DATA @ ;
```

Referring once again to Fig. 8.5, note that the binary output of the ADC is available to Forth at the address 167774. The 12-bit ADC impresses its output on the lower 12 bits of the bit-mapped parallel interface, allowing the word CONVERT to fetch the contents of the output buffer to the Forth stack. But the definition of convert also includes the Forth word CWAIT. Why?

Almost all A/D procedures call for a regular, orderly sequence of conversions which occur at intervals appropriate for the task at hand. And almost all ADC systems provide some sort of timing control circuitry. In the present case, the Analogic 12-bit converter is equipped with a clock pulse input which enables the user to initiate each A/D conversion, or to initiate a sequence of conversions by pulsing the input. The Analogic ADC is designed to carry out an A/D procedure only after receipt of an INITIATE-CONVERSION command from either the computer or an external clock.

Once a conversion has been completed, the Analogic ADC so indicates by setting an internal voltage level called the *end-of-conversion* flag. This flag is made available to the DRV11, and thence to the PDP-11 bus as bit 15 of the parallel interface's status register. The Forth system can monitor the progress of the conversion by interrogating this particular bit.

To visualize how this occurs, refer to the definition of CWAIT above. An indefinite loop, CWAIT *begins* the process of AND ing the status register with octal 100000, killing time *until* bit 15 becomes a 1, signifying the end of conversion. When included in the definition of CONVERT, CWAIT ensures that the interface buffer cannot be fetched to the Forth stack until the conversion has been completed. This system design places all responsibility for the conversion timing in the hands of the external clock, freeing Forth to fetch the data from the interface buffer.

Analog Signals: Data Acquisition and Device Control

What form do the data take? Exactly the form required by a DAC to generate a corresponding analog signal. For instance, suppose your 12-bit ADC is configured to convert input analog signals over a range of -10.00 to $+10.00$ V. The lowest possible binary output value, 0000_8, corresponds to the lowest possible analog input, -10.00 V, while $+10.00$ V will produce an octal value of 7777 at the ADC output. Shorting the input leads of an A/D so configured (0.00 V) results in a value of 3777 at the output. These octal integer values correspond to decimal 0, 4095, and 2047, and hex 0, FFF, and 7FF, respectively. The best illustration of this is a sample application, the use of a Forth/ADC system as a voltmeter.

Forth Voltmeter

Presume that you have a 12-bit ADC configured to convert voltages ranging from -10.00 to $+10.00$ V, as above. You need a word to output the voltage in actual voltage units, rather than a binary integer representation. Consider this definition:

```
: .V 2047 - 1000 2047 */ .WITH ?##. ##" ;    ( n ... )
```

The function of .V is conversion of a single integer to an actual voltage format. First, 2047 is subtracted from the value on top of the stack, then */ (star slash) is used to scale the value. Try it with a dummy value on the stack.

```
2047 .V<ret> 0.00 ok

4095 .V<ret> 10.00 ok

   0 .V<ret> -10.00 'ok
```

If this new word is included in a definition along with CONVERT, the resulting word will read and output voltage values.

```
: ?VOLTS BEGIN CONVERT .V 13 EMIT ?TERMINAL UNTIL ;
```

?VOLTS is an indefinite loop definition that continually fetches values from the ADC (CONVERT) and prints the corresponding voltage at the terminal (.V) over and over until ?TERMINAL sets a flag for UNTIL. The 13 EMIT appears in the definition to force the terminal to issue a line feed after each conversion. On a CRT this works well, since each new value erases the old. If you have a hard-copy terminal, use CR instead.

8.3 Saving Data on the Disk

The combination of `CONVERT` and `.V` fetches and displays the value of the converted voltage, but provides no means for storing the value for subsequent processing. What if we need to record an entire array of such voltages as a representation of some physical characteristic of a system, such as a visible or infrared spectrum. To accomplish this we need to combine words like `CONVERT` with a numeric storage facility derived from `ALLOT`.

Storing Data in an Array

Consider the consequences of entering this Forth phrase:

```
0 VARIABLE ARRAY 8000 ALLOT
```

The variable `ARRAY` has been entered into Forth's dictionary along with an additional 4000 cells. (Remember, `ALLOT` allocates 8-bit bytes and the cells have 16 bits.) Choice of a 4000-cell array is arbitrary in this case, but not unusual in data-acquisition systems.

Now all we have to do is create the Forth words to fill these locations successively with data obtained with `CONVERT`. To do this we will need an additional variable to keep track of the number of points we will be `CONVERT`ing (unless we always `CONVERT` 4000). Enter these definitions:

```
0 VARIABLE #POINTS
: POINTS    #POINTS ! ; ( n ... )


: ACQUIRE   ARRAY 2 - #POINTS @ 0 DO
            2+ DUP CONVERT SWAP ! LOOP DROP ; ( ... )
```

The definition of `POINTS` is obvious. It allows us to use phrases like this:

```
4000 POINTS ACQUIRE
```

to fill `ARRAY` with a series of 16-bit integers obtained by using `CONVERT`. Fewer than 4000 values can be obtained, of course, but the size of the array `ALLOT`ed in the entry of `ARRAY` cannot be exceeded.

The definition of `ACQUIRE` is straightforward. Do a stack analysis to see how it works if you are uncertain.

The data in the array can be displayed as easily as it was obtained, incidentally. Here is a word that will use the DAC to do so:

Analog Signals: Data Acquisition and Device Control

```
: SHOWDATA ARRAY 2 - #POINTS @ 0 DO 2+ DUP @ I SWAP SCOPE
           LOOP DROP ;
```

The D/A equivalent of ACQUIRE, SHOWDATA sequentially fetches and SCOPEs previously stored data. If you want to create a standing display on an oscilloscope, you must get SHOWDATA to execute over and over, an obvious application for an indefinite loop.

```
: DISPLAY BEGIN SHOWDATA ?TERMINAL UNTIL ;
```

Here you have all the software tools necessary to store and retrieve an entire array of data. Figure 8.6 summarizes this incredibly compact data-storage and -retrieval system for a PDP-11 DAC/ADC system. Forth characteristically offers this remarkable compactness. Also, it is possible to use this same approach in Forth assembler code. A code version of SHOWDATA is presented in App. F, "A Forth Assembler."

```
Block  # 191
   0 ( Data Acquisition:  Figure 8.6,           first half ........ )
   1
   2 Octal    170444 constant dacx      ( Channel 2 D/A register )
   3          170442 constant dacy      ( Channel 1 D/A register )
   4          167770 constant statreg   ( DRV11 status register )
   5          167774 constant data   decimal ( DRV11 input buffer )
   6
   7
   8 : scope dacy ! dacx ! ;                     ( xpos ypos ... )
   9
  10 0 variable array 8192 allot ( data array, 4096 cells, 8 blocks )
  11
  12 1 variable #points    : points #points ! ;         ( counter )
  13
  14
  15

Block  # 192
   0 ( Data Acquisition:  Figure 8.6,         second half ... )
   1
   2 : Showdata array 2 - #points @ 0 do 2 + dup @ i swap scope
   3                  loop drop ( leftover address ) ;
   4
   5 : Display  begin showdata ?terminal until ;
   6
   7  octal : Cwait begin statreg @ 100000 and until ;   decimal
   8
   9 : Convert   cwait data @ ;   ( n ... )
  10
  11 : Acquire   array 2 - #points @ 0 do 2+ dup convert
  12             swap ! loop drop ( drop duped address ) ;
  13
  14 : >disk    0 do 2dup 0 r/w 1+ swap 1024 + swap loop 2drop ;
  15 : Disk>    0 do 2dup 1 r/w 1+ swap 1024 + swap loop 2drop ;
```

Figure 8.6 Data-storage and data-retrieval routines

Hardware Control with Forth

But the simplicity and compactness have not yet fully exerted themselves. By adding only two more simple definitions, you can also use Forth to save your CONVERTed data on the disk and retrieve it for subsequent analysis and display.

Storing Binary Data on the Disk

Remember BLOCK? This powerful word, charged with control of transfer of information to and from disk blocks, is actually defined in terms of a very useful lower-level word named R/W (pronounced "R slash W").

Heretofore we have used Forth's disk routines for handling ASCII encoded material (mostly Forth words). But with R/W and our ability to deal with arrays of binary data, an entire new prospect arises. We can acquire large arrays of data, temporarily saving them in RAM, and then save these arrays in a sequence of disk blocks. Indeed, with R/W we can save nearly anything on the disk.

On many Forth systems R/W is a primitive, and on others, it is nearly so. The stack notation for R/W is

```
R/W ( addr blk# flag ... )
```

As its name implies, R/W is used for both reading and writing blocks, where addr specifies the memory address of the source or destination, blk# represents the block number of the destination or the source, and a flag = 1 represents a read (disk =>RAM) while a 0 flag represents a write (RAM => disk). R/W deals with one Forth block at a time. To store or retrieve more data, R/W must appear in a looping word. Define these words on your system:

```
: >DISK 0 DO 2DUP 0 R/W 1+ SWAP 1024 + SWAP LOOP 2DROP ;

        ( From-addr to-start block count-blks ... )

: Disk> 0 DO 2DUP 1 R/W 1+ SWAP 1024 + SWAP LOOP 2DROP ;

        ( To-addr From-start block count-blks ... )
```

>DISK writes to the disk while DISK> copies from disk to memory. In a sense, these definitions could have been named DISK! and DISK@ with equal effectiveness, were it not that such names would have erroneously implied single-block transfers. In either case, they allow you to transfer a region of memory to disk (regardless of the RAM's contents)

and then retrieve it for subsequent analysis. For example, it is easy to carry out the following data-acquisition exercise, which stores 4000 points in array and displays them on a scope.

```
4000 POINTS ACQUIRE DISPLAY<ret>
```

Storing the data on a disk before its display is added to the routine with

```
4000 POINTS ACQUIRE ARRAY 200 8 >DISK<ret>
```

where eight Forth blocks of data are copied, starting at ARRAY's address and filling Forth blocks 200 through 207.

Retrieving the data for display purposes is as easily accomplished with

```
ARRAY 200 8 DISK> DISPLAY<ret>
```

Here eight blocks, starting at 200, are read to RAM, starting at ARRAY's address.

Note that eight blocks is actually enough storage for 4096 cells. R/W will write in 1024-byte, or 512-cell, blocks only. In these examples a little bit of the Forth dictionary (96 cells' worth to be exact) that follows ARRAY gets written to the disk along with the data. That is perfectly OK, as long as it is not retrieved later and assumed to be data. The ability to send the Forth dictionary to the disk raises a very interesting prospect for those users who might want to save their applications in compiled or interpreted form. See Prob. 8 at the end of this chapter for a lead into this technique.

This chapter has dealt with the techniques of data acquisition and display by focusing on mainly the hardware aspects of the A/D and D/A processes. By the time you finish doing the problems below, you will be prepared for Chap. 9, where you will learn the fundamental principles underlying the design of useful and effective data-handling software.

8.4 Problems

1. To really fine-tune words like MS you can use two slightly different "empty loops" to offset one another in time. For example, consider this definition of MS:

```
: A-STALL 16 0 DO              LOOP ; ( ... )

: B-STALL 16 0 DO I DROP       LOOP ; ( ... )

: MS          0 DO A-STALL B-STALL LOOP ; ( n ... )
```

If the limits in A-STALL and B-STALL are changed to 15 and 17, respectively, MS will take slightly longer than with 16 and 16.
　　　Write a version of MS that is accurate to 1 sec in 10 min.

2. Write a Forth routine to generate a 10-Hz square wave with an amplitude of 5 V.

3. The demonstration word PARA generates only one side of a parabolic arc. Write other versions that actually display whole parabolas with either upward- or downward-facing minima.

4. Write a Forth word to generate a sawtooth waveform with a maximum amplitude of 7.5 V and a frequency of 1 Hz.

5. Write a Forth word to store a parabola in an 8-block, 4095-cell array.

6. Create a Forth word to save the parabola from Prob. 8.4 in blocks 200 to 207 of a Forth disk.

7. Write a Forth word to display the aforementioned parabola, not by creating it in situ, but by reading it from the disk.

8. For advanced users: Write a word that uses R/W to store your Forth dictionary on disk. Another word will be necessary to get it back, of course, so you should write that one as well. Remember to study your system's dictionary structure carefully and use the appropriate user variables as pointers to the various key places in your dictionary.

Chapter 9

Signal-Processing Fundamentals

Now that you have become accustomed to the hardware-intensive aspects of data acquisition and device control, you need to learn how to deal with the data that you have collected. In this chapter we will focus on the Forth applications for reducing and analyzing data which have been obtained through analog-to-digital conversion procedures. But first we must discuss the fundamentals of data sampling, beginning with the sampling theorem.

9.1 The Sampling Theorem

In designing a data-acquisition application, one must ask this question: "How often must the system sample the data in order to avoid losing information?" It is obvious that extremely rapid sampling of very slowly varying data will result in capturing all or most of the useful information in a signal. It should be equally obvious that information can be expected to disappear during the slow digitization of a fairly rapid process. But what is considered "rapid" in this context, and what do we really mean by terms like "relatively slowly?" Obviously, we need quantitative criteria to use in the selection of sampling times. Once such criteria have been set, we can incorporate them into our data-acquisition applications and Forth code.

Consider the sine waves represented in Fig. 9.1. Sampling relatively frequently, as in Fig. 9.1a, results in a fairly accurate representation of the original analog signal. But when the sampling process operates at a slower rate, as in Fig. 9.1b, the result, a far less accurate representation of the visual aspects of the signal, gives rise to a serious potential for misinterpretation of the data as well. This problem arises because of the creation of an illusory signal image called an *alias*, illustrated by the dotted line in Fig. 9.1b. This phenomenon is not unique to electronics or scientific data processing, by the way. It is regularly encountered in everyday life as well. Consider, for example, the wood-spoked wagon wheels that apparently turn backward in old Western films. This illusion illustrates an optical aliasing created by the camera's frame-by-frame digitization of the wheel's analog rotation.

In the same way, quantitative analysis of the data points in Fig. 9.1b for evaluation of the signal's frequency components would result in the determination of an erroneous, or alias, frequency for the signal. The potential for frequency aliasing is not unique to sine waves, of course. Complex signals consisting of numerous contributing waveforms are susceptible to aliasing as well. Thus it appears that one of the first tasks that confronts the data analyst is establishment of criteria to guarantee that the results of the analysis will truly reflect the parameters of the original signal. This is the domain of the sampling theorem.

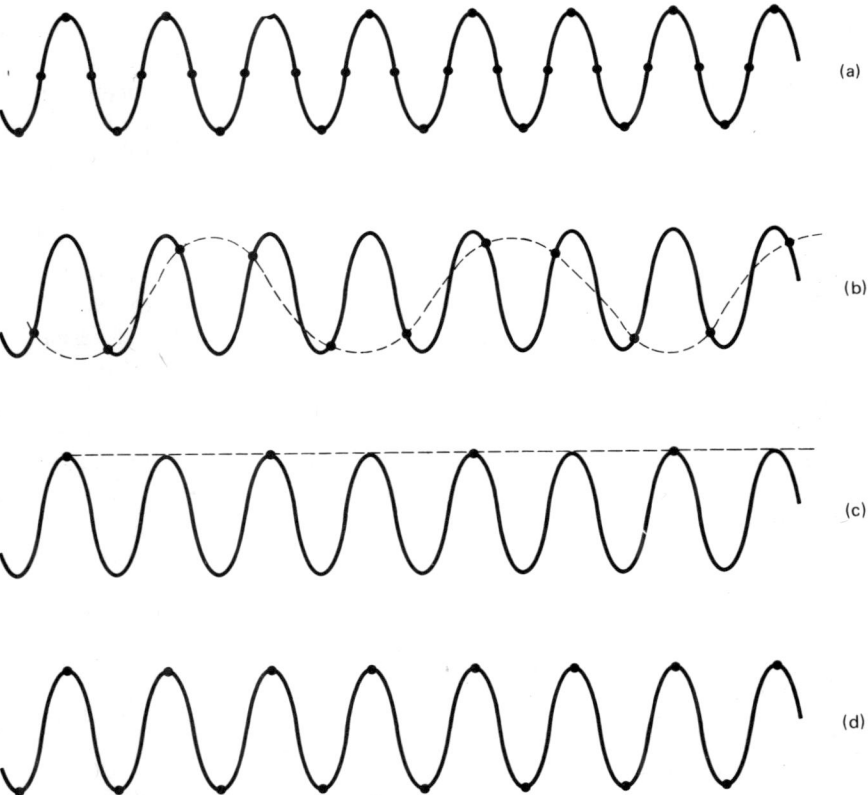

Figure 9.1 Sine waves sampled at various frequencies

Consider a sine wave sampled at a rate exactly equal to its own frequency, as in Fig. 9.1c. As far as reconstruction of the signal from the digitized data is concerned, the input signal appears to be a direct-current voltage level, and not a periodic function at all. This stroboscopic sampling rate is analogous to a wagon wheel's rotating at precisely the correct velocity to appear motionless to the cinema viewer.

If the same periodic signal is sampled twice as fast, however, as in Fig. 9.1d, reconstruction of the signal from the data points, while not representing the exact visual form of the original signal, does properly reflect the *frequency* and *amplitude* of the input data. These are the only criteria necessary for the representation of a sine wave, and thus the only parameters necessary for proper reconstruction of the signal.

Here, then, is the crux of the sampling theorem:

> Accurate reconstruction of a signal requires sampling the data at a frequency at least twice that of the highest-frequency component in the original signal.

If the condition of the sampling theorem is not met, aliasing will occur.

To an experimentalist, given the job of designing a data-acquisition package for a particular application, the sampling theorem provides clear guidance in the determination of sampling parameters. The A/D process must run at least twice as fast as the fastest component in the composite signal if characteristic frequency determinations are to be made. Furthermore, the theorem merely sets a lower limit on digitization speed. In cases in which the intent of the A/D process is an accurate reconstruction of the *visual* components of the signal without regard for possible frequency analysis (as in continuous-wave infrared spectral analysis, for instance), the sampling rate must be faster still.

Another aspect of digitization that must be addressed by the data-acquisition programmer involves the problems arising from electronic noise.

9.2 Noise

Every optical and electronic device is subject to various levels of undesired signals that arise from sources both external and internal to the data-acquisition device. Such signals are called *noise*. In astronomy, for example, one contributor to noise in stellar observation is sunlight scattered by dust in the earth's atmosphere. In radio and television broadcasting, the static we hear and the "snow" we see on the screen are another form of electronic noise. In some cases we have control of some of the parameters that produce noise, and in others we do not, but in all cases we need to learn to deal with its effects.

Many data-acquisition applications involve the identification of maxima and minima within an array of data gathered from some device. In analog readout devices such as strip-chart recorders, the presence of such peaks and valleys is nearly always clear to human observers, who excel at recognition of patterns in visual images. But when it comes to computers, such pattern-recognition processes are nontrivial tasks, requiring fairly sophisticated programming.

Consider the data displayed in Fig. 9.2. We can clearly see that the data correspond to one maxima superimposed on a fairly noisy baseline. In addition, there may also be another peak near the right-hand extreme. Whether or not that suspect peak is truly there and what its exact position is, as well as the position of the maximum that is obviously present, cannot be determined until we look closely at the quantitative aspects of noise.

The *mean noise* of a digitized signal is defined as the sum of the absolute values of the differences between adjacent points (s_i; s_{i+1}) divided by the total number of points (n).

$$\text{Mean\_noise} = \frac{\Sigma |s_i| - |s_{i+1}|}{n}$$

A relatively quiet signal, i.e., a smoothly changing function with few, if any, precipitous variations in intensity from one signal to the next, is characterized by a relatively low value of mean noise. Noisy signals, on the other hand, are expected to be characterized by higher mean noise values.

We can operationally define *peaks* as collections of values that exceed the level of the mean noise by some predetermined amount. Indeed, it is not uncommon to define peaks as ranges of values, however wide, that

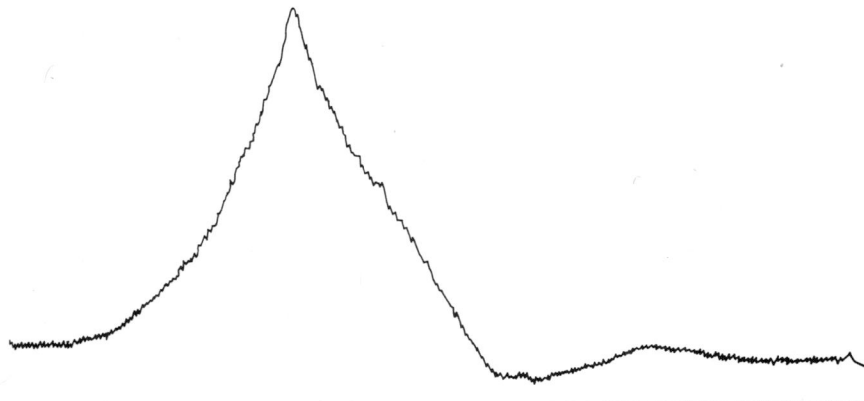

Figure 9.2 Peaks superimposed on a noisy baseline

individually exceed the level of the noise by a factor of 3. By that definition, in an array of data exhibiting a mean noise of 20 (the dimensions of mean noise are the dimensions of the parameter under observation), any observed values exceeding 60 constitute components of a peak.

A more conservative definition of a peak might restrict consideration to values exceeding 5 times the mean noise, while a very liberal data-interpretation scheme might include in the category of real peaks all values equal to or greater than twice the mean noise. In this chapter we will arbitrarily use the "3-times-the-noise" criterion to identify peaks in Forth routines. In your later applications, circumstances may well dictate choice of another standard.

Now that we have a way to calculate the noise level of a given signal, we can use that information in the process of identification of significant components within a particular signal.

9.3 Forth in Identification of Peaks

Suppose you have a computer equipped with an ADC which has been configured with a conversion range of -10.00 to $+10.00$ V. Assume further that your task is the digitization and analysis of signals such as those shown in Fig. 9.3. Whereas the magnitude of the signal at any time might be either positive or negative, as the left-hand axis in Fig. 9.3 illustrates, the binary values generated by the ADC are always positive. As shown in Chap. 8, there is no sign bit associated with the output of the ADC, and

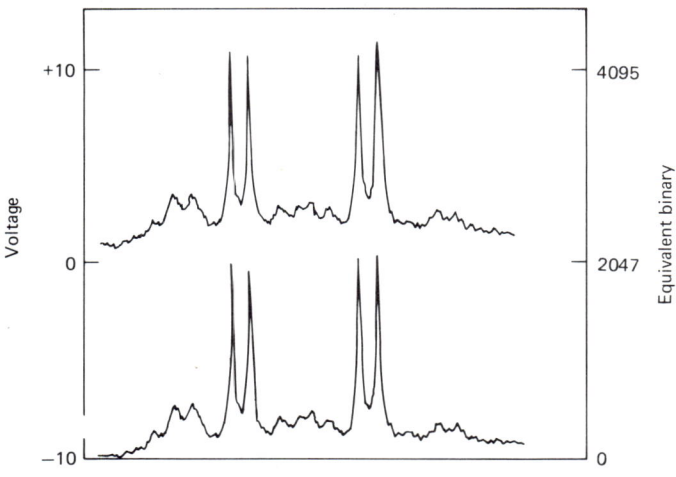

Figure 9.3 Representative signal for digitization and analysis

```
Block # 170
  0 ( TOOLS ...Maximum and Minimum locators                    )
  1
  2 0 variable largest  0 variable where  0 variable least
  3
  4 : maximum 0 largest ! 0 do dup @ dup largest @ > if
  5             largest ! dup where ! else drop then 2+ loop drop ;
  6
  7 : minimum 32767 least ! 0 do dup @ dup least @ < if
  8             least ! dup where ! else drop then 2+ loop drop ;
  9
 10                  ( addr   cell-count   ...   )
 11
 12
 13
 14
 15


Block # 171
  0 ( Signal processing...page 1 of 4                       DLT )
  1
  2 0 0 2variable sum_noise   0 variable mean_noise 0 variable pbeg
  3   0 variable  on_peak   0 0 2variable area    0 variable plast
  4
  5 : ?noise     ( addr count ... )
  6              0 0 sum_noise 2! swap over 1 do dup 2@
  7              - abs 0 sum_noise 2@ d+ sum_noise 2!
  8              2+ loop drop >r sum_noise 2@ r> 1 - u/ swap drop
  9              mean_noise ! ;
 10
 11 : adjust    ( addr count ... )
 12              2dup minimum least @
 13              -1 * swap 0 do swap 2dup +! 2+ swap loop 2drop ;
 14
 15


Block # 172
  0 ( Signal processing...page 2 of 4                           )
  1
  2 : spec_header cr ." Mean noise: " Mean_noise ?   cr cr
  3              ." From       To         Center     Height     Area" ;
  4
  5
  6 : Integrate ( ... )
  7              0 0 area 2! plast @ pbeg @ do i @ 0 area 2@
  8              d+ area 2! 2 +loop ;
  9
 10
 11 : Pprint (  ...  )
 12              cr plast @ pbeg @ 2dup . 4 spaces . 4 spaces
 13              swap over - 2 / maximum where ? 4 spaces largest ?
 14              integrate area 2@ 4 spaces d. ;
 15
```

the programmer must always be aware of the range of values corresponding to positive and negative signal levels.

To use Forth, or any computer language, to determine the position and magnitude of peaks in such a signal such as that represented by Fig. 9.3 is fairly easy. First you divide the task into several simple processes. Although there are many ways to approach such a job, the simplest is as follows:

1. Determine the mean noise of the signal of interest.
2. Offset the entire signal so that the smallest value in the entire array of data has a value of 0.
3. Locate all regions in the array which have magnitudes exceeding 3 times the mean noise of the entire signal.

```
Block  # 173
  0 ( Signal Processing ................. page 3 of 4          )
  1
  2 : ?Peak    ( addr ... )
  3             dup @ mean_noise @ 3 * >  ( do the comparison    )
  4             if                        ( value bigger than noise? )
  5                on_peak @ 0= ( not)    ( If so, are we on a peak  )
  6                if                     ( or not?  If not, set flag )
  7                    1 on_peak !
  8                    dup pbeg !         ( and save address of point )
  9                then
 10             else                      ( otherwise val is < noise  )
 11                on_peak @              ( are we on the end of peak? )
 12                if 0 on_peak ! dup plast ! ( if so, indicate,     )
 13                    pprint             ( print peak statistics     )
 14                then
 15             then drop ;               ( & drop the residual address)

Block  # 174
  0 ( Signal processing .............page 4 of 4   DLT )
  1
  2 : Peaks    ( address cellcount ... )
  3             spec_header cr over pbeg ! 0 on_peak !
  4             2 * over + swap do i ?peak 2 +loop ;
  5
  6
  7 : Analyze  ( address cellcount ... )
  8             2dup ?noise 2dup adjust peaks ;
  9
 10 : ?spectrum ( ... )  array #points @ analyze ;
 11
 12 : spectrum  ( ... )  4000 points acquire page
 13             ?spectrum  cdisplay ;
 14
 15 : Kwang-pu  4000 points acquire page ?spectrum cdisplay ;
```

Figure 9.4 Mean noise and peak identification routines

This technique necessarily assumes that the baseline of the signal of interest is linear and that the mean baseline value is near 0 (after the offset adjustment) as well.

This division of the process into component tasks makes the implementation of a peak identification process very simple in Forth. Figure 9.4 consists of a series of five Forth blocks that do exactly that. In addition to the identification process, the Forth words in these blocks carry out the labeled output of the identified peaks, including their positions, maximum intensities, and areas.

The key words in this example application package are:

`?NOISE ( addr count ... )`

and

`?PEAK ( addr ... )`

but they are supported by a series of other words that need explanation as well, so we will inspect them all, at least briefly.

Let us assume that we wish to accumulate a 4000-cell array of data in RAM beginning at a location identified by the variable **ARRAY**. (You will recall that this is exactly the procedure we used in Chap. 8 with the A/D procedures we created at that point.) Further assume that we wish to identify any and all peaks that may be found in that 16-bit, 4000-cell array of data. The highest-level application word in Fig. 9.4 is obviously **SPECTRUM**, a straightforward word for which the definition is merely:

`4000 POINTS ACQUIRE ?SPECTRUM`

The next lower level in the application is represented by **?SPECTRUM**, a word with a name chosen to imply its role in elucidating the details of the sought-for spectrum. This word fetches the address of the data in memory and the number of points of interest and then calls **ANALYZE**, a key word whose definition clearly demonstrates the three fundamental tasks outlined above:

`: ANALYZE ( address count ... ) 2DUP 2DUP ?NOISE ADJUST PEAKS ;`

Each of the key words in the defintion of **ANALYZE**, **?NOISE** (pronounced "Q-noise"), **ADJUST**, and **PEAKS**, has the same stack notation, requiring the address and count of an array on the stack and explaining the presence of **2DUP** twice in the definition. We will take the key words in order, looking first at the inner workings of **?NOISE**, the word that calculates the signal's mean noise.

Calculation of Mean Noise

As mentioned above, the mean noise calculation requires summation of the differences between absolute values of adjoining data points. Although this may seem at first to be a fairly straightforward procedure, the possibility of overflow of the contents of a 16-bit variable location used as summation accumulator makes that task a bit more complicated. For instance, in the 4000-cell sample array in the example, an average difference of only 20 binary units will result in a sum of 80,000 (before division by the number of points). This value obviously exceeds the limit for a single-length, unsigned integer.

To preclude such overflow from leading to erroneous results, the definition of ?NOISE uses 32-bit integer arithmetic. Look at the listing of block 171. The summation is carried out in the 32-bit, double-length variable named SUM_NOISE. After summation, the resultant mean noise is computed by mixed-mode division of the 32-bit accumulated noise by the 16-bit cell count. The resulting parameter is stored in the 16-bit variable MEAN_NOISE, in preparation for later use. It would also be possible, but wasteful of computing time, to use floating-point operations at this point. Once the mean noise has been determined, the next process in the analysis of the data in the designated array is carried out by Adjusting the data.

ADJUSTing an Array

The definition of ADJUST is found in block 171. Expecting to find an address and a cell count on the stack, ADJUST begins by searching for the smallest 16-bit value in the array. ADJUST then subtracts this value from the contents of every cell in the array. The result is an array with its baseline "shifted" to the lowest possible values.

The key to ADJUST is the definition of MINIMUM found in block 170 of Fig. 9.4. As its name implies, this word searches an array of specified length for the smallest value therein, storing the minimum value in the variable LEAST and its location in WHERE. MAXIMUM functions analogously, leaving its finds in LARGEST and WHERE, respectively. Incidentally, these words are useful in all sorts of applications and you might want to include them in a tools block. Their stack notations are identical to those of ?NOISE, ANALYZE, and ADJUST, i.e., (address cell-count ...).

Once the array containing the sampled signal has been ADJUSTed, execution of the Forth code in ANALYZE passes to PEAKS, the peak identification routine.

Identifying Peaks

In anticipation of printing the locations of the peaks that it finds, PEAKS begins by printing a header (SPEC_HEADER in block 172 of Fig. 9.4) and initiates a definite loop that examines the contents of every cell in the array. The examination is carried out by the Forth word ?PEAK, defined in block 173 of Fig. 9.4.

Determination of whether or not a particular value is part of a peak appears at first to be straightforward, but there are a few wrinkles that complicate the process. Let us begin the conceptualization of a word to do this job with a few thoughts on its design. We will begin by assuming that the word will begin at the first entry in the array, examining each value of the array in turn.

1. Any value greater than 3 times the mean noise is, or is part of, a peak. Values less than this are considered part of the noise.
2. When the level of the signal increases to a degree that the previous definition qualifies the point under examination as the first point in a peak, we will store the address of that array element and set a flag to indicate that we are now on a peak.
3. When the level of the signal falls back down into the noise, we will store that location as well, marking the end of the peak, and initiate the analysis and printout of the peak just passed. We must also clear the flag that indicates we are on a peak.
4. Analysis will terminate with the examination of the contents of the last address.

All this is necessitated by the computer's inability to look at the entire array of data simultaneously. Indeed, as Forth inspects the points, one by one, cell by cell, there are four distinct possibilities that emerge for each point. To see what they are, let us first introduce the variables that are needed in this analytical process:

0 VARIABLE ON_PEAK	The flag that is set to indicate a peak
0 VARIABLE PBEG	The address of the beginning of the peak
0 VARIABLE PLAST	The address of the last cell in the peak

The various actions that Forth must take as it examines the contents of a cell during the peak identification process can be summarized in this fashion:

Conditions	Action	Comment
`ON_PEAK`=`false` and `Contents` ≤ 3 * `noise`	None.	In the noise
`ON_PEAK`=`false` and `Contents` > 3 * `noise`	Store address in PBEG; set ON_PEAK true.	First point of a peak
`ON_PEAK`=`true` and `Contents` > 3 * `noise`	None.	On a peak
`ON_PEAK`=`true` and `Contents` ≤ 3 * `noise`	Store address in `PLAST`; set `ON_PEAK` `false`; analyze and print peak status.	Last point of a peak

The distillation of this logic is seen in the definition of `?PEAK` in block 173 of Fig. 9.4 (shown in this fashion for those who have not yet discovered that Forth is indeed a "structured" language). Note that the process of peak analysis and printout is triggered by the data falling below the level of the noise. This application uses the Forth definition `PPRINT` to generate a printout of the data on a peak-by-peak basis.

Also note the use of `MAXIMUM` in `PPRINT`. It is equally feasible to store the peak locations and magnitudes in additional arrays for further analysis, disk storage (e.g., condensation of spectra), or archival.

Using the fundamental applications vocabulary in Fig. 9.5, the results of an analysis of a periodic function (xxx Hz sine wave sampled at yyy ms/sample) are illustrated in Fig. 9.5.

One common task in scientific data processing, and a subject which we

```
Mean noise: 21

From     To      Center    Height   Area
18690    19078    18886    2358    248167
19124    19512    19318    2357    248055
19556    19946    19752    2357    248111
19990    20380    20188    2356    248191
20424    20812    20622    2357    248199
20858    21246    21054    2357    248198
21292    21680    21488    2358    248221
21726    22114    21922    2358    248259
22160    22548    22356    2358    248303
22594    22982    22788    2358    248324
23028    23416    23222    2358    248256
23460    23850    23656    2357    248270
23894    24284    24090    2357    248212
24328    24718    24522    2356    248247
24762    25152    24956    2356    248299
25196    25584    25390    2357    248286
25630    26018    25824    2357    248452
26064    26452    26260    2359    248425
```

Figure 9.5 Example of peak printout

need to consider before bringing this chapter to a close, involves determination of the areas under the peaks with which we have been dealing.

Peak Integration

Once a peak has been identified, the easiest way to determine the area under it is through simple summation of the contents of all the memory locations that contain the relevant data. In the above example application, where the starting and ending memory locations representative of the peak are stored in variables, this method of integration is quite direct. As illustrated in Fig. 9.6a, this technique approximates the area under the curve of interest as a series of adjacent rectangles, summing the areas of the rectangles. In this application, the word that does the job is INTEGRATE (in block 172 of Fig. 9.4).

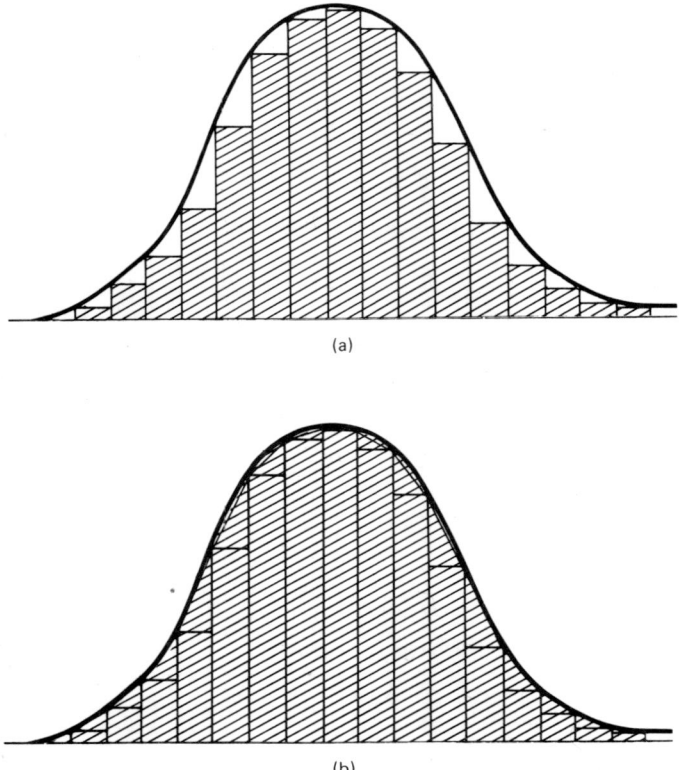

Figure 9.6 Peak integration examples

After initializing the 32-bit variable AREA, INTEGRATE fetches the contents of PBEG and PLAST to be used as limit and index of a 2 +LOOP. The respective contents of all the locations spanning PBEG to PLAST are summed (using 32-bit arithmetic) into AREA. The possibility of an area exceeding the capacity of a 16-bit cell necessitates the use of double integers, exactly as seen before in ?NOISE.

As might be expected, the accuracy of this integration-by-summation technique is highest when the number of samples distributed across the peak is large. When the sampling rate is slow relative to the signal, it is necessary to use more sophisticated techniques, such as the trapezoidal approximation illustrated in Fig. 9.6b. In this method the peak is approximated as a series of adjoining trapezoids, the areas of which are summed to give a better estimate of the area. This involves inclusion of the little trianglelike areas in the integral summation.

Where the most accurate estimate of peak areas is desirable, it is necessary to resort to elegant techniques. One possibility is Romberg integration, in which various combinations of data locations are chosen to utilize varying step sizes in the integral estimation. Discussions of these and other relevant techniques beyond the scope of this book can be found in most numerical analysis textbooks.

These definitions have been presented to encourage the use of Forth in signal-processing and spectral-analysis applications, and should not be construed as an implication that such data-reduction processes are always (if ever) this simple. Indeed, molecular spectra consisting of overlapping peaks that never see the baseline, and complex waveforms gathered in the frequency domain that require Fourier analysis, are equally subject to Forth's attentions as these elementary examples. Now that you have become accomplished in the uses of Forth as a data-acquisition and information-processing tool, you will be able to readily write data-handling applications along the lines developed in this chapter.

Appendix

Software Tools

The following block listings (Figs. A.1, A.2, and A.3) contain a few definitions that have proved useful. As your proficiency develops, you will add your own entries. Because these definitions follow the Forth Interest Group (Fig-Forth) standards, minor variations in some of the definitions will be required if you are using a Forth-79 or poly-Forth system (see App. C). Of course, one of the most useful sets of software tools is your terminal personality block, described in Chap. 7, specifically Fig. 7.7.

```
Block  # 90
   0 ( TOOLS ... stack & miscellaneous )
   1 0 variable cnt    ( used as a counter by decout, below )
   2
   3 : depth     s0 @ sp@ - 2 / 1 - ;   ( calculates depth for .s )
   4
   5 : .s        depth if cr sp@ 2 - s0 @ 2 - do i @ . -2 +loop
   6             else ." stack's empty " quit then ;
   7
   8 : room      s0 @ dp @ - . ." bytes available " ;
   9
  10 : decout    0 cnt ! begin 1 cnt +! 10 /mod dup 0= until drop
  11             cnt @ 0 do 48 + emit loop ;
  12
  13 : ms        0 do 32 0 do  loop loop ;    ( adjust as needed )
  14 : sec       0 do 1000 ms  loop ;
  15 : min       0 do   60 sec loop ;
```

Figure A.1 Block 90: tools, stock, and miscellaneous

```
Block  # 91
   0 ( TOOLS ... various base converting I/O definitions: )
   1
   2 : O.     octal . decimal ;  ( type octal equivalent of decimal )
   3
   4 : H.     hex   . decimal ;  ( type hexadecimal equivalent )
   5
   6 : B.     binary . decimal ; ( type binary equivalent )
   7
   8
   9
  10
  11
  12
  13
  14
  15
```

Figure A.2 Block 91: tools, various base-converting I/O definitions

```
Block  # 92
   0 ( TOOLS ...binary disk storage & limits searcher )
   1
   2 0 variable largest 0 variable where  0 variable least
   3 : maximum 0 largest ! 0 do dup @ dup largest @ > if
   4             largest ! dup where ! else drop then 2+ loop drop ;
   5
   6 : minimum 32767 least ! 0 do dup @ dup least @ < if
   7             least ! dup where ! else drop then 2+ loop drop ;
   8
   9                                    ( addr cell-count )
  10
  11 : >Disk    0 do 2dup 0 r/w 1+ swap 1024 + swap loop 2drop ;
  12              ( from[addr]    to[init block#]   blkcnt ...    )
  13
  14 : Disk>    0 do 2dup 1 r/w 1+ swap 1024 + swap loop 2drop ;
  15              ( to[addr]     from[init blk#]   blkcnt ...     )
```

Figure A.3 Block 92: tools, binary disk storage, and limits searcher

Appendix B

Floating-Point Support

The floating-point support definitions used in the PDP-11, Fig-Forth environment in the author's laboratory rely on the machine-level floating-point instruction sets (FP-11 and FIS) that Digital Equipment Corporation supplies with the KEF11-AA and KEV11 chip sets for the PDP-11/23 and the PDP-11/03 computers, respectively. Listings of the PDP-11 specific assembly codes are available from the author, c/o Department of Chemistry, California State University, Northridge, CA 91330.

At the Forth level, the interface between 16-bit integer, 32-bit integer, and 32-bit floating-point values is handled by the straightforward definitions in Fig. B.1. An illustrative high-level floating-point square-root definition is included as well.

```
Block # 94
   0 ( Floating Point Math Support .....................22-Apr-83 )
   1 : places place ! ;
   2 : float s->d d>f ;          ( s...f )
   3
   4 : fix  f>d drop  ;          ( f...s )
   5
   6 : f< f- swap drop 0< ;      ( f f... flag )
   7
   8 floating  1.0E-5  2constant eps ( convergence crit. for fsqrt )
   9
  10 : fsqrt      2dup 0.5903 f* 0.4173 f+ begin
  11              2over 2over f/ 2over f+ 0.5 f*
  12              2swap 2over f- fabs eps f< until
  13              2swap 2drop ;
  14
  15 : sqdemo  100 1 do i dup . float fsqrt f. cr loop ;
```

Figure B.1 Block 94: floating-point math support

Appendix C

Forth Dialects

The Forth dialect used in this book derives from the Forth Interest Group's version of International Standard Forth. This dialect is commonly referred to as "Fig-Forth," a name which stems from its adoption as the standard dialect by that group in 1978. It is the most widely available version of Forth in the public domain, having been implemented on a host of machines under various operating systems, and in stand-alone versions as well.

In addition to Fig-Forth, there are slightly different variants available from a wide variety of sources. The most advanced, poly-Forth, is a high-performance, high-priced offering from Forth Incorporated. A related, public-domain Forth dialect which is also supported by the Forth Interest Group is Forth-79. This version is so similar to Fig-Forth that most applications written for one will run on the other with little or no modification. Some of the differences, however, are significant enough to call for attention here.

Dialectical differences come in two types, words that have the same name in one or more dialects but behave more or less differently (akin to homonyms), and dictionary entries that exhibit different names for essentially the same definitions (similar to synonyms).

When transporting applications written in one dialect to another, homonyms are usually identifiable by close inspection of their stack effects. The most perplexing differences here come with two very common definitions, `VARIABLE` and `MOVE`.

Word	Fig-Forth	Forth-70	poly-Forth
VARIABLE	(n ...)	(...)	(...)
MOVE	(a a c ...)	(a a c ...)	(a a b ...)

At compile time Fig-Forth's `VARIABLE` expects to find a value on the stack with which to initialize the variable. Forth-79 and poly-Forth create the dictionary entry in the same manner, but the variable must be initialized *after* its creation as a dictionary entry. Thus `0 VARIABLE DATA` in Fig-Forth is equivalent to `VARIABLE DATA 0 DATA !` in the other two dialects.

When it comes to moving characters around in memory, poly-Forth is the variant. Fig-Forth and Forth-79 expect to find a source and destination address on the stack, followed by a 16-bit *cell* count; poly-Forth has been written to expect a *byte* count. Thus, conversion of poly-Forth applications to Fig Forth applications requires halving the count in `MOVE` instructions.

When it comes to synonyms, a similar set of problems arise. In Fig-Forth, the pointer to byte offset within the incoming text buffer is called `IN`, whereas in Forth-79 and poly-Forth it is `>IN`. Fig-Forth calls its dictionary pointer `DP` and its pointer to the terminal input buffer `TIB`, whereas poly-Forth uses `H` and `S0`, respectively.

There are other, more subtle differences, but they are largely at the lower levels. Although these differences can cause problems, the problems can be overcome with a modest amount of attention to the details of your system.

Appendix D

Number Formatting

The following two Forth Blocks (Figs. D.1 and D.2) contain the necessary definitions to implement the high-level number formatting system (.WITH and D.WITH) described in Chap. 6. These definitions follow the Forth Interest Group conventions that interrogate a variable called STATE to determine whether the system is in COMPILE mode. This allows .WITH and its 32-bit partner to be used either interactively or in a colon definition. If you wish to examine these definitions closely as an exercise in Forth programming concepts, you will benefit by doing a side-by-side comparison with the definition of . " (dot quote).

```
Block    # 26
   0 ( Formatted Output   16 & 32 bit integers,     block 1/2 )
   1   0 variable digits   0 variable cnum    0 variable slots
   2   0 variable sig
   3 : clear   pad 64 32 fill ;
   4 : ?slots  0 slots ! cnum @ 0 do pad i + c@ 35 = if 1 slots +!
   5           then   loop ;
   6 : ?sign   dup 0< if dminus 45 sig ! else 32 sig ! then ;
   7 : ?count  count dup cnum ! ;
   8 : dec>    ?sign  0 digits ! begin 1 digits +! 10 m/mod over
   9           0= until 2drop ;
  10 : >out    cnum @ 0 do pad i + c@ dup 35 = if swap 48 + emit
  11           drop else dup 63 = if sig @ emit drop else emit
  12           then then loop ;
  13 : ovrflo  0 do 42 emit loop digits @ 1+ 0 do drop loop ;
  14 : mask    pad 1 - begin 1 +   dup c@ 35 = if dup 32 swap c! swap
  15           1 - swap then over 0= until 2drop ;    ( n ==>  )
```

Figure D.1 Block 26: formatted output of 16- and 32-bit integers

```
Block  # 27
  0 ( Formatted Output                              block 2/2  )
  1 : ready     clear pad swap cmove ?slots ;
  2
  3 : display   slots @ digits @ - dup 0< if cnum @ ovrflo else dup
  4             0= if drop >out else mask >out then then ;
  5 : =cells    dup 1 and + ; ( Req'd to avoid odd add rf on LSI-11)
  6 : (d.with)  R ?count dup 1+ =cells R> + >R ready dec> display ;
  7
  8 : (.with)   R ?count dup 1+ =cells R> + >R ready s->d dec>
  9             display ;
 10 : d.with    34 state @ if compile (d.with) word here c@ 1+ =cells
 11             allot else  word here ?count ready dec>
 12             display then ;      immediate
 13 : .with     34 state @ if compile (.with) word here c@ 1+ =cells
 14             allot  else word here ?count ready s->d dec>
 15             display then ;      immediate
```

Figure D.2 Block 27: formatted output

Appendix

The Universal Screen Editor

The Universal Screen Editor (U.S.E.) provides Forth programmers with the wherewithal to create and edit Forth blocks on the screen of their terminals. It provides for cursor control, swapping of lines in a Forth block, automatic text insertion, and character deletion. It is patterned after several editors which are distributed with Digital Equipment Corporation's RT-11, RSX-11M+, and VMS operating systems in its use of escape codes and special-function keys that are provided on the DEC VT-52 and VT-100 terminals, but it is not restricted to those terminals. Indeed, U.S.E. will operate on any terminal that has the ability to (1) clear its screen and home the cursor and (2) accept cursor position commands. It should be loaded after a terminal personality block which defines these features, as shown in Figs. E.1 and E.2 (see also Fig. 7.7).

To use the editor, copy it to a sequence of blocks, load a terminal per-

```
Block  # 2
    0 ( Terminal Personality Block....H19-A VT52 emulation..        )
    1 decimal      : pesc 27 emit emit ;   ( Send an escape code    )
    2 : home 72 pesc ;
    3 : page home 74 pesc ;                          ( clear screen )
    4 : putcur 89 pesc 31 + emit 31 + emit ;  ( home is 1,1 not 0,0 )
    5 : revvid 112 pesc ;              ( terminal to reverse video  )
    6 : vid     113 pesc ;             ( terminal to normal video   )
    7 : graph   70 pesc ;                    ( enter graphics mode  )
    8 : nograph 71 pesc ;                    ( exit graphics mode   )
    9 : nocur 120 pesc 53 emit ;                     ( Cursor off   )
   10 : cur   121 pesc 53 emit ;                     ( Cursor on    )
   11 : getchr drop key ;            ( disregard chr following <esc> )
   12
   13
   14 : list lp @ 0 = if page then list ;
   15
```

Figure E.1 Block 2: terminal personality block for H19-A VT52 emulation

```
Block # 3
   0 ( Terminal Personality Block....Intecolor VT52 emulation...  )
   1 decimal       : pesc 27 emit emit ;        ( send an escape code )
   2 : home 72 pesc ;                           ( cursor to upper left )
   3 : page home 74 pesc ;                           ( clear screen )
   4 : putcur 89 pesc 31 + emit 31 + emit ; ( home is 1,1 not 0,0 )
   5
   6 ( : graph    40 pesc 48 emit )        ( enter graphics mode)
   7 ( : nograph  40 pesc 66 emit )        ( exit graphics mode )
   8
   9 : nocur ;   : cur ; ( Too bad! Intecolor can't do either one! )
  10
  11 : getchr drop key ;     ( to ignore the char. following <esc> )
  12 : revvid ;
  13 : vid ;            ( fill in later )
  14 : list lp @ 0 = if page then list ;
  15
```

Figure E.2 Block 3: terminal personality block for Intecolor VT 52 emulation

sonality block like 2 or 3 (Fig. E.1 or E.2), and then load the editor. The terminal personality block should have LIST defined as : LIST PAGE LIST ; , by the way, if U.S.E. is to function properly. To invoke the editor, simply put the number of the block to be edited on the stack and enter EDIT<ret>. The screen should clear and the target block should appear. Try it on a blank block first.

Many modern terminals and keyboards have "special-function" keys that actually send more than one character to the processor. These character sequences are usually escape codes (Fig. E.3). On the Zenith-19 terminal, for example, these are blue-and-white keys that send the escape sequences <esc><P> and <esc><R>, respectively. Whatever those keys accomplish in a particular application can be accomplished almost as easily by pressing the escape key and then the uppercase P or Q key. In addi-

```
Block # 20
   0 ( The Universal screen editor....Introduction:    Block 1/5  )
   1
   2 (         This Editor uses escape codes to carry out cursor
   3           positioning and screen clearing functions.
   4           It uses the DEC KED editor commands where appropriate.
   5           Load a terminal personality block first.  See block 2.
   6           David L. Toppen, Data Acquisition Lab, Chemistry, CSUN)
   7
   8 Vocabulary Editor Immediate
   9 Editor Definitions
  10 0 variable escr      ( Block being edited )
  11 0 variable nline     ( Current line )
  12 0 variable linaddr   ( address of the current line in buffer )
  13 0 variable nchr      ( curr chr in line )
  14 0 variable cursor    ( address of cursor in buffer )
  15 0 variable dflag   0 variable reflag ( done and refresh flags )
```

Figure E.3 Block 20: introduction to the Universal Screen Editor

```
Block # 21
  0 ( Universal Screen Editor ...                      Block 2/5 )
  1 : zcur 0 nchr ! 0 nline ! 0 cursor ! ;  : done dflag @ ;
  2 : scrcur   nchr @ nline @   3 + swap 5 + swap putcur ;
  3 : @line    linaddr @ pad 64 cmove ;    ( store line in pad )
  4 : !line    pad linaddr @ 64 cmove ;    ( fetch line from pad )
  5 : lfix     nocur pad dup 64 + swap nchr @ + do i c@ emit loop
  6            scrcur cur ;
  7 : ldelete scrcur pad nchr @ + 64 nchr @ - 32 fill lfix !line ;
  8 : scratch  1 21 putcur !line ." block not saved " ;
  9 : ex       1 21 putcur !line ."  saved" update flush ;
 10 : finish   dflag @ 1 - if scratch else ex then ;
 11 : nextline !line linaddr @ 64 + dup linaddr ! cursor !
 12            0 nchr ! nline @  15 < if 1 nline +! @line else
 13            7 emit then scrcur ;
 14 : command 1 reflag !  scrcur pad nchr @ + c@ emit 1 19 putcur
 15            ." Command? "  10 19 putcur quit ;
```

Figure E.4 Block 21: Universal Screen Editor

tion, there are "arrow" keys on nearly all terminals which control the motion of the cursor. On the Z-19, cursor motions up, down, right, and left are generated with the appropriate keys *or* with routines <esc><A>, <esc><B>, <esc><C>, and <esc><D>, respectively. To move the cursor to line 3, for example, just enter the "down" sequence twice, or use the "down" key.

To enter Forth definitions, just type them. The cursor will move accordingly. To insert text, move the cursor over the character to the right of the point of insertion and type away. The existing text will move to the right as the insertion takes place. Character deletion is equally easy, but be careful (Fig. E.4). The character to the left of the cursor will disappear when the delete key (not the backspace key) is pressed, and the text will fill to the left. The convention of deleting to the left of the cursor, rather than deleting the character under the cursor, is common in sophisticated word-processing applications, by the way.

The white key on the Z-19 (<esc><R>) deletes an entire line at a time.

In this editor, the blue key (or the sequence <esc><P>, or whatever special-function key produces that sequence on your system) calls for the COMMAND mode. In that mode the cursor moves to the bottom of the block and prompts the user for a command (Figs. E.5 and E.6). There are only a few commands:

EXIT<ret>	(...)	Save the block and return to Forth.
SAVE<ret>	(...)	A synonym for EXIT.
QUIT<ret>	(...)	Return to Forth; do not save the block.
RESTORE<ret>	(...)	Refresh the screen with a new image of the block (rarely used).
TRADE<ret>	(n n ...)	Trade the lines whose numbers appear on the stack.

```
Block  # 22
  0 ( Universal Screen Editor ...                       Block  3/5 )
  1 : rightmove    nchr @ 63 < if 1 cursor +! 1 nchr +!
  2              else     7 emit   scrcur then ;
  3 : leftmove  nchr @ 0 > if -1 cursor +! -1 nchr +!
  4              else     7 emit   scrcur then ;
  5 : newline    !line dup cursor +! linaddr +! @line ;
  6 : downline nline @ 15 < if 64 newline 1 nline +! else 7 emit
  7             scrcur then ;   : upline    nline @ 0 > if -64 newline
  8             -1 nline +! else 7 emit scrcur then ;
  9 : curmove dup 66 = if downline else    dup 65 = if upline else
 10             dup 80 = if !line drop command else
 11             dup 67 = if rightmove else   dup 82 = if ldelete else
 12             dup 68 = if leftmove  else
 13    dup 84 = if scratch escr @ 1 - dup escr ! 1 reflag ! zcur else
 14    dup 83 = if scratch escr @ 1+  dup escr ! 1 reflag ! zcur else
 15       7 emit  then  then  then  then  then  then  then  drop ;
```

Figure E.5 Block 22: Universal Screen Editor

```
Block  # 23
  0 ( Universal Screen Editor                           Block  4/5 )
  1 : rblk    nocur nline @ 3 + putcur 32 emit scrcur cur   ;
  2
  3 : insert dup 13 = if scrcur drop nextline else pad nchr @ +
  4          dup dup 1+ 63 nchr @ - <cmove c! nchr @ 63 = if nextline
  5     else 1 nchr +! 1 cursor +! lfix 69 rblk then then ;
  6 : delete   drop nchr @ dup 0 > if pad + dup 1 - 64 nchr @ - cmove
  7           -1 nchr +! -1 cursor +! lfix 68 rblk
  8            32 pad 63 + c! else drop 7 emit scrcur then ;
  9 : refresh dup block nline @ 64 * + linaddr ! page list
 10           @line scrcur  0 reflag ! ;
 11 : ?insert   dup 8 = if delete else insert then ;
 12 : await   0 dflag ! begin reflag @ if escr @ refresh then
 13           key dup 27 = if getchr curmove
 14           else ?insert then done until finish 0 18 putcur ;
 15 : restore escr @ refresh await ;
```

Figure E.6 Block 23: Universal Screen Editor

```
Block  # 24
  0 ( Universal Screen Editor ...                       Block  5/5 )
  1 : select   zcur dup escr ! refresh await ;
  2
  3              0 variable line1 0 variable line2
  4
  5 : trade    escr @ block 2dup swap 64 * + line1 !
  6            swap drop swap 64 * + dup line2 ! pad 64 cmove
  7            line1 @ line2 @ 64 cmove pad line1 @ 64 cmove
  8            restore ;
  9 : advance ex escr @ 1+ dup escr ! select ;
 10 : backup  ex escr @ 1 - dup escr ! select ;
 11 : exit ex [compile] forth ;   : save exit ;
 12 : quit scratch [compile] forth ;
 13   Forth Definitions
 14 : edit [compile] editor editor select ;
 15   Forth Definitions
```

Figure E.7 Block 24: Universal Screen Editor

The key definitions in the editor are AWAIT, ?INSERT (pronounced "Q insert"), and CURMOVE. The interface to the dictionary and the entry point to the editor is provided by EDIT, and EXIT provides a way out (Fig. E.7). This screen editor provides an excellent set of example definitions for a student of Forth system design. Experiment with it, expand it, improve it. For example, you might wish to add search routines to the definitions.

Appendix F

A Forth Assembler

As illustrated in Chap. 8, a Forth assembler can be used to write "code" definitions that run at machine speed. This public-domain PDP-11 assembler was created for the Forth Interest Group by John S. James (see Figs. F.1 to F.8). The block numbered 85 (Fig. F.7) contains examples of code written for this assembler.

Using a Forth assembler requires more than just a casual understanding of the architecture of the machine in use. For example, the numerous addressing modes in the PDP-11's instruction set create a richness and flexibility for the experienced programmer and simultaneously a bewildering maze of symbols for the novice. If your application requires regular use of assembly-level programming in addition to high-level Forth, you will benefit from first reading a text on the assembly language of your machine of choice.

```
Block  # 10
   0 ( ASSEMBLER)                              OCTAL
   1 VOCABULARY ASSEMBLER IMMEDIATE        0 VARIABLE OLDBASE
   2 : ENTERCODE [COMPILE] ASSEMBLER   BASE @ OLDBASE ! OCTAL    SP@ ;
   3 : CODE CREATE ENTERCODE ;
   4 ASSEMBLER DEFINITIONS
   5   ' ENTERCODE 2 -      ' ;CODE 10 +    !    ( PATCH ';CODE')
   6 : FIXMODE ( COMPLETE THE MODE PACKET)
   7      DUP -1 = IF DROP ELSE DUP 10 SWAP U< IF 67 ENDIF ENDIF ;
   8 : OP <BUILDS , DOES> @ , ;
   9 : ORMODE ( MODE ADDR -> .    SET MODE INTO INSTR.)
  10      SWAP OVER @ OR SWAP ! ;
  11 : ,OPERAND ( ?OPERAND MODE -> ) DUP 67 = OVER 77 = OR IF ( PC)
  12      SWAP HERE 2 + - SWAP ENDIF   DUP 27 = OVER 37 = OR ( LITERAL)
  13      SWAP 177760 AND 60 = OR ( RELATIVE) IF , ENDIF ;
  14 : 1OP <BUILDS , DOES> @ , FIXMODE   DUP HERE 2 -
  15      ORMODE ,OPERAND ;                          DECIMAL
```

Figure F.1 Block 10: assembler, octal

222

```
Block  # 11
   0 ( ASSEMBLER, CONT.)                              OCTAL
   1 : SWAPOP ( -> .   EXCHANGE OPERANDS OF 3-WORD INSTR, ADJ. PC-REL)
   2      HERE 2 - @ HERE 6 - @ 6700 AND 6700 = IF ( PC-REL) 2 + ENDIF
   3      HERE 4 - @ HERE 6 - @ 67 AND 67 = IF ( PC-REL) 2 - ENDIF
   4      HERE 2 - ! HERE 4 - ! ;
   5 : 20P <BUILDS , DOES> @ ,
   6      FIXMODE   DUP HERE 2 -   DUP >R ORMODE  ,OPERAND
   7      FIXMODE   DUP 100 * R ORMODE      ,OPERAND   HERE R> - 6 =
   8      IF SWAPOP ENDIF ;
   9 : ROP <BUILDS , DOES> @ , FIXMODE DUP HERE 2 - DUP >R ORMODE
  10      ,OPERAND DUP 7 SWAP U< IF ."     ERR-REG-B " ENDIF
  11      100 * R> ORMODE ;
  12 : BOP <BUILDS , DOES> @ ,   HERE -   DUP 376 >
  13      IF ."  ERR-BR+ " . ENDIF   DUP -400 < IF ."  ERR-BR- " .
  14      ENDIF      2 / 377 AND HERE 2 - ORMODE ;
  15                                                  DECIMAL
```

Figure F.2 Block 11: assembler, octal *(continued)*

```
Block  # 12
   0 ( ASSEMBLER - INSTRUCTION TABLE)         OCTAL
   1 010000 20P MOV,    110000 20P MOVB,     020000 20P CMP,
   2 120000 20P CMPB,   060000 20P ADD,      160000 20P SUB,
   3 030000 20P BIT,    130000 20P BITB,     050000 20P BIS,
   4 150000 20P BISB,   040000 20P BIC,      140000 20P BICB,
   5 005000 10P CLR,    105000 10P CLRB,     005100 10P COM,
   6 105100 10P COMB,   005200 10P INC,      105200 10P INCB,
   7 005300 10P DEC,    105300 10P DECB,     005400 10P NEG,
   8 105400 10P NEGB,   005700 10P TST,      105700 10P TSTB,
   9 006200 10P ASR,    106200 10P ASRB,     006300 10P ASL,
  10 106300 10P ASLB,   006000 10P ROR,      106000 10P RORB,
  11 006100 10P ROL,    106100 10P ROLB,     000300 10P SWAB,
  12 005500 10P ADC,    105500 10P ADCB,     005600 10P SBC,
  13 105600 10P SBCB,   006700 10P SXT,      000100 10P JMP,
  14 074000 ROP XOR,    004000 ROP JSR,
  15 : RTS, 200 OR , ;                       DECIMAL
```

Figure F.3 Block 12: assembler instruction table, octal

```
Block  # 13
   0 ( ASSEMBLER - CONT.)                    OCTAL
   1 000400 BOP BR,     001000 BOP BNE,      001400 BOP BEQ,
   2 100000 BOP BPL,    100400 BOP BMI,      102000 BOP BVC,
   3 102400 BOP BVS,    103000 BOP BCC,      103400 BOP BCS,
   4 002000 BOP BGE,    002400 BOP BLT,      003400 BOP BLE,
   5 101000 BOP BHI,    101400 BOP BLOS,     103000 BOP BHIS,
   6 103400 BOP BLO,    003000 BOP BGT,      000003 OP BPT,
   7 000004 OP IOT,     000002 OP RTI,       000006 OP RTT,
   8 000000 OP HALT,    000001 OP WAIT,      000005 OP RESET,
   9 000241 OP CLC,     000242 OP CLV,       000244 OP CLZ,
  10 000250 OP CLN,     000261 OP SEC,       000262 OP SEV,
  11 000264 OP SEZ,     000270 OP SEN,       000277 OP SCC,
  12 000257 OP CCC,     000240 OP NOP,       006400 OP MARK,
  13 : EMT, 104000 + , ;
  14
  15                                         DECIMAL
```

Figure F.4 Block 13: assembler, octal *(continued)*

224 Appendix F

```
Block  # 14
    0 ( ASSEMBLER - REGISTERS, MODES, AND CONDITIONS)    OCTAL
    1 : C CONSTANT ;         0 C R0    1 C R1    2 C R2    3 C R3    4 C R4
    2       5 C R5    6 C SP   7 C PC    2 C W    3 C U    4 C IP    5 C S    6 C RP
    3 : RTST ( R MODE -> MODE)   OVER DUP 7 > SWAP 0 < OR
    4      IF ."   NOT A REGISTER: " OVER . ENDIF + -1 ;
    5 : )+ 20 RTST ;         : -) 40 RTST ;         : I) 60 RTST ;
    6 : @)+ 30 RTST ;        : @-) 50 RTST ;        : @I) 70 RTST ;
    7 : # 27 -1 ;            : @# 37 -1 ;
    8 : () DUP 10 U< IF ( REGISTER DEFERRED) 10 + -1
    9      ELSE ( RELATIVE DEFERRED) 77 -1 ENDIF ;
   10 ( NOTE - THE FOLLOWING CONDITIONALS REVERSED FOR 'IF,', ETC. )
   11 001000 C EQ     001400 C NE      100000 C MI     100400 C PL
   12 102000 C VS     102400 C VC      103000 C CS     103400 C CC
   13 002000 C LT     002400 C GE      003000 C LE     003400 C GT
   14 101000 C LOS    101400 C HI      103000 C LO     103400 C HIS
   15                                                  DECIMAL
```

Figure F.5 Block 14: assembler for registers, modes, and conditions (octal)

```
Block  # 15
    0 ( ASSEMBLER - STRUCTURED CONDITIONALS)   OCTAL
    1
    2 : IF, ( CONDITION -> ADDR ) HERE SWAP , ;
    3 : IPATCH ( ADDR ADDR -> . )  OVER - 2 / 1 -    377 AND
    4     SWAP DUP @ ROT OR SWAP ! ;
    5 : ENDIF, ( ADDR -> ) HERE IPATCH ;    : THEN, ENDIF, ;
    6 : ELSE, ( ADDR -> ADDR ) 00400 ,    HERE IPATCH    HERE 2 - ;
    7 : BEGIN, ( -> ADDR )   HERE ;
    8 : WHILE, ( CONDITION -> ADDR )   HERE SWAP , ;
    9 : REPEAT, ( ADDR ADDR -> ) HERE 400 ,  ROT IPATCH HERE IPATCH ;
   10 : UNTIL, ( ADDR CONDITION -> )  , HERE 2 - SWAP IPATCH ;
   11 : C; CURRENT @ CONTEXT !   OLDBASE @ BASE !    SP@ 2+ =
   12    IF SMUDGE ELSE ." CODE ERROR, STACK DEPTH CHANGED " ENDIF ;
   13
   14 : NEXT, IP )+ W MOV,    W @)+ JMP, ;
   15 FORTH DEFINITIONS                           DECIMAL
```

Figure F.6 Block 15: assembler for structured conditionals (octal)

```
Block  # 85
    0 ( Assembler examples ........................................... )
    1
    2 Code Cdup    S () S -) MOV, NEXT, C;
    3
    4 (      Cdup is an assembler version of DUP. S is defined in the
    5       assembler to refer to the Forth stack. () represents a
    6       register deferred memory reference, while -) is an
    7       autodecrement memory instruction. Thus, the result of
    8       Cdup is to copy the contents of the stack to one location
    9       lower in memory (Forth's stacks grow down, Fig. 7.3 ).
   10
   11 Code Ramp 10000 # R1 MOV, BEGIN, R1 DEC, GT WHILE,
   12           R1 DACX MOV, R1 DACY MOV, REPEAT, NEXT, C;
   13
   14 (     Ramp begins copying reg 1 to both DACs, decrements the reg
   15       regularly and stops when its contents become zero .)
```

Figure F.7 Block 85: assembler examples

```
Block # 194
   0 ( Assembler version, Data Display Routines, Appendix F )
   1
   2 Code cdata 0 # r1 mov, array # r0 mov,  ( init registers )
   3      begin,
   4           r1 inc, 10000 # r1 cmp,  ( increment cntr & compare)
   5      gt while,                     ( if not done yet... )
   6           r0 )+ dacy mov,          ( send data to Y dac )
   7           r1    dacx mov,          ( and position to X dac )
   8      repeat,                       ( and go back for another )
   9      next, c;                      ( terminate the code def. )
  10
  11 : Cdisplay   begin cdata ?terminal until ;
  12
  13      ( Note the use of the code definition within the high level
  14        definition of Cdisplay. )
  15
```

Figure F.8 Block 194: assembler version of data display routines

Subject Index

A/D (analog-to-digital) conversion, 186–195
ADC (analog-to-digital converter), 174, 186
Alias frequency, 197
Alternate execution, 88–89
ANSI (American National Standards Institute) standard (3.64) for escape codes, 169–171
Area (exercise), 16–18
Arithmetic operations:
 double-length, 49, 58–61
 floating-point, 52–58
 single-length, 46–47
Arrays, 79–84
 byte, 83–84
 double-integer, 82–83
 floating-point, 82–83
 single-integer, 79–82
 storing data in, 192–194
ASCII character code, 105–110
 nonprinting characters, 106–109
 printing characters, 109–110
 values, 108
Assembler code, 184, 222–225
Atomic weights (exercise), 84

Babbage, Charles, 147–148
Baud rate, 156
Baudot, M., 156
Blanks, removing, 115
Block buffers, 111, 125–126, 129–131
Blocks, 120–133
 buffers and, 111, 125–126, 129–131
 editing, 126–131
 emptying, 130
 indexing, 123–125
 listing, 121–123
 loading, 131–133
 saving, 129–131
Boole, George, 86

Boolean logic, 87, 99–101
Buffers, 111–112
 block, 111, 125–126, 129–131
 data, 161
 scratchpad, 111
 terminal input (TIB), 111, 153
Bus:
 PDP-11, 148–149
 S-100, 149, 150
Bytes, 41
 addressing, 66–68

Cells, 41–46
 addressing, 66–68
 bytes and, 41, 83
 super (32-bit), 48–51
Characters (8-bit):
 ASCII (*see* ASCII character code)
 input (*see* Input)
 moving in memory, 118–120
Colon (:), 16, 30
Command String Introducer Pair, 170
Comparison operations, 86–87
Compile-time behavior, 30–31
Conditionals, 87–88
Constants, 73–78
 double-length, 75–76
 floating-point, 76–78
 single-length, 73–74

D/A (digital-to-analog) conversion, 174–186
DAC (digital-to-analog converter), 174
DCE (data-communication equipment), 155–156
Decisions, 85–89
Delimiters (spaces), 9
Dialects:
 Fig-Forth, 213
 Kitt Peak, 24
 poly-Forth, 24, 213

Dictionary, 7, 22–29, 150–152
Digitization, 188
Disk storage, 120–126
  (*See also* Blocks)
DMA (direct-memory access) peripherals, 150
Dot (.), 7
DTE (data-terminal equipment), 155–156
DUP (duplicate), 11

Editor:
  skeleton, 126–131
  universal screen, 170, 217–221
EIA (Electronics Industry Association) standard RS-232C, 155
ELSE, 89
Encoding:
  hexadecimal, 43
  octal, 42
Escape sequences, 166–173
Execution-time behavior, 30

Falling bodies (exercise), 34, 73
Fetching numbers (@), 66
Forth dialects (*see* Dialects)

Gas laws (exercise), 63, 68, 76
Gas pressure (exercise), 70

Hexadecimal arithmetic, 39–40
Hexadecimal encoding, 43
High-level languages, 5
High-level words, 23

IF ... THEN construction, 86
Immediate words, 31–33
Input:
  ASCII (*see* ASCII character code)
  floating-point, 53
  multiple-character, 116–120
  numeric, 44
  single-character, 110–116
Interlingual applications, 33
Interpreter, 7
I/O (input/output):
  interface, 156
  memory-mapped, 152

I/O (input/output) (*Cont.*):
  parallel, 154
  serial, 154–156

Languages, 5
LIFO (last-in, first-out) data structure, 6
Logic:
  bit, 101
  Boolean, 87, 99–101
Loops:
  definite, 90
  early termination, 93
  indefinite, 96
  quit, 7
  32-bit, 94
Low-level languages, 5
Low-level words, 23

Machine language, 5
Memory:
  moving characters in, 118–120
  organization, 150–153
    Forth, 152–153
    PDP-11, 151–152
  random access, 125
  virtual, 120–126
  (*See also* Blocks; Buffers)
Moore, Charles, 3
Multiplexor, 149

Names for Forth words, 23–25
Noise, 199–201
Numbers:
  binary, 37, 39
  decimal, 134–137
  double-precision, 50
  fixed-point, 39, 49
  floating-point, 49–50, 52–58, 212
  formatting display of (*see* Numeric output, formatted)
  hexadecimal, 39–40
  input, 44
  integer: double-length, 48, 49
    single, 41
  octal, 39
  output (*see* Numeric output)
  signed, 43
  storage of, 40–41, 68
Numeric output, 133–142
  decimal, 134–137

SUBJECT INDEX

Numeric output (*Cont.*):
  floating-point, 53
  formatted, 137–142, 215–216
    right-justified, 138–139
    32-bit, 141–142
    with .WITH, 139

Octal arithmetic, 39
Octal encoding, 42

Pad, 111–116
  reading from, 114–116
  writing to, 112–114
Peak, signal:
  identification of, 201–208
  integration of, 208–209
Perimeter (exercise), 18–19
Personality blocks:
  printer, 172
  terminal, 170, 217
Plus store (+!), 68
Pointers, 25, 151
Pop, 6
Postfix notation, 8
Power dissipation (exercise), 35
Pressure, gas (exercise), 70
Printer personality block, 172
Printing, 7, 46, 121, 156–160
Push, 6, 44

Quit loop, 7
Quoting strings (."), 17

Radix conversions, 61–62
RAM (random access memory), 125
Reinitialization, 71–73
Relativistic mass (exercise), 62
Resistance, electrical (exercise), 65–66
Reynolds number (exercise), 58
RS-232 standard, 155
Run-time behavior, 30–31

Sample-and-hold technique, 188
Sampling frequency, 189
Sampling theorem, 197–199
Scratchpad (*see* Pad)
Settling time, 176

Signal processing, 197–209
Stack:
  double integer on, 49
  floating-point numbers on, 54
  notation, 10, 12, 54
  parameter, 6, 49, 54, 153
  return, 6, 91–93, 153
Status registers, 161–162
Stefan's law (exercise), 57
Storing numbers (!), 68

Terminal personality block, 170, 217
TIB (terminal input buffer), 111, 153
Timing:
  in A/D, 189, 190
  in D/A, 180
Top-down programming, 157–160
Trailing blanks, clearing, 115

UART (universal asynchronous receiver-transmitter), 154
Unit-factor conversions, 63
Unsigned print, 46

Variables, 64–66
  double-length, 74, 75
  floating-point, 76
  single-length, 66
  user, 78–79
Virtual memory, 120–126
VLIST (vocabulary list), 22
Vocabularies, 29–34
VOCABULARY, 32
Voltage:
  gradations: in A/D, 187
    in D/A, 175
  measurement, 191
  reference, 175, 187
  resolution, 175, 187

Waveforms, 178–180
  linear, 178
  nonlinear, 186
Word length, 41
Words, 7, 16–34
  high-level, 23
  immediate, 31–33
  low-level, 23
  names for, 23–25

Forth Vocabulary Index

Arithmetic and logic:
  + (n1 n2 ... n1+n2), 6, 11
  − (n1 n2 ... n1−n2), 43
  * (n1 n2 ... n1*n2), 43
  / (n1 n2 ... n1/n2), 43
  D+ (d1 d2 ... d1+d2), 49
  D− (d1 d2 ... d1−d2), 49
  F* (f1 f2 ... f1*f2), 52
  F+ (f1 f2 ... f1+f2), 52
  F− (f1 f2 ... f1−f2), 52
  F/ (f1 f2 ... f1/f2), 52
  M* (n1 n2 ... d(prod)), 49
  M/ (d n ... n(quot)), 49
  /MOD (u1 u2 ... u(rem) u(quot)), 47
  AND (n1 n2 ... and), 99
  FSQRT (f1 ... sqr(f1)), 56
  MOD (u1 u2 ... u(rem)), 47
  OR (n1 n1 ... or), 100
  XOR (n1 n2 ... xor), 100

Comparison:
  = (equals) (n1 n2 ... f), 87
  > (n1 n2 ... f), 87
  < (n1 n2 ... f), 87
  O= (or NOT) (n ... f), 87
  O> (n ... f), 87
  O< (n ... f), 87

Data analysis:
  ?NOISE (add cnt ...), 204
  ?PEAK (addr ...), 204
  ADJUST (add cnt ...), 205
  ANALYZE (add cnt ...), 205
  INTEGRATE (...), 208
  MAXIMUM (add cnt ...), 202
  MINIMUM (add cnt ...), 202

Data analysis (*Cont.*):
  SPECTRUM (...), 205
Defining words:
  : (colon) (...), 16
  ; (semicolon) (...), 16
  2CONSTANT (d ...), 75
  2VARIABLE (d ...), 75
  CONSTANT (n ...), 73
  VARIABLE (n ...), 66
Device control and data acquisition:
  W! (n add ...), 165
  ACQUIRE (...), 192
  CONVERT (... n), 190
  CWAIT (...), 190
  DECOUT (n ...), 135
  DISPLAY (...), 193
  MS (n ...), 181
  OUTPUT (add n ...), 158
  POINTS (n ...), 192
  RAMP (...), 179
  SCOPE (n1 n2 ...), 177
  TOOT (...), 31
  WAIT (...), 102
Dictionary and vocabularies:
  ALLOT (n ...), 79
  DEFINITIONS (...), 32
  EDITOR (...), 170
  FORGET (...), 20, 27
  FORTH (...), 34
  HERE (... add), 117
  IMMEDIATE (...), 31
  ROOM (...), 26, 210
  SMUDGE (...), 29
  VLIST (...), 22
  VOCABULARY (...), 32
Disk operations:
  >DISK (from to blkcnt ...), 194
  DISK > (to from blkcnt ...), 194

Disk operations (*Cont.*):
  R/W (add blk f ...), 194
  BLOCK (n ... add), 125
  EMPTY-BUFFERS (...), 130
  FLUSH (...), 126
  INDEX (n1 n2 ...), 123
  LIST (n ...), 121, 168
  LOAD (n ...), 131
  LTYPE (add ...), 122
  SAVE (...), 123
  SAVE-BUFFERS (...), 126
  SCR (... add), 122, 153
  UPDATE (...), 128
  VIZ (n ...), 122

Editor applications:
  EXIT (...), 219
  L (...), 123
  P (n ...), 123
  QUIT (...), 219
  RESTORE (...), 219
  SAVE (...), 219
  TRADE (n1 n2 ...), 219

Input-output formatting:
  D.WITH (...), 139
  .WITH (...), 139
  FLOATING (...), 51
  INTEGER (...), 51
  NUMBER (add ... d), 51
  PLACES (n ...), 53

Loop structures and conditional executions:
  BEGIN ... UNTIL, 97
  BEGIN ... WHILE ... REPEAT, 98
  DO ... LOOP, 90
  DO ... +LOOP, 95
  I, 92
  IF ... ELSE ... ENDIF, 89
  IF ... ENDIF, 86
  IF ... THEN, 86
  LEAVE, 93

Memory:
  @ (add ... n), 66
  ! (n add ...), 68
  +! (n add ...), 68
  ? (add ...), 72
  2@ (add ... d), 74

Memory (*Cont.*):
  2! (d add ...), 74
  C@ (add ... c), 217
  C! (c add ...), 217
  CLEAR (the pad) (...), 112
  CMOVE (from to u ...), 119
  FILL (add u c ...), 119

Number bases:
  BASE (... add), 78
  BINARY (...), 46
  DECIMAL (...), 46
  HEX (...), 61
  OCTAL (...), 78

Stack manipulation:
  >R (n ...), 91
  R> (...), 91
  2DROP (d ...), 12
  2DUP (d ... d d), 12, 19
  2OVER (d1 d2 ... d1 d2 d1), 12
  2ROT (d1 d2 d3 ... d2 d3 d1), 12
  2SWAP (d1 d2 ... d2 d1), 12
  DROP (n ...), 12
  DUP (n ... n n), 11
  OVER (n1 n2 ... n1 n2 n1), 12
  ROT (n1 n2 n3 ... n2 n3 n1), 12
  SWAP (n1 n2 ... n2 n1), 12

Terminal input-output:
  . (dot) (n ...), 7, 139
  ." ... " (...), 17
  D. (d ...), 139
  D.R (d width ...), 139
  F. (f ...), 53
  .R (n width ...), 138
  ?TERMINAL (... f), 97
  −TRAILING (add n1 ... add n2), 115
  U. (u ...), 139
  UD. (ud ...), 139
  UD.R (ud width ...), 139
  U.R (u width ...), 139
  COUNT (add ... add+1 u), 118
  CR (...), 107
  EMIT (c ...), 29, 105
  EXPECT (add n ...), 116
  KEY (... c), 110
  TEXT (c ...), 119
  TYPE (add u ...), 23, 114, 158
  WORD (c ...), 116